MOURNE COUNTRY

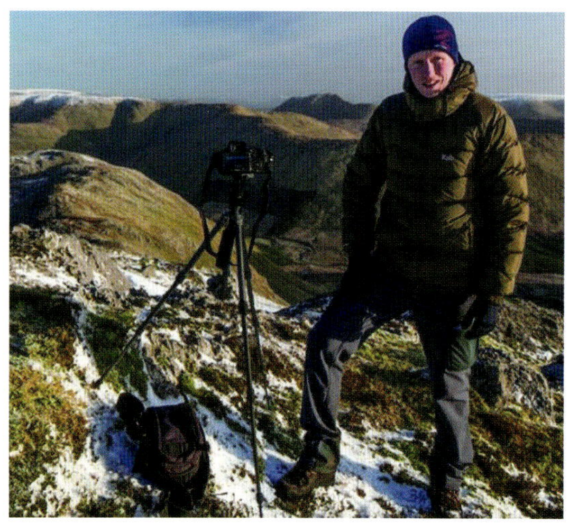

GARETH McCORMACK is a landscape photographer and writer, hailing from County Tyrone but now living in the west of Ireland. Known for his use of dynamic framing and light, he has shot far-flung landscapes around the world and worked for dozens of commercial and editorial clients. Gareth has been visiting the Mournes for more than twenty years. garethmccormack.com

First published 2022 by The O'Brien Press Ltd.,
12 Terenure Road East, Rathgar, Dublin 6, D06 HD27, Ireland.
Tel: +353 1 4923333. Fax: +353 1 4922777
Email: books@obrien.ie. Website: obrien.ie
The O'Brien Press is a member of Publishing Ireland.

ISBN 978-1-78849-177-8

10 9 8 7 6 5 4 3 2 1
26 25 24 23 22

Printed and bound by Drukarnia Skleniarz, Poland
The paper in this book is produced using pulp from managed forests.

Published in

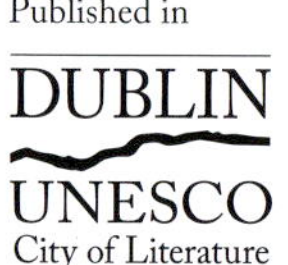

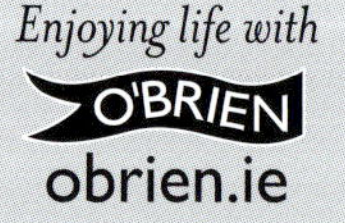

MOURNE COUNTRY

Gareth McCormack

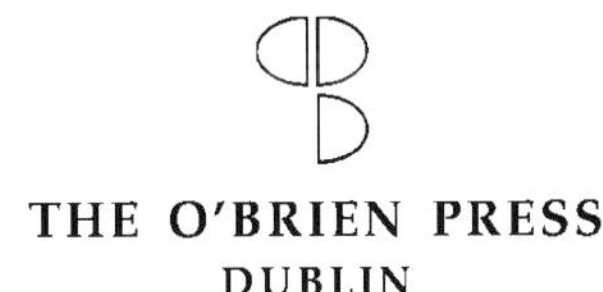

THE O'BRIEN PRESS
DUBLIN

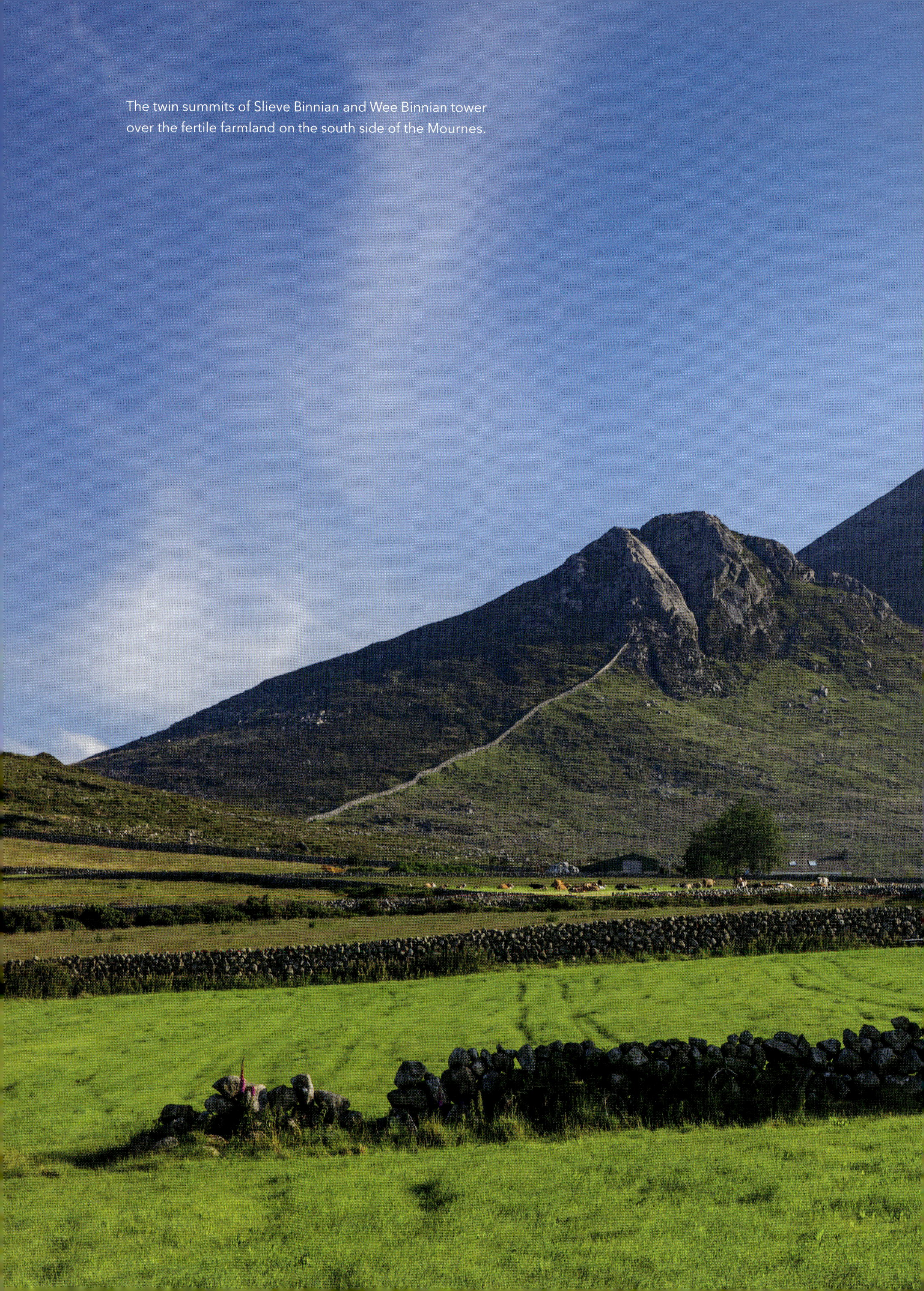
The twin summits of Slieve Binnian and Wee Binnian tower over the fertile farmland on the south side of the Mournes.

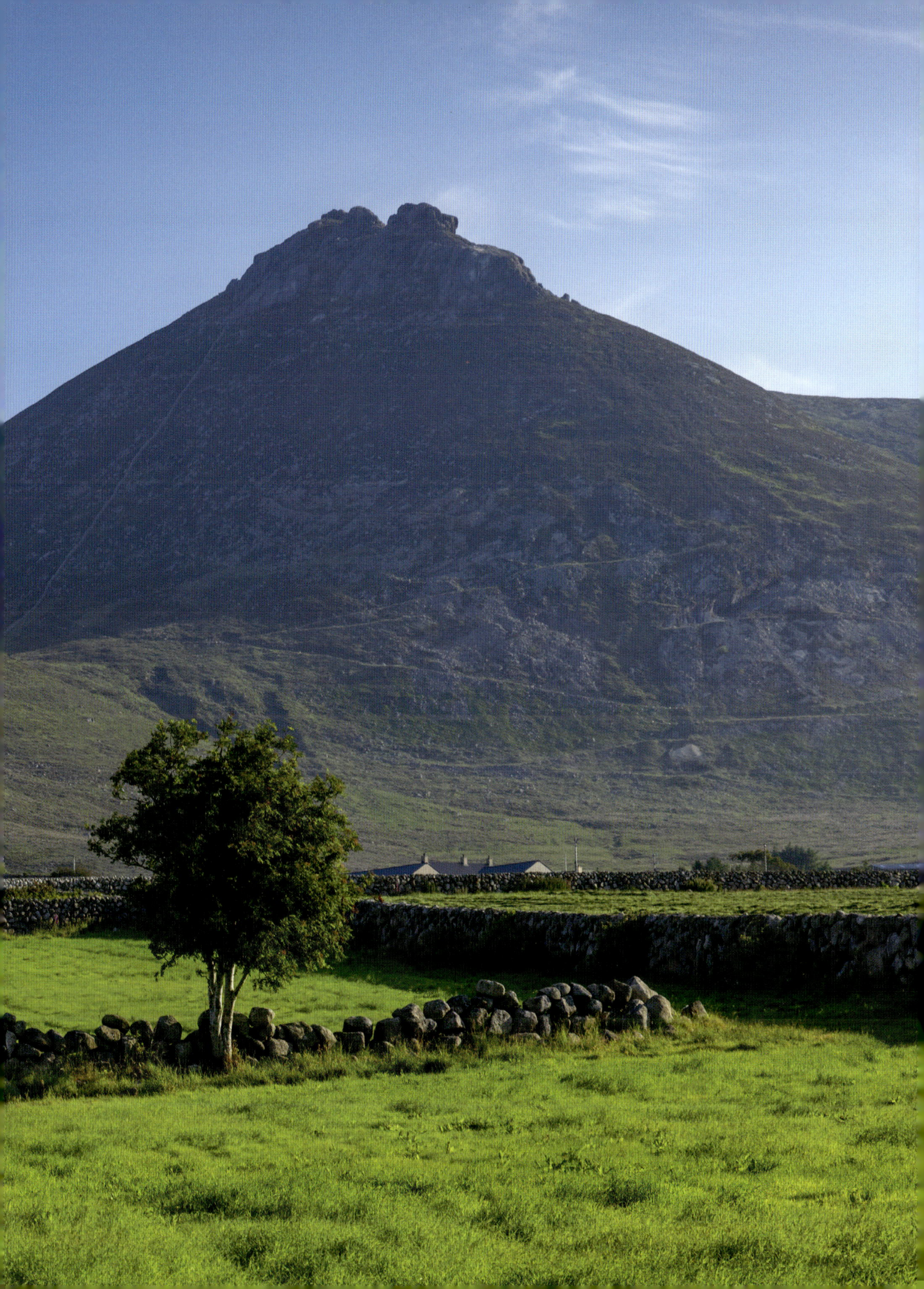

MOURNE COUNTRY

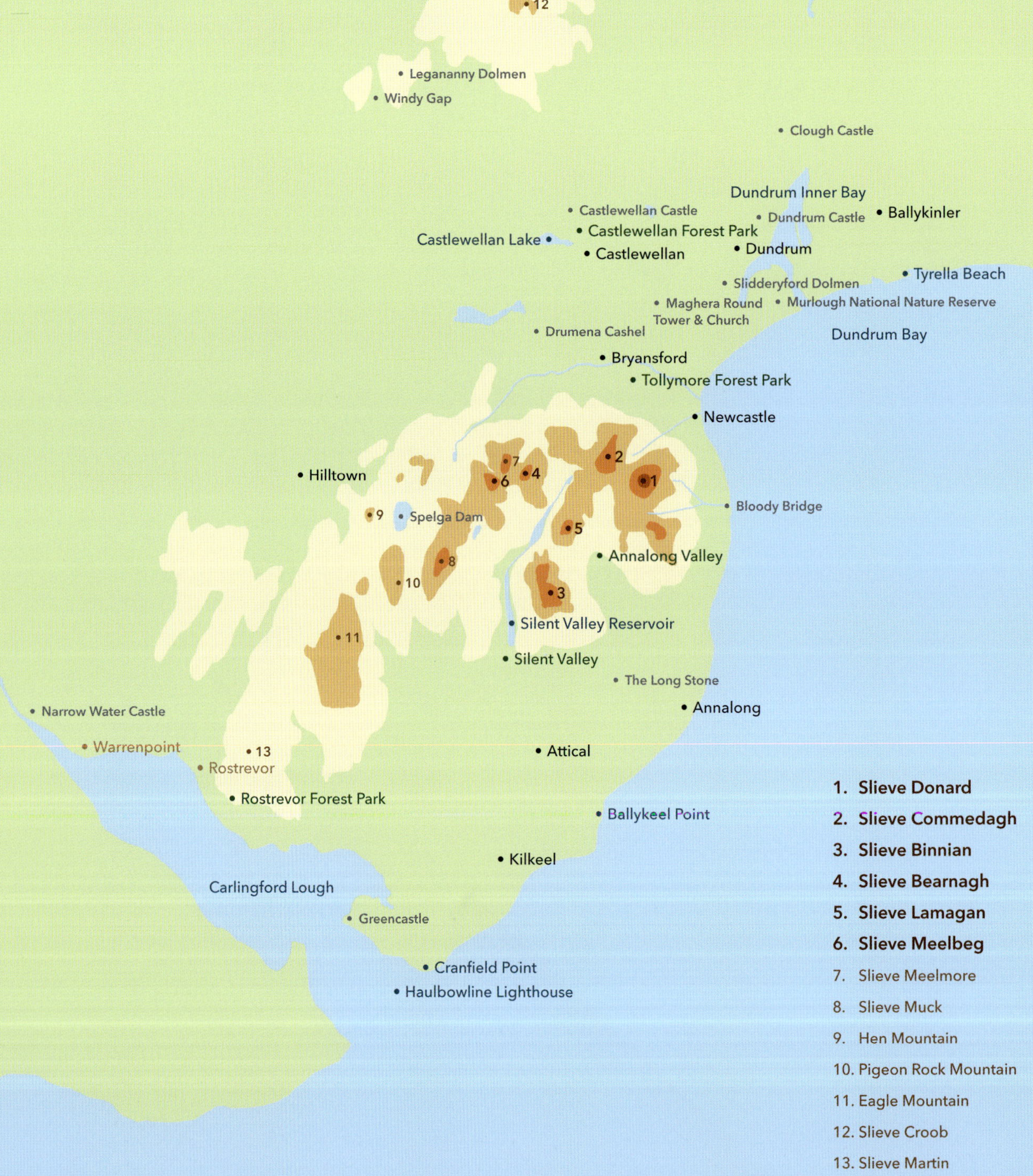

1. Slieve Donard
2. Slieve Commedagh
3. Slieve Binnian
4. Slieve Bearnagh
5. Slieve Lamagan
6. Slieve Meelbeg
7. Slieve Meelmore
8. Slieve Muck
9. Hen Mountain
10. Pigeon Rock Mountain
11. Eagle Mountain
12. Slieve Croob
13. Slieve Martin

CONTENTS

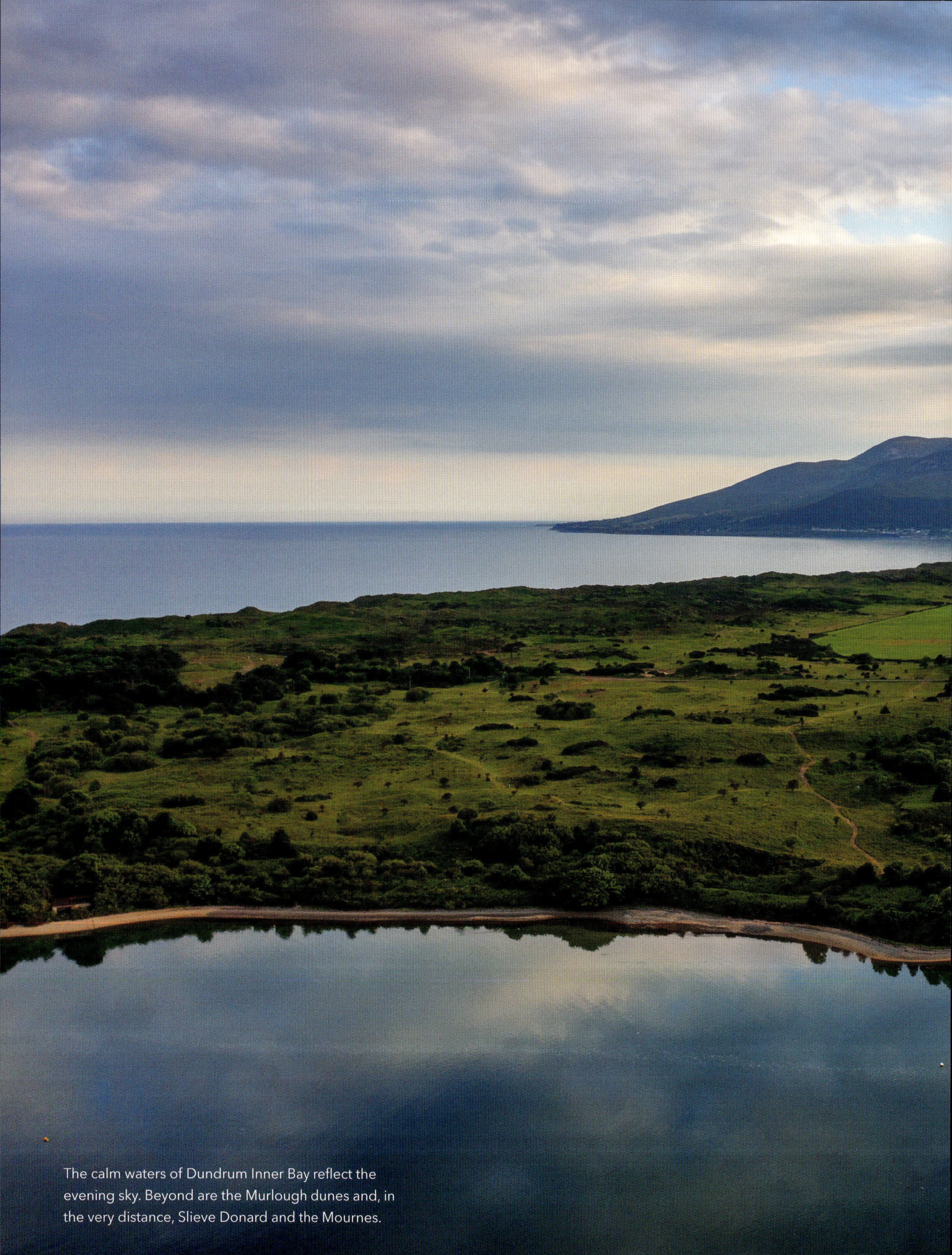

The calm waters of Dundrum Inner Bay reflect the evening sky. Beyond are the Murlough dunes and, in the very distance, Slieve Donard and the Mournes.

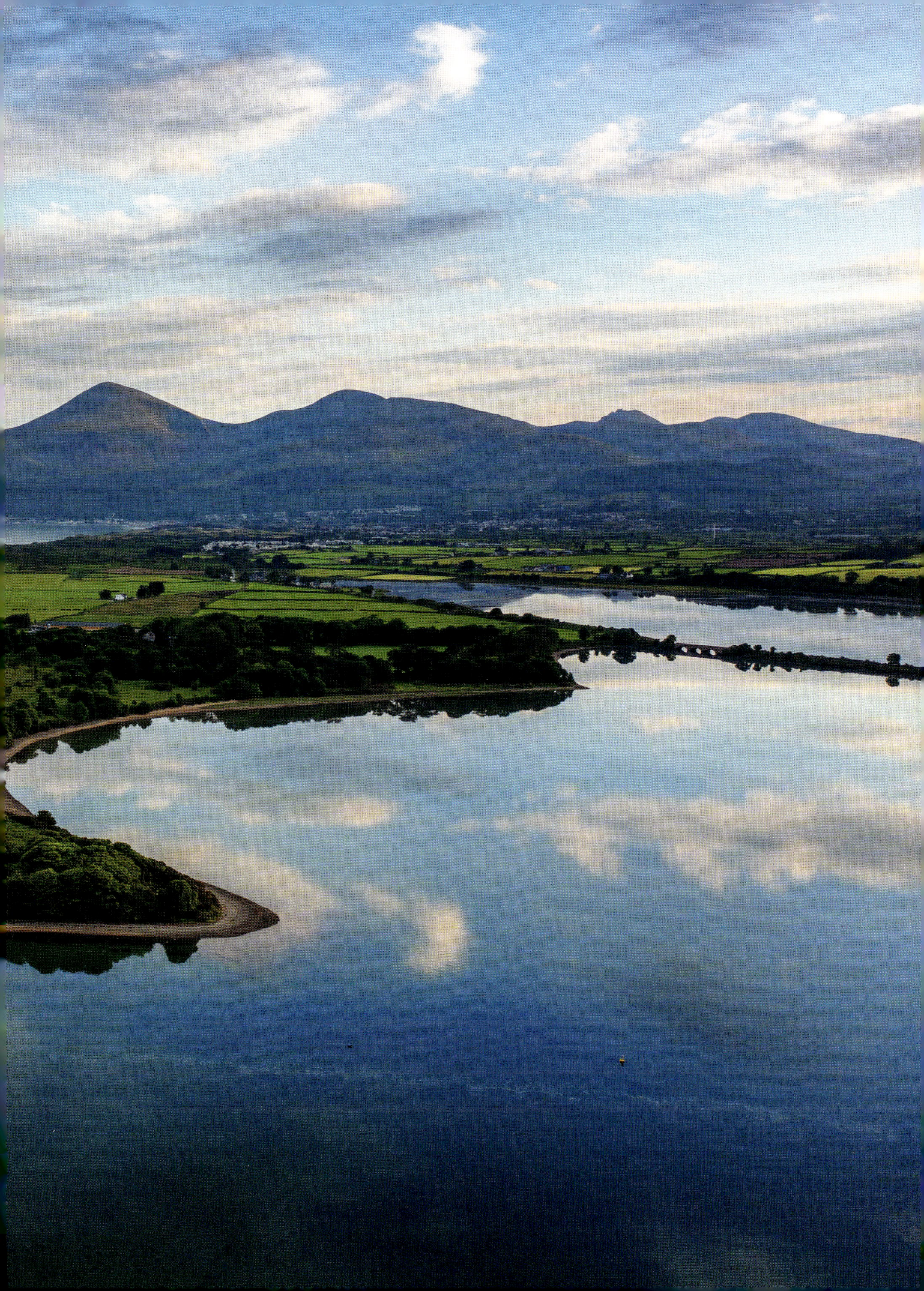

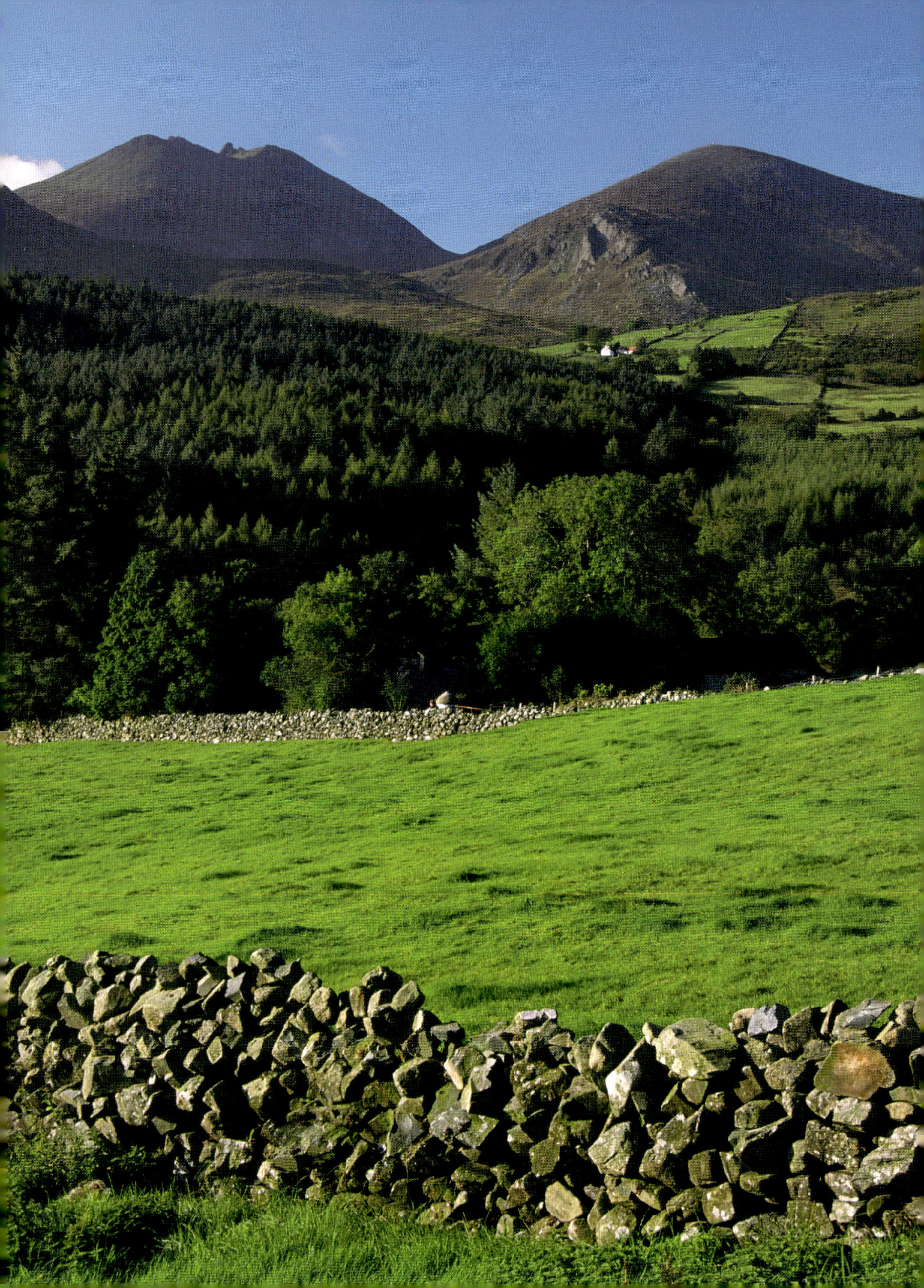

INTRODUCTION

'Where the Mountains o' Mourne sweep down to the sea ...'
Percy French

The Mourne mountains occupy the southern corner of County Down, approximately an hour's drive south of Belfast city. Their highest summit, Slieve Donard, is, at 850m, the tallest in Northern Ireland and Ulster. They are probably the most distinctive mountains in Ireland, clustered tightly together in a compact knot of summits, with graceful, sweeping slopes crowned by characteristic granite tors – set amid the patchwork woodlands and verdant farmland of the wider Mourne region.

The Mournes were originally known in Irish as *Beanne-Boirche* ('Boirche's Peaks'), a name variously attributed to a shepherd called Boirche from the 3rd century, or Bécc Bairrche

Left: The lush pastures of the Trassey Valley. The two summits in the background are Slieve Bearnagh on the left and Slieve Meelmore on the right.

Below: Looking across Dundrum Castle and Dundrum village towards the Mourne mountains. Slieve Donard is the prominent summit on the left.

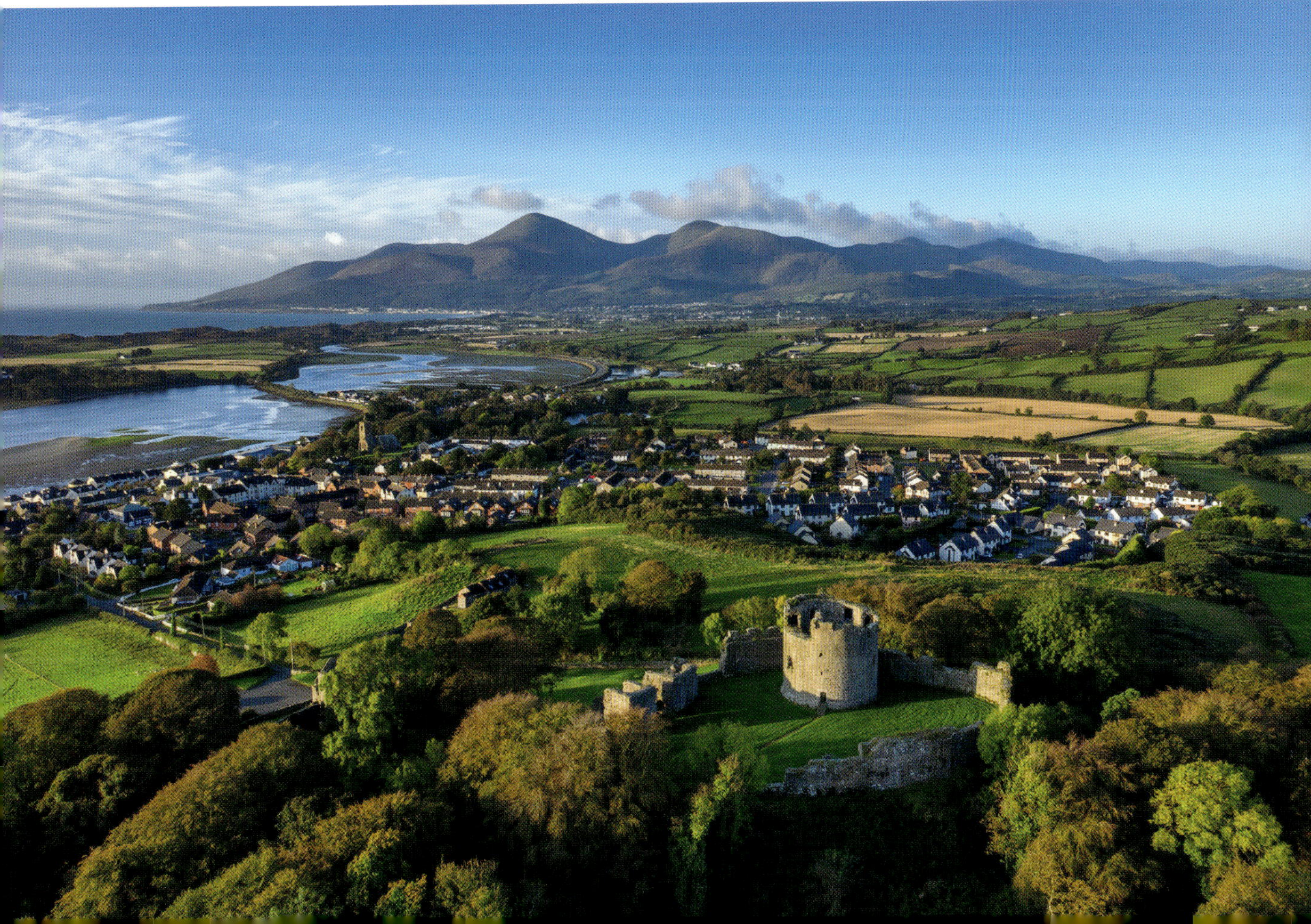

mac Blathmaic, a king of Ulster from the 7th and 8th centuries. But from sometime around the 13th century, the wider area in which the mountains stand became known as *Múrna*, from a Celtic or pre-Celtic tribe, the Mugdorna, who moved into the area from County Monaghan towards the end of the 12th century. The anglicisation of Múrna to Mourne took place when the area of the Mournes and the coastal plain to the south became the Barony of Mourne.

Today the Mourne district is widely considered to be much greater in extent than the Barony of Mourne or the ancient territory of Múrna. In 1986, an area of 570 km² was designated as the Mourne Area of Outstanding Natural Beauty, encapsulating all of the original barony and also the western foothills of the Mournes as far as Warrenpoint, a great swathe of

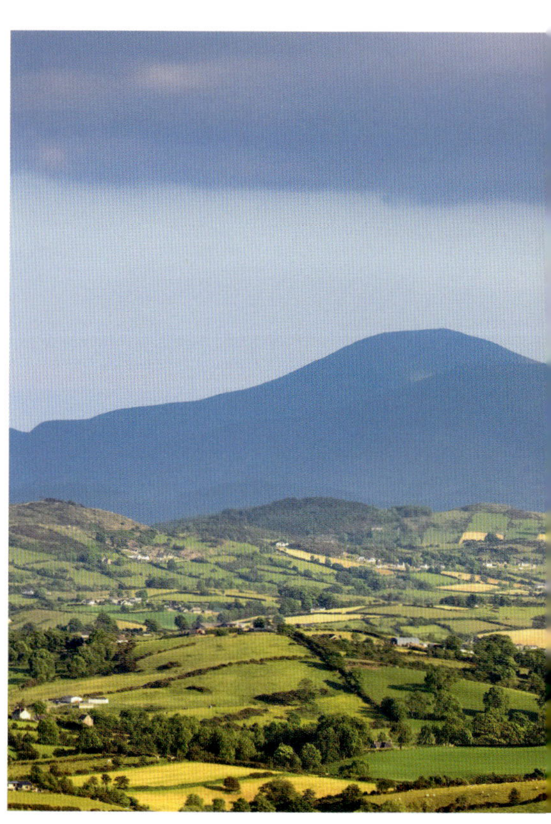

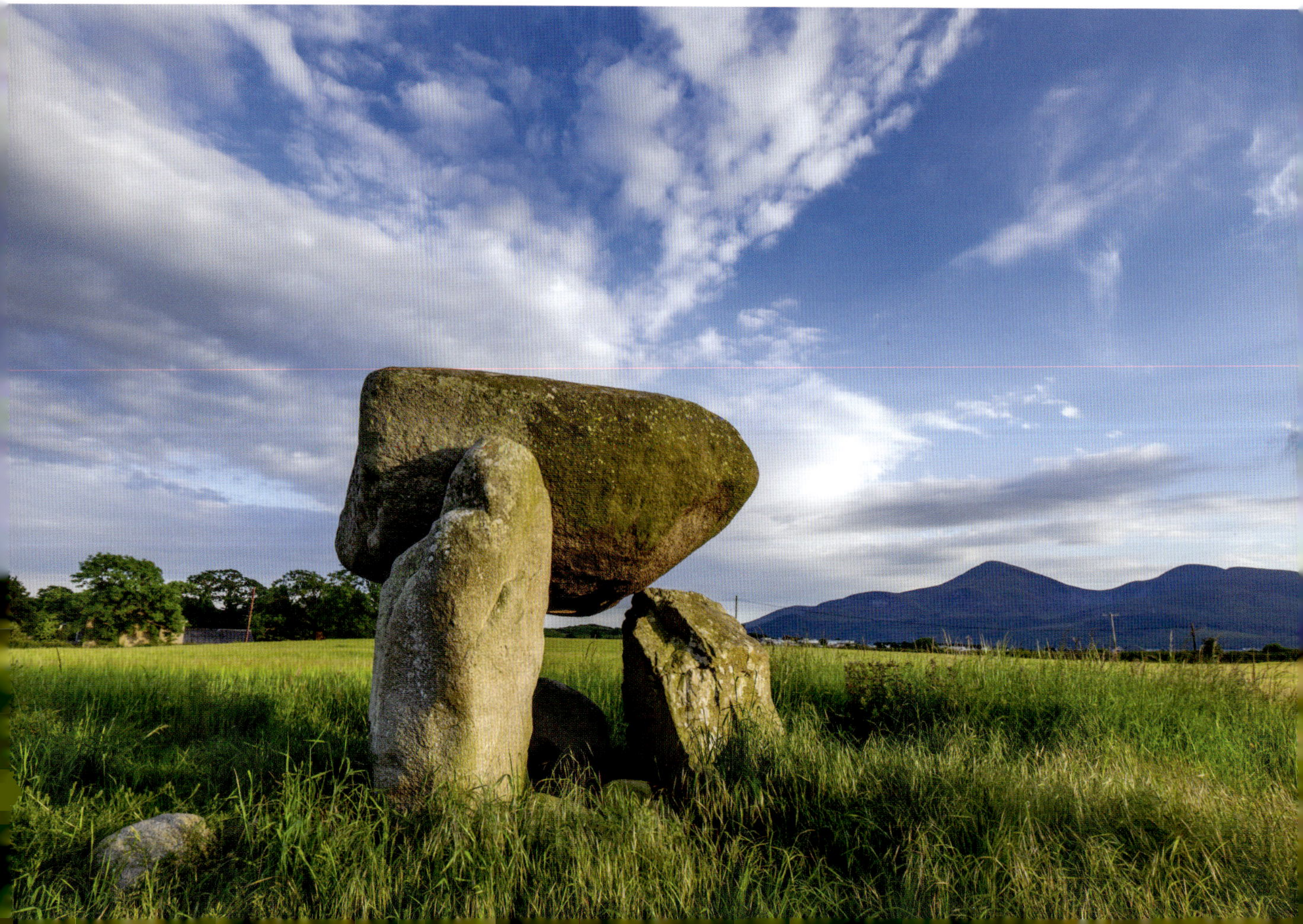

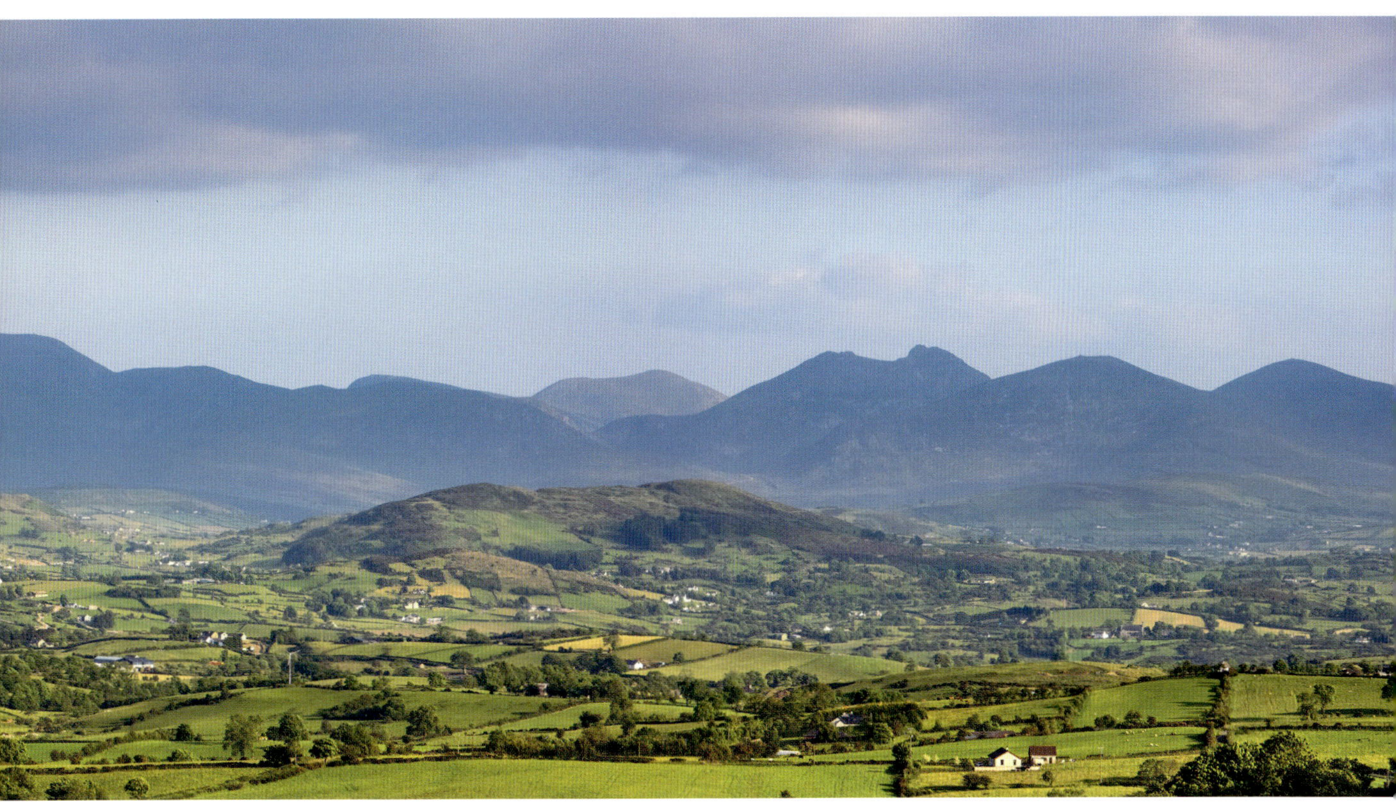

Left: Slidderyford Dolmen, a fine example of a Neolithic burial tomb located just south of Dundrum village.

Above: A panoramic view of the Mournes from Windy Gap, with Slieve Donard prominent on the left of the picture and Slieve Bearnagh the conspicuous mountain with a gap in it on the right. In the foreground are some of the extensive drumlins left behind by retreating ice sheets at the end of the last ice age.

valley, forest and mountain to the north as far as Slieve Croob, and also the coastal area around Newcastle and Dundrum.

This greater area boasts an incredible diversity of beautiful landscapes, from windswept uplands to rich farmland, extensive forestry and woodland, to vast beaches and coastal heath. There are large seaside towns like Newcastle, small villages like Dundrum and busy fishing communities like Kilkeel. Scattered throughout the landscape are many monuments documenting millennia of settlement in the Mourne area, from prehistoric dolmens to Norman castles. And all this with the ever-present backdrop of the High Mournes.

* * * *

I first visited the Mournes as a student with the Queen's University Belfast Mountaineering Club. We stayed in a derelict old farmhouse in the shadow of Slieve Binnian and spent our days climbing on the rough Mourne granite or walking among the high peaks. I remember a long and unpleasant winter's night bivouacked in the shelter of the Mourne Wall. I remember fingers numb and bloodied by the scourges of the climb. I remember fear and exhilaration in equal measure. I remember long, arduous days in the hills with friends, finishing by a pub fire in the evening.

Below: Conor Gilmour climbing 'Electra', a classic Mournes route on the North Tor of Slieve Binnian.

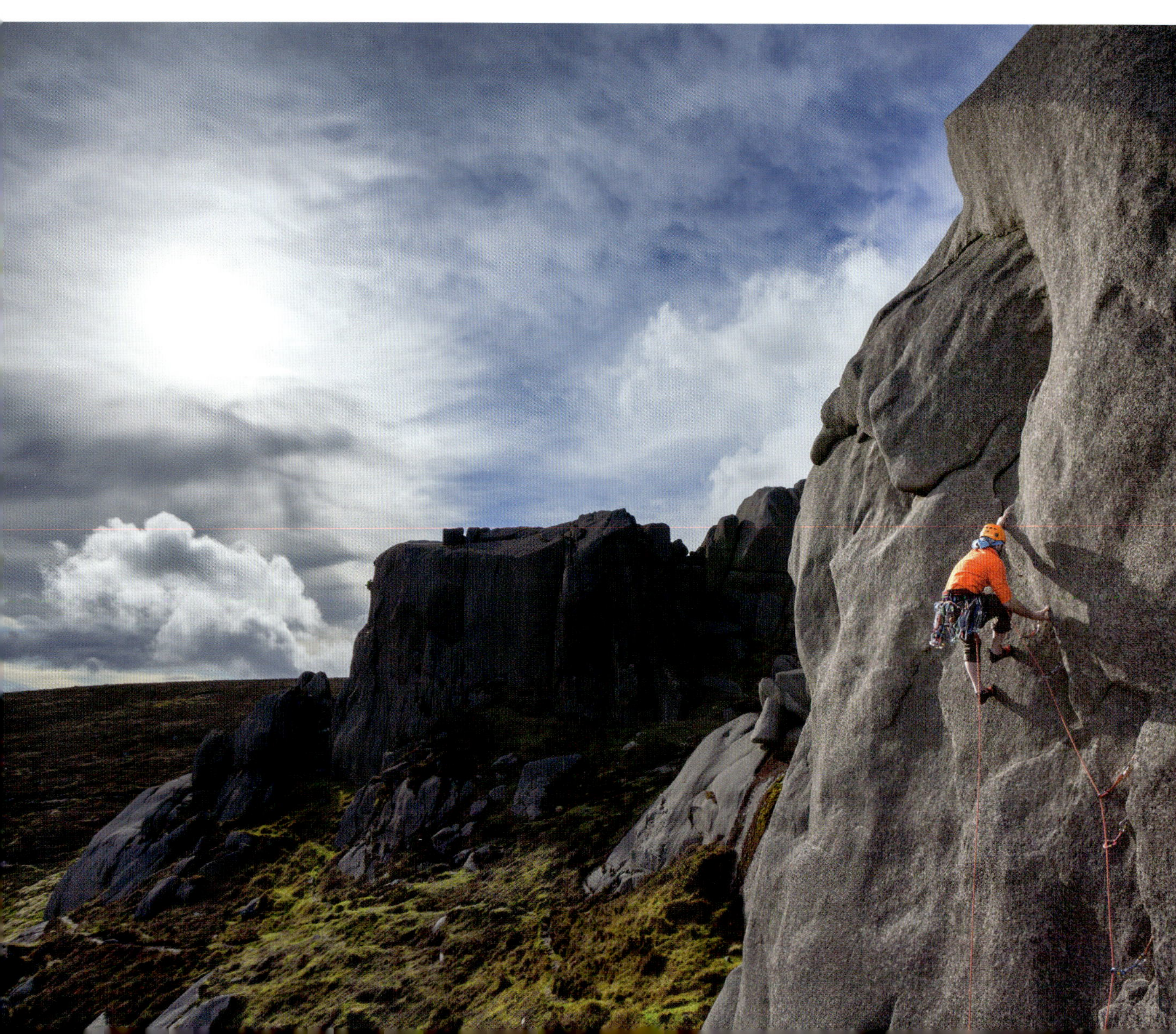

Right: Slieve Binnian rises above the rich farmland of the coastal plains between Annalong and Kilkeel.

Below: The summit tors of Slieve Bearnagh peeping through the 'V' of the Carrick Little Valley.

As much as those memories have persisted, it is the beauty of the Mourne landscape that has drawn me back there again and again. There is a variety and character to the Mournes that is rare. In a small, concentrated area you can find so many different topographies, from austere mountain cliffs to pastoral farmland, from coastal heath and sweeping beaches to rich woodland. History, culture and heritage permeate the fabric of the landscape in something as simple as the Mourne stonewalls, built from the spoil of the mountainsides in a style found nowhere else in Britain or Ireland.

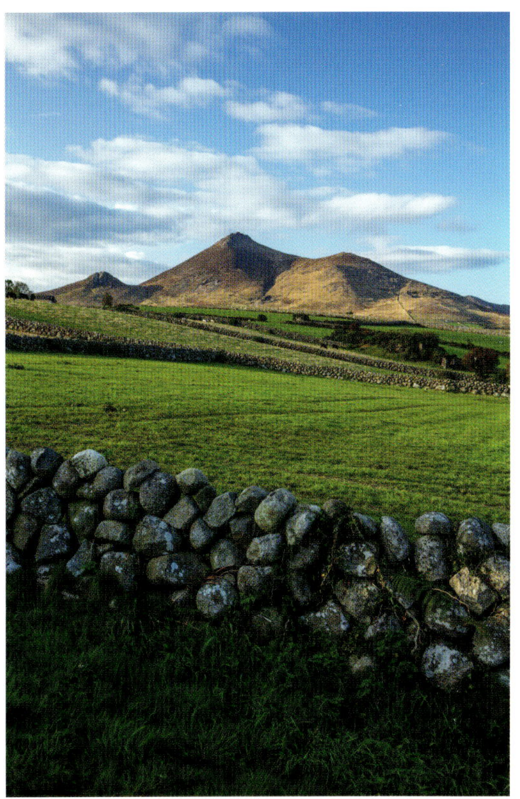

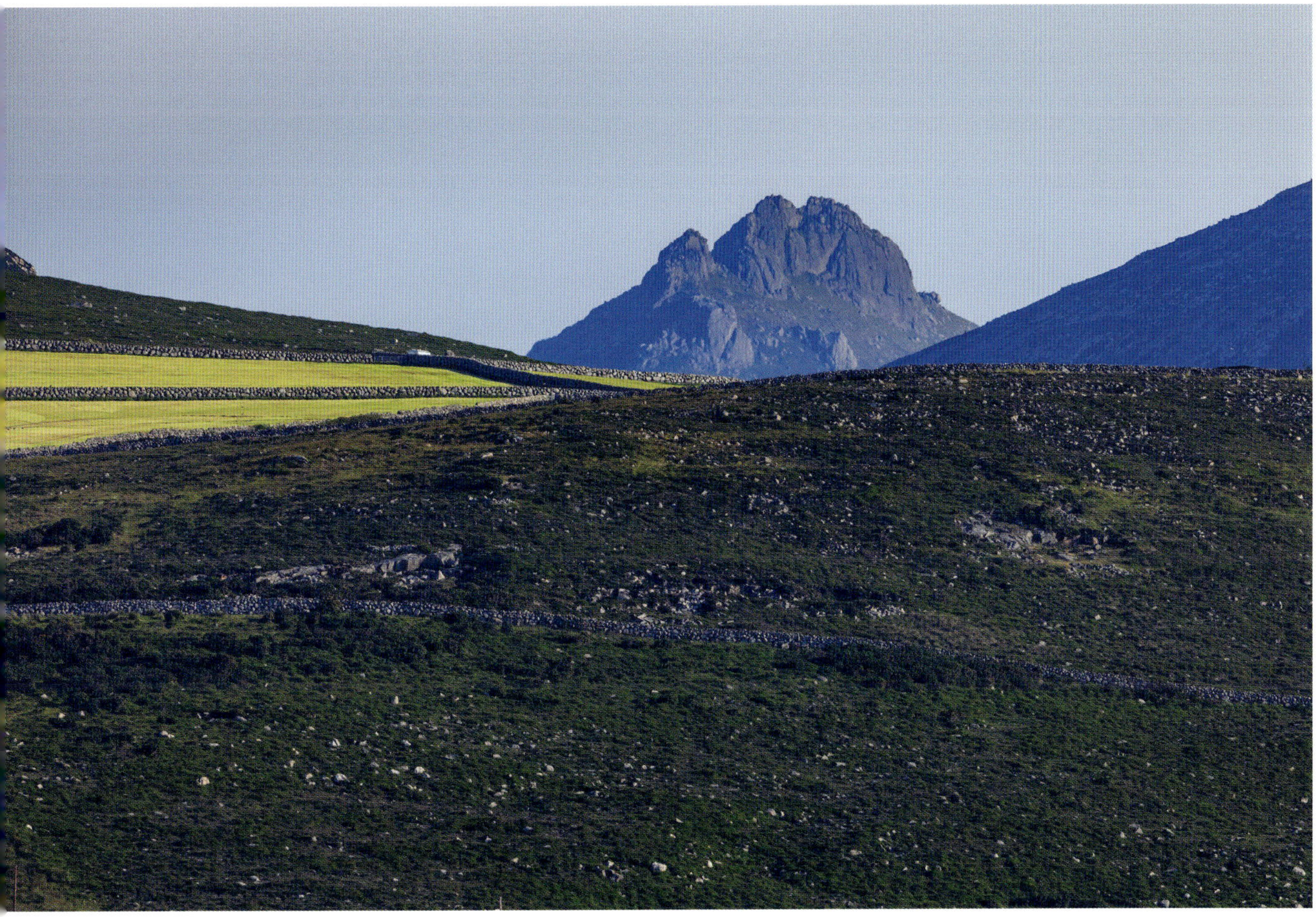

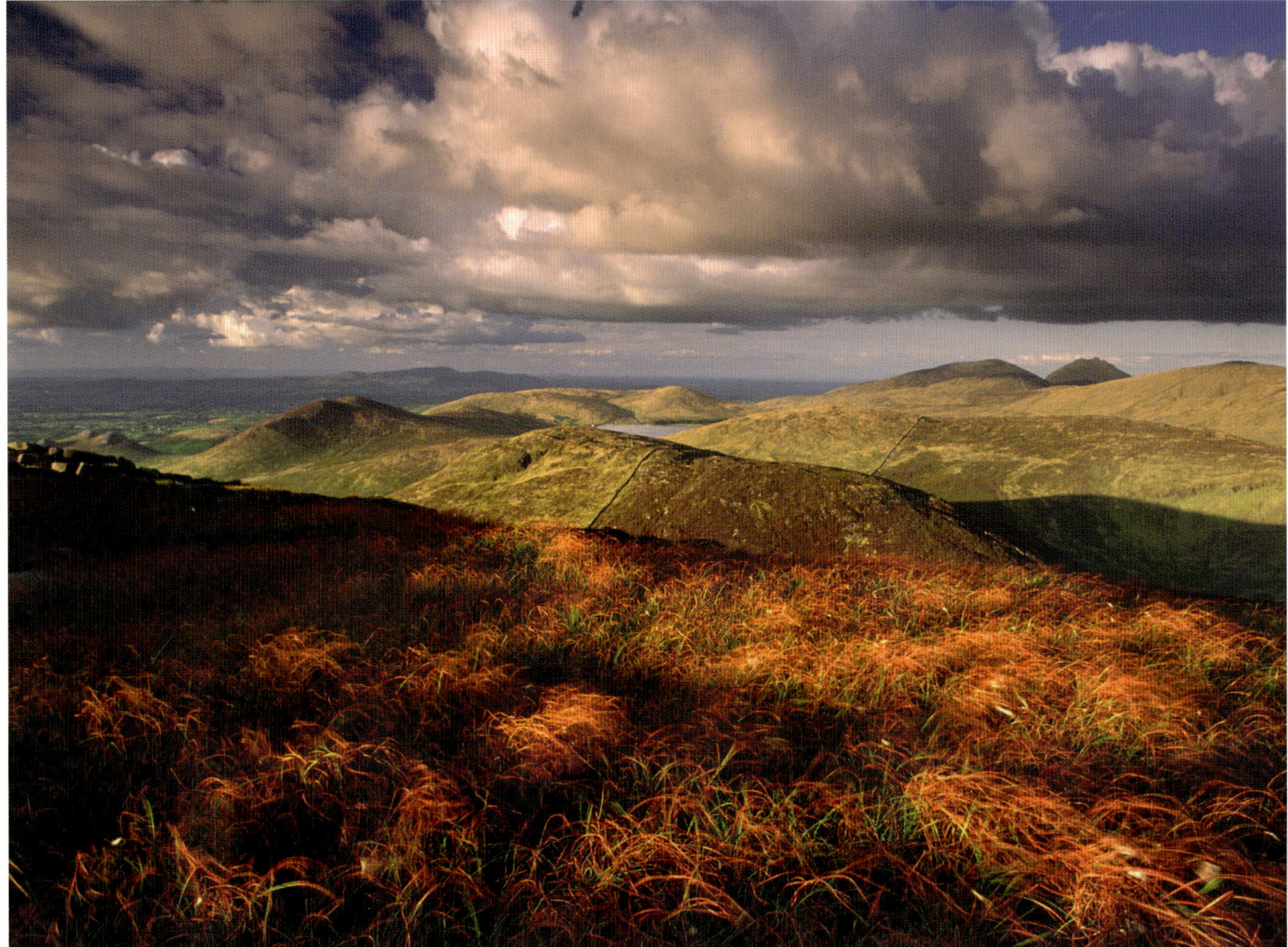

My work on this book has brought me to new and unexpected corners of the Mournes. Of course, I knew the High Mournes very well, but the woods of Tollymore, the dunes of Murlough, the Norman castles and the prehistoric archaeology of the area were all new and rich experiences.

One of the highlights of my research trips was a chill autumn morning photographing the woodland along the banks of the Shimna River in Tollymore. I found my way to the sprawling limbs of an ancient and gnarled oak, right where the river pours over a small rapid. The early sun was rising though the trees, filtering a beautiful golden light across the water. So absorbing was the scene that two hours seemed to pass in the blink of an eye. I hope some of this sense of wonder has found its way onto the pages of this book.

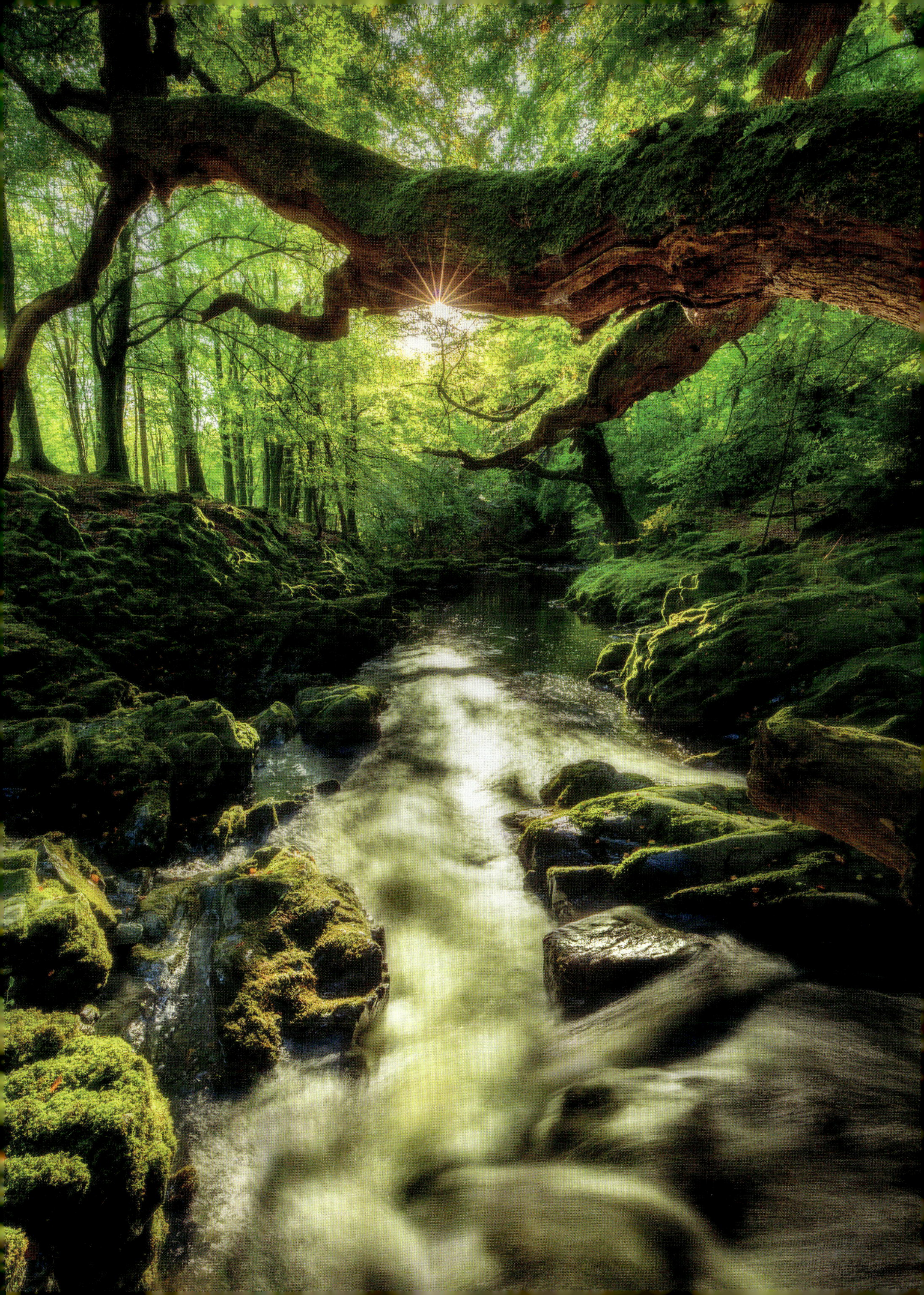

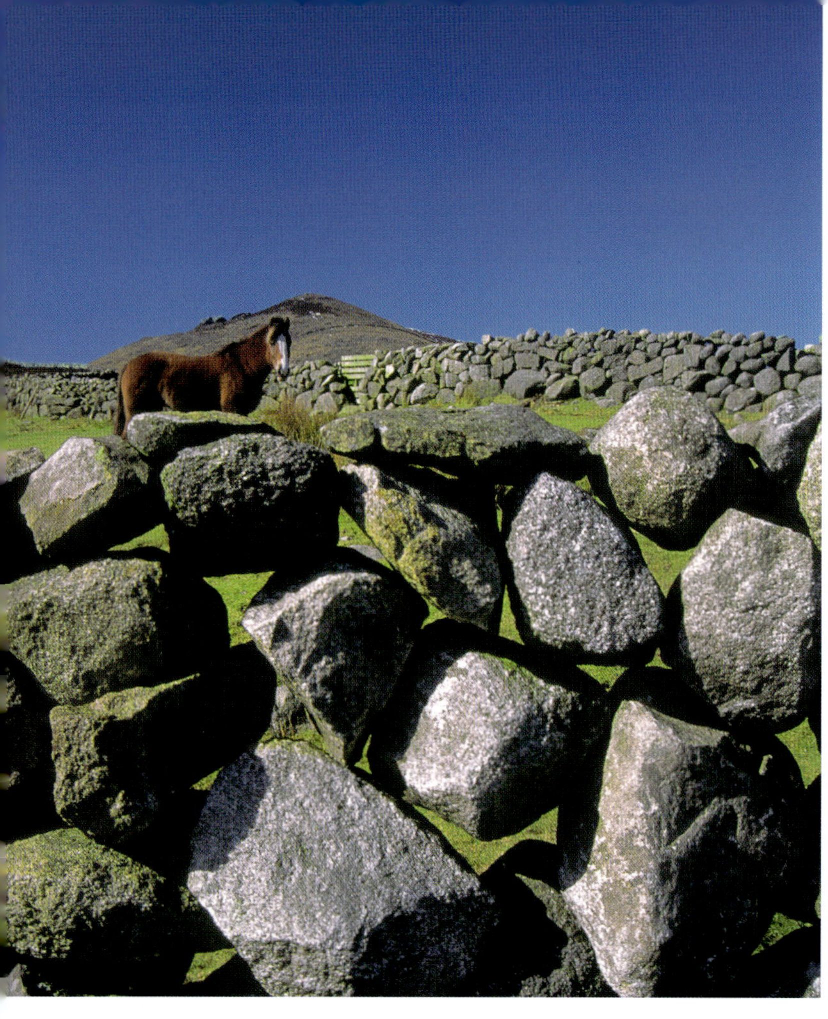

Left: A horse peering over a stone wall near Annalong. Dry-stone walls are a characteristic feature of the Mourne landscape.

Right: A classic view of Slieve Bearnagh and Spellack across the Trassey Valley from the Newcastle to Hilltown road.

Below: Winter's evening panorama looking north across the summit tors of Slieve Binnian. The mountains in the distance are, from right to left, Slieve Donard, Slieve Commedagh, Slieve Bearnagh and the Meelmores.

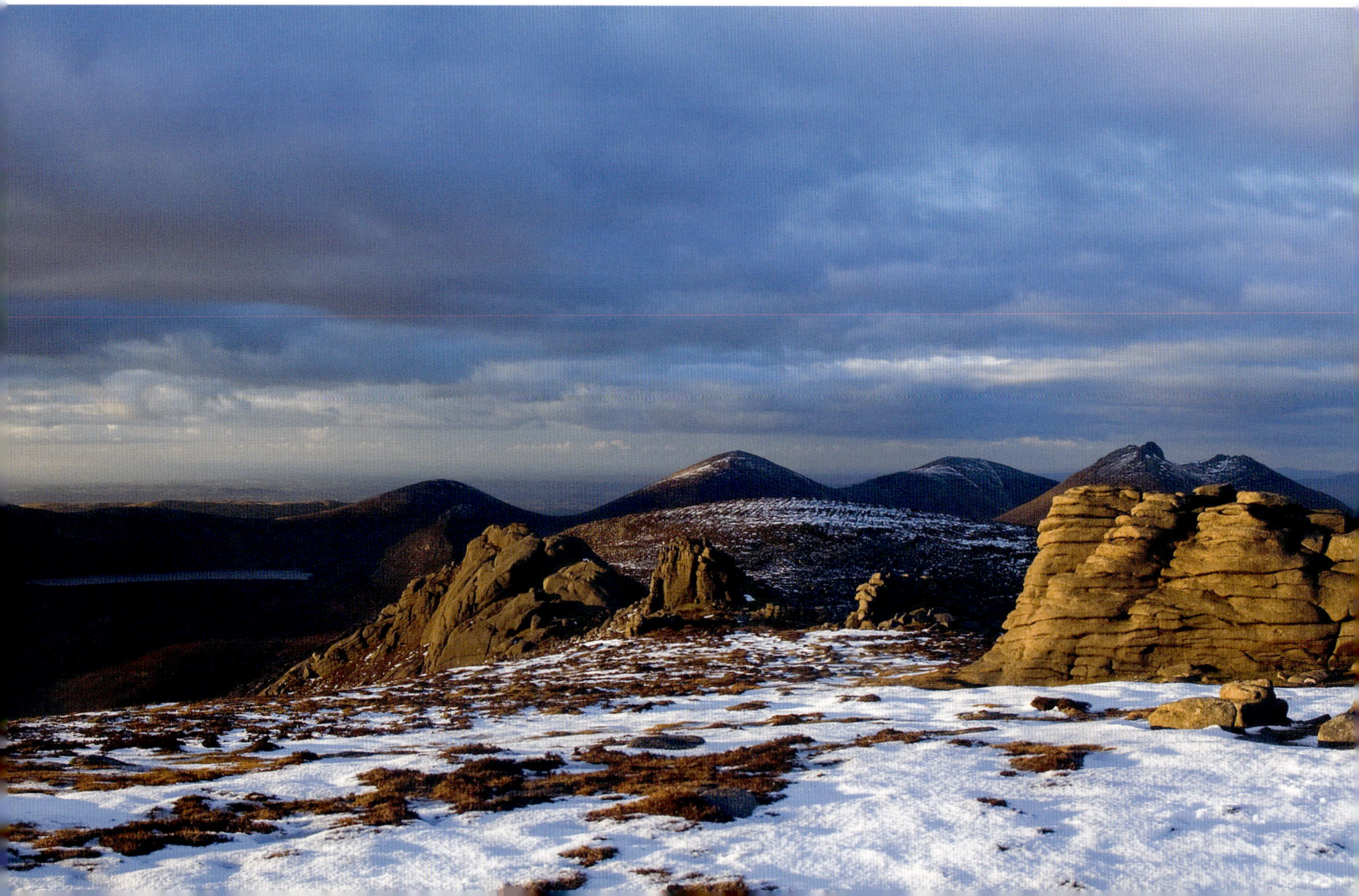

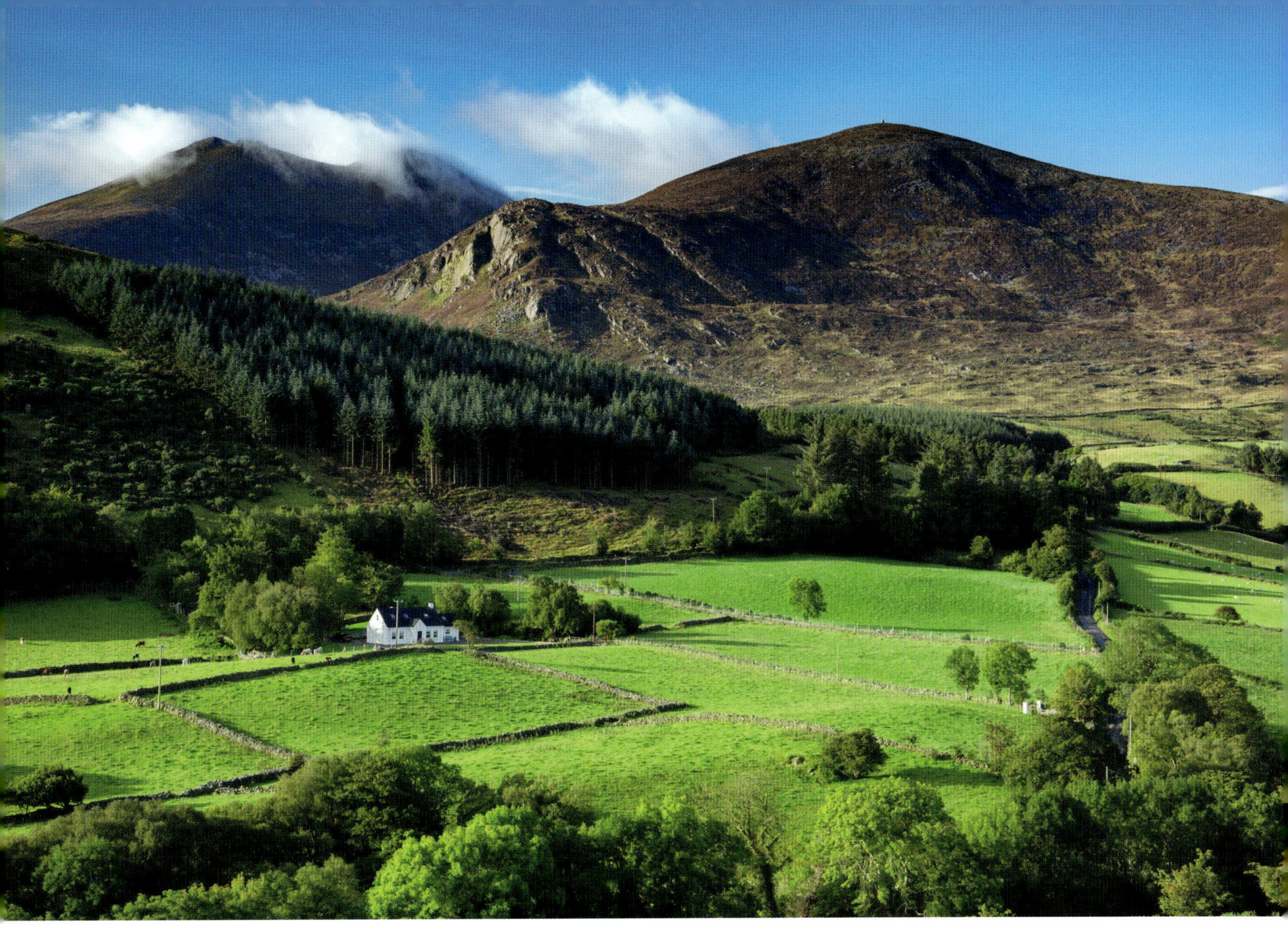

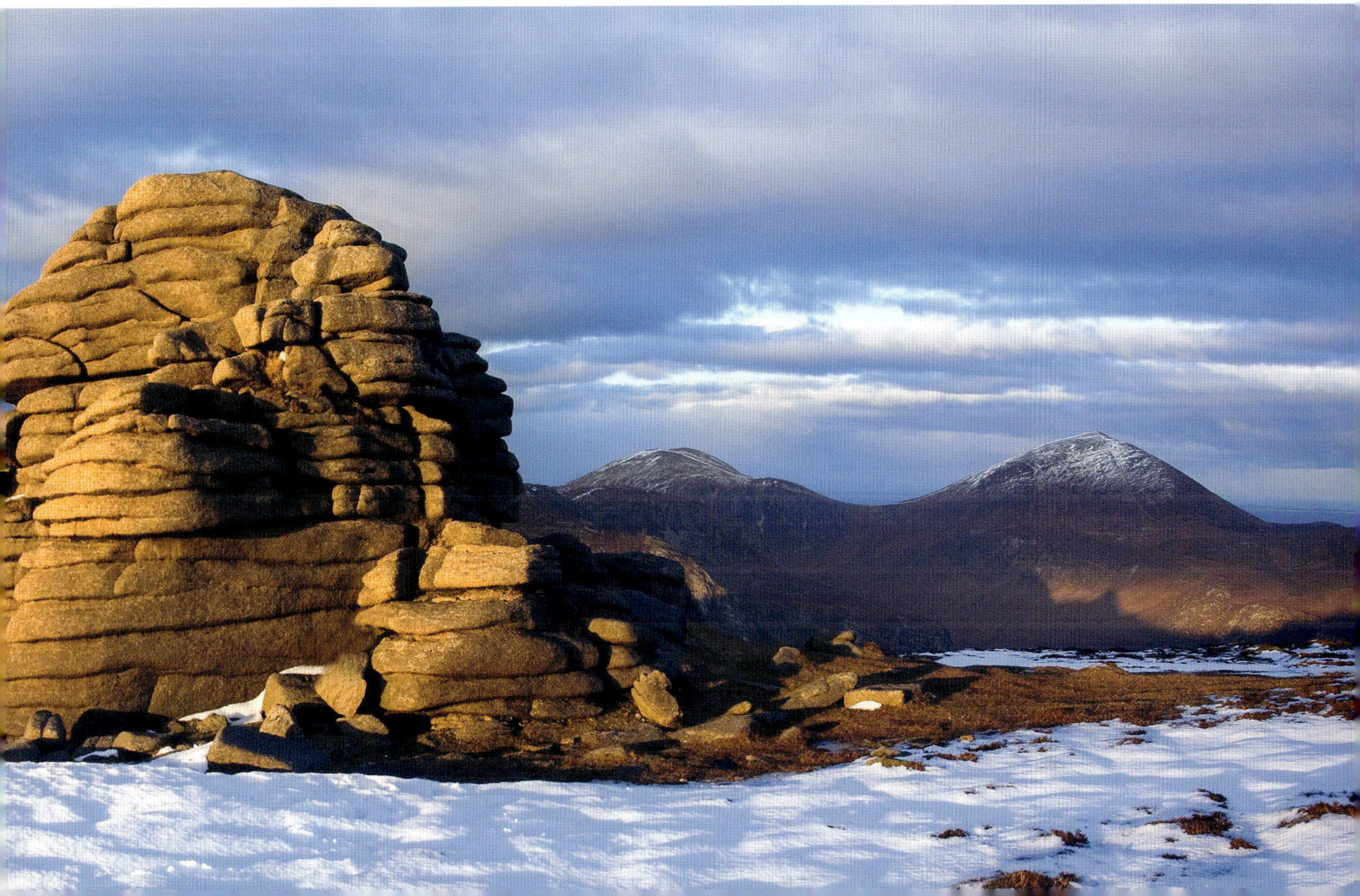

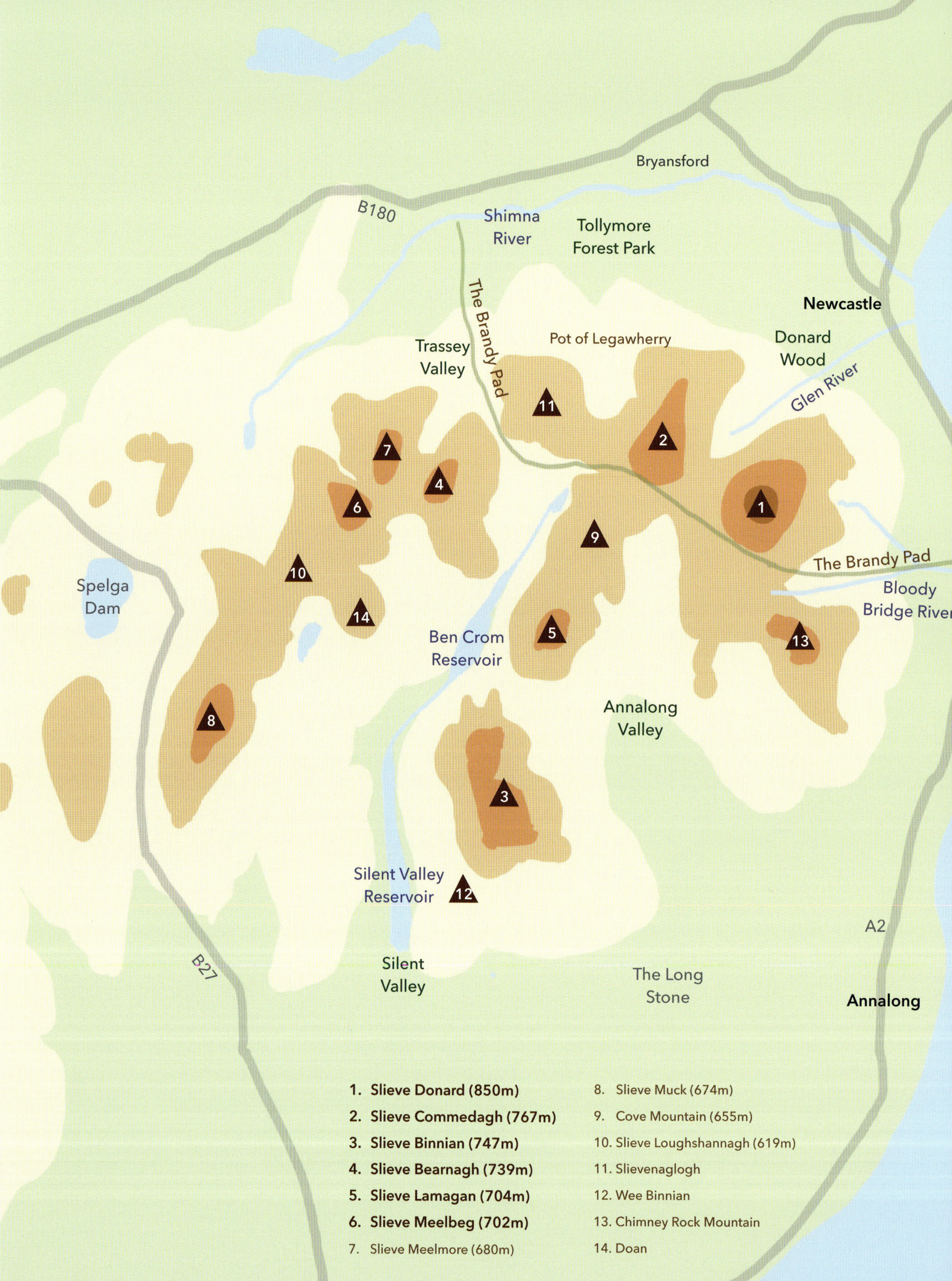

1. **Slieve Donard (850m)**
2. **Slieve Commedagh (767m)**
3. **Slieve Binnian (747m)**
4. **Slieve Bearnagh (739m)**
5. **Slieve Lamagan (704m)**
6. **Slieve Meelbeg (702m)**
7. Slieve Meelmore (680m)

8. Slieve Muck (674m)
9. Cove Mountain (655m)
10. Slieve Loughshannagh (619m)
11. Slievenaglogh
12. Wee Binnian
13. Chimney Rock Mountain
14. Doan

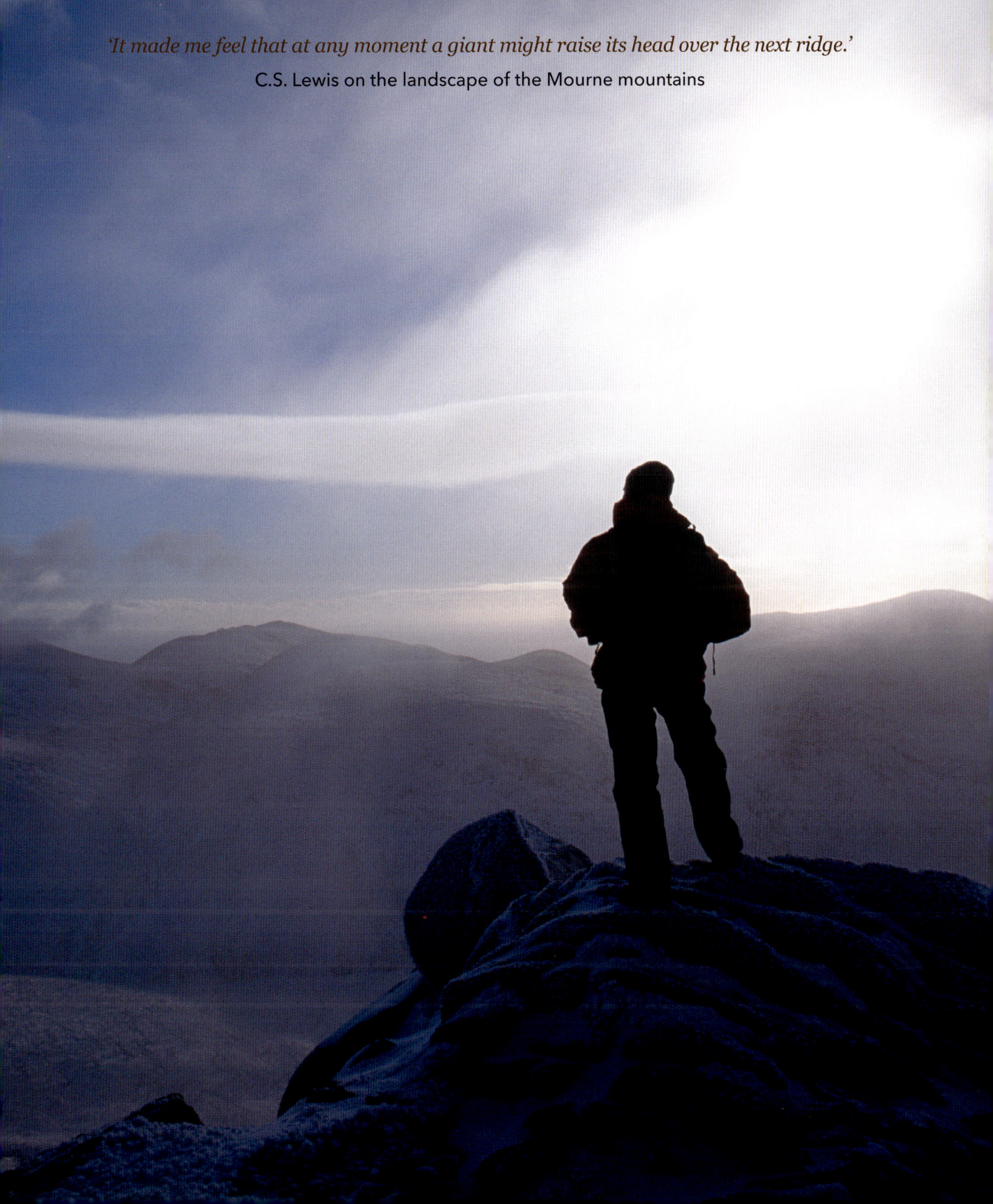

THE HIGH MOURNES

'It made me feel that at any moment a giant might raise its head over the next ridge.'

C.S. Lewis on the landscape of the Mourne mountains

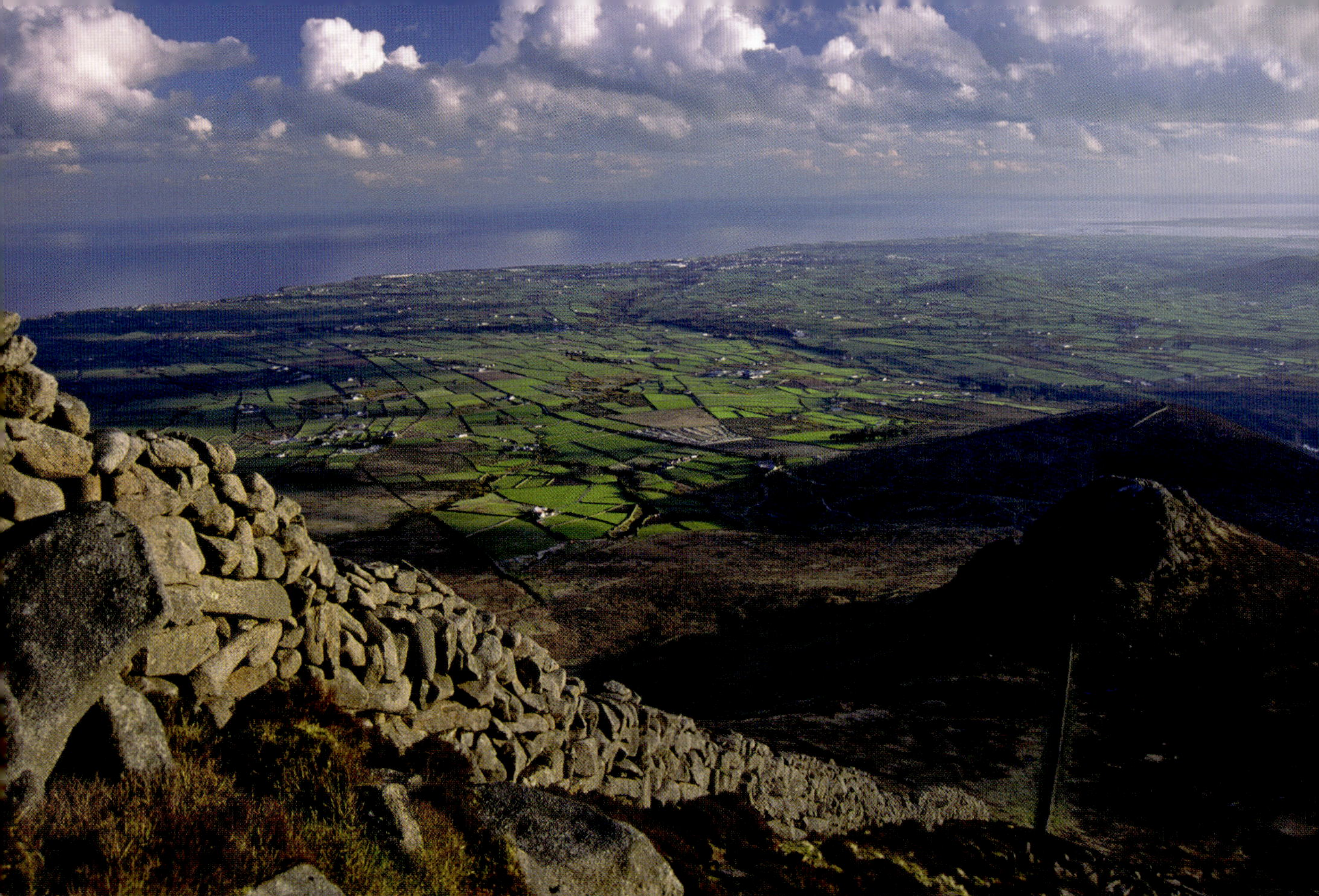

The Mourne mountains are one of the great ranges of Ireland. This compact knot of inspirational summits is crowned by Slieve Donard, at 850m; in all, fourteen summits in excess of 600m and thirty in excess of 500m occupy an area similar to that of Belfast City. They are also one of the most distinctive ranges, with several of the peaks, most notably Slieve Binnian and Slieve Bearnagh, crowned with jagged granite tors, lending the mountains their characteristic skyline when viewed from the wider Mourne area.

They have an evocative mystique enhanced by such foreboding names as The Devil's Coach Road, Bloody Bridge and the Silent Valley. Most of the mountains' names begin with the word Slieve, an anglicisation of 'Sliabh', the Irish word for mountain. Those that don't are often named within a curiously avian theme: Eagle Mountain, Pigeon Rock, Hen Mountain, Cock Mountain and Buzzard's Roost.

The spectacular High Mournes lie to the east of the area and form a broad 'm' of ridges and summits, encircling the Annalong and Silent valleys. The latter was dammed in the early 20th century to create a reservoir, supplying the water needs of Belfast city. The entire catchment is enclosed by the Mourne Wall, up to two metres high and more than thirty kilometres long, running like a miniature Great Wall of China right across the highest ridges and summits of the Mournes.

Previous page: A winter walk on the summit of Slieve Bearnagh.

Left: Looking southwest along the Mourne Wall as it plunges down the slopes of Slieve Binnian towards Wee Binnian, with the patchwork fields of the Mourne coastal plain beyond.

Below: Summit tors on Slieve Binnian.

Being an hour from Belfast and two hours from Dublin, this is, unsurprisingly, a very popular recreational area. The Mournes are served by the best network of paths and tracks of any mountain range in Ireland, affording good access to walkers and explorers of all abilities. The biggest draw is understandably Slieve Donard, which attracts over 90,000 people each year to climb its slopes from the Newcastle side. On a clear day, the panorama from the summit includes a large part of Northern Ireland and extends south beyond Dublin to the Wicklow Mountains and east across the Irish Sea to the Isle of Man and parts of the Scottish coast. Magnificent as this may be, for many this is surpassed by the surreal summit tors of Slieve Binnian and Slieve Bearnagh, formations that look as if they could have been plucked from the desert landscapes of the American Southwest. Despite their popularity,

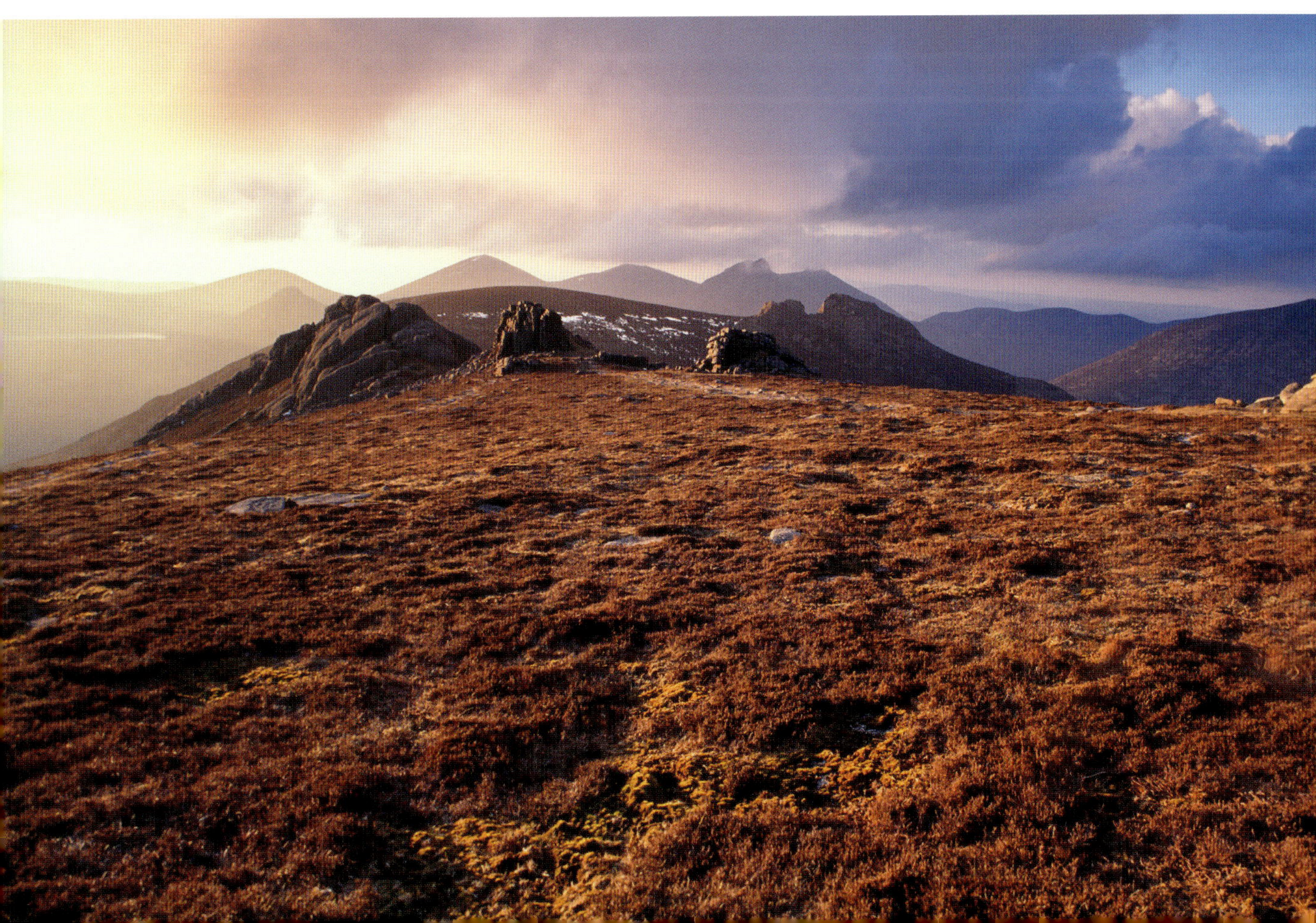

there is still plenty of scope in the Mournes to walk all day and not see another soul.

Mourne granite is superb for rock-climbing, and the many crags and tors host several hundred high-quality rock-climbing routes at all difficulty levels. In 1995, internationally renowned Yorkshire climber John Dunne succeeded on what was for several years regarded as one of the hardest pitches of traditional rock climbing anywhere in the

Below: A low winter sun peeps through the clouds near the summit of Slieve Bearnagh.

Below right: Bog asphodel (*Narthecium ossifragum*).

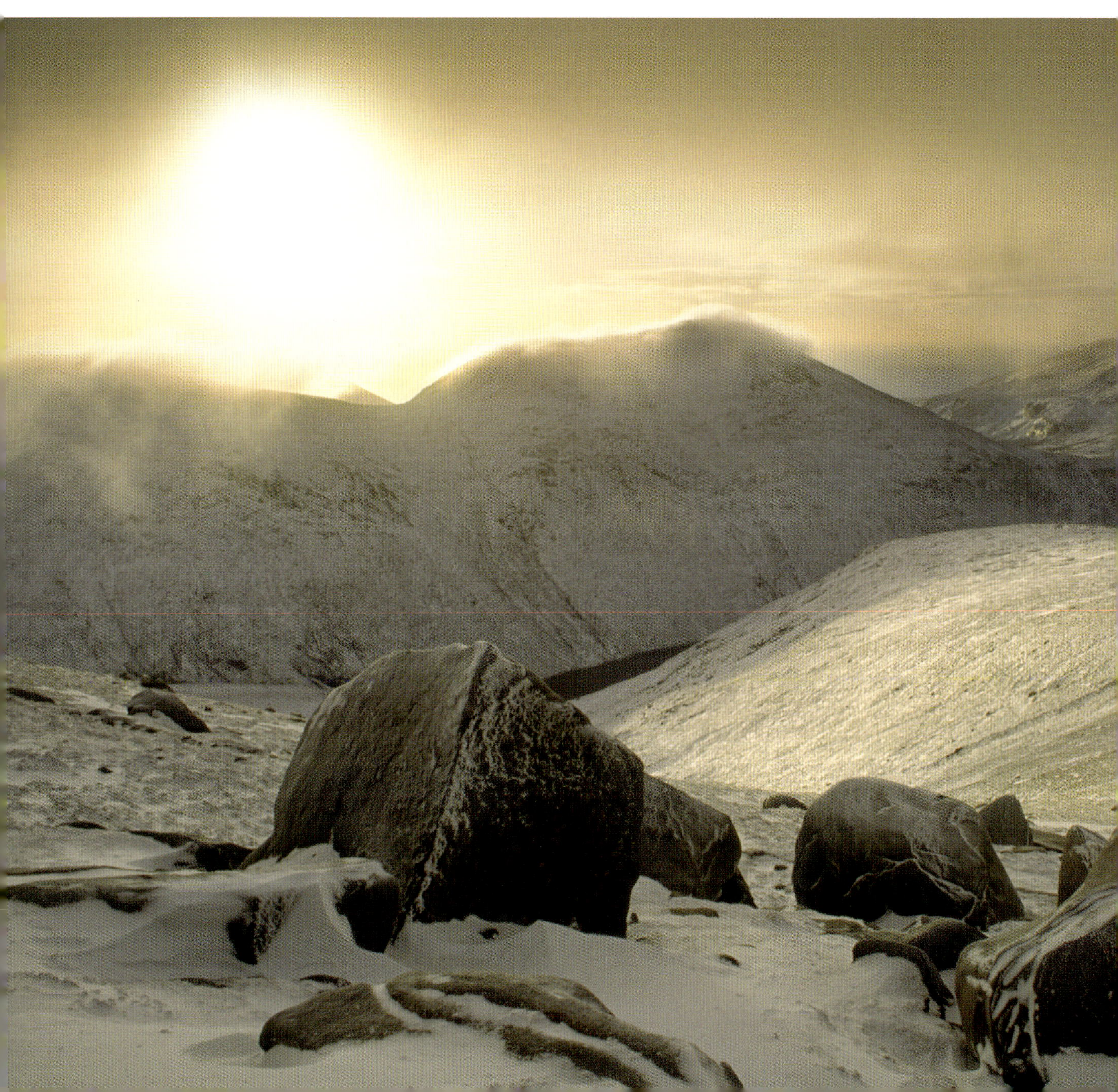

world. Dunne's route – called 'Divided Years' – climbs the audacious overhanging prow of Buzzard's Roost, a brooding crag perched high on the northern slopes of Slieve Binnian. In the years since Dunne's first ascent, it has seen only a handful of others, two of them by local climbers, and has cemented its reputation as one of the hardest and finest climbing routes in Ireland or Britain.

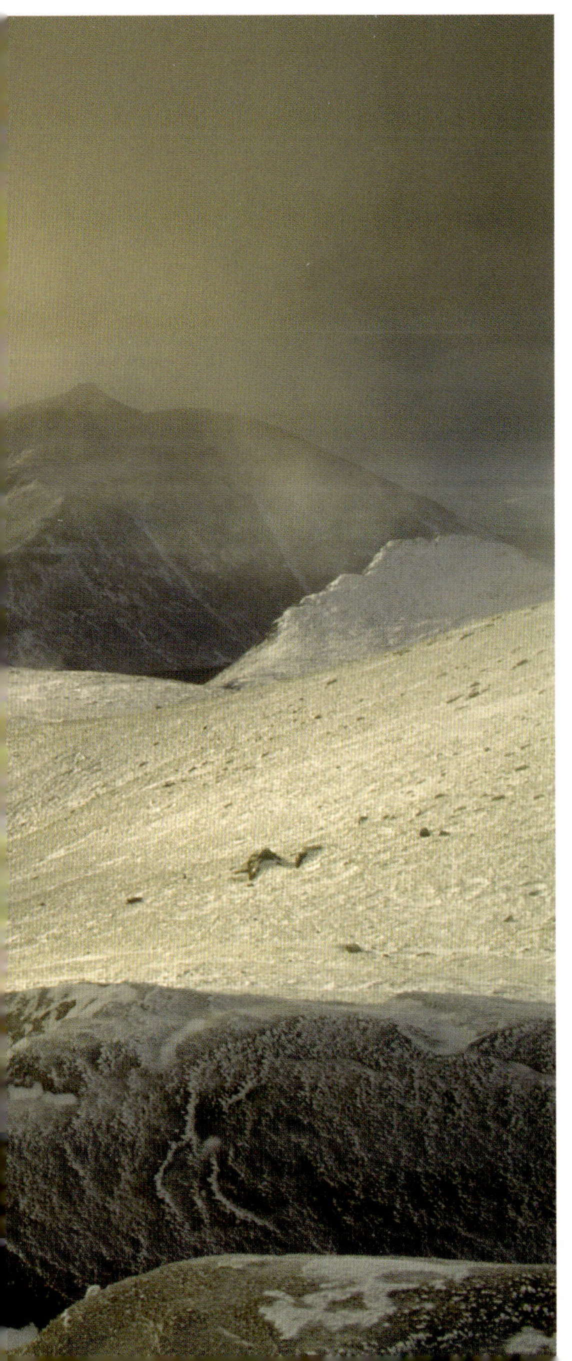

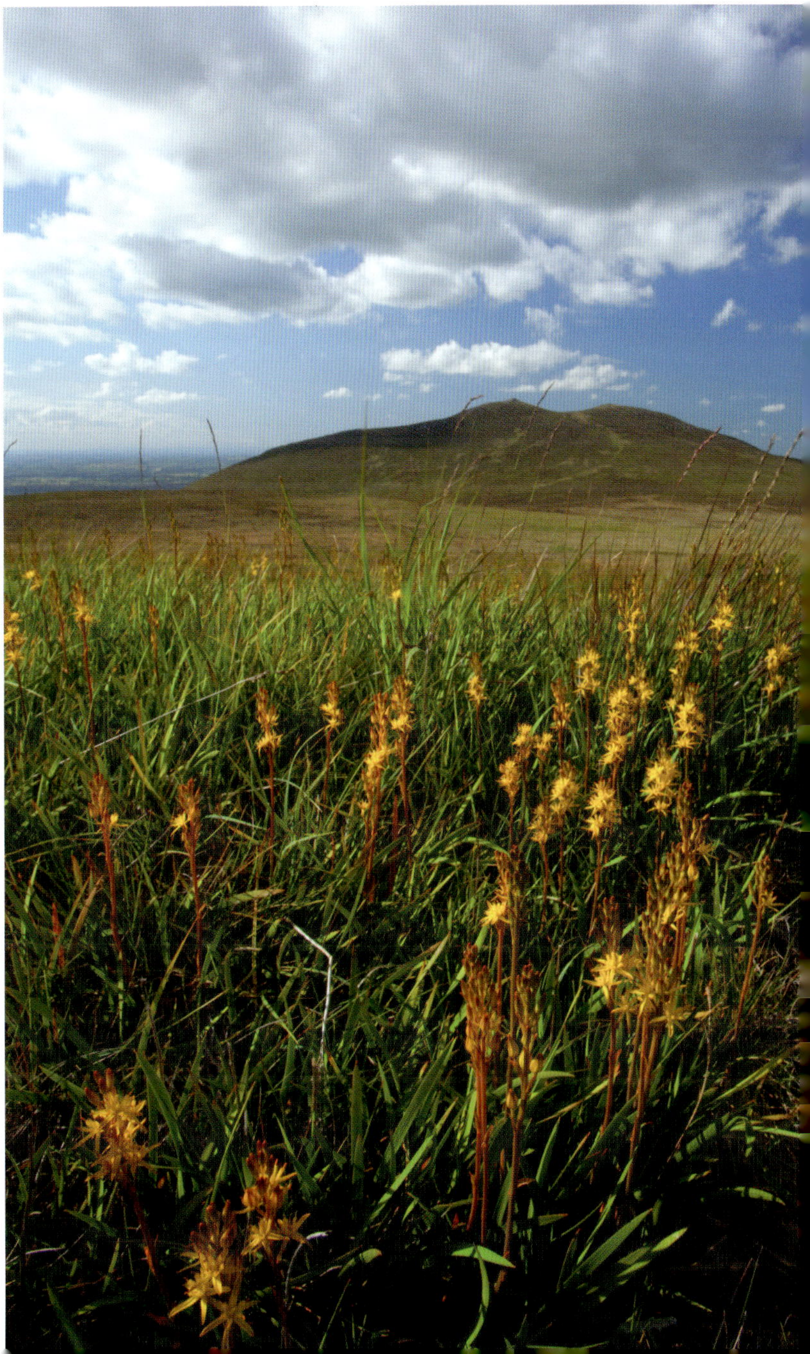

THE GEOLOGY OF THE MOURNES

The Mourne region is dominated by the granite of the High Mournes. However, the underlying geology is actually quite complex. Many of the surrounding lowland areas are composed of Silurian rocks of shale, mudstone and greywacke, which formed more than 400 million years ago from the sediments lying at the bottom of the ancient Iapetus Ocean. Of a similar age are the granites of the outlying hills and mountains such as Slieve Croob, which formed during the closure of the Iapetus Ocean.

The granite of the High Mournes did not form until relatively recently; a mere fifty to sixty million years ago. At this time, what we now know as the Atlantic Ocean was growing as the North American and European continental plates were torn apart. The intense volcanic activity associated with this upheaval was responsible for many iconic landscapes in Northern Ireland including the Giant's Causeway and the rocks of Fair Head in north Antrim. In the Mournes, this new granite formed from molten magma that rose up into a cavity left under a thin 'roof' of Silurian rocks as a huge block of shale subsided. Over the last two million years, successive ice ages stripped away the covering of softer Silurian rocks to reveal the granite of the High Mournes.

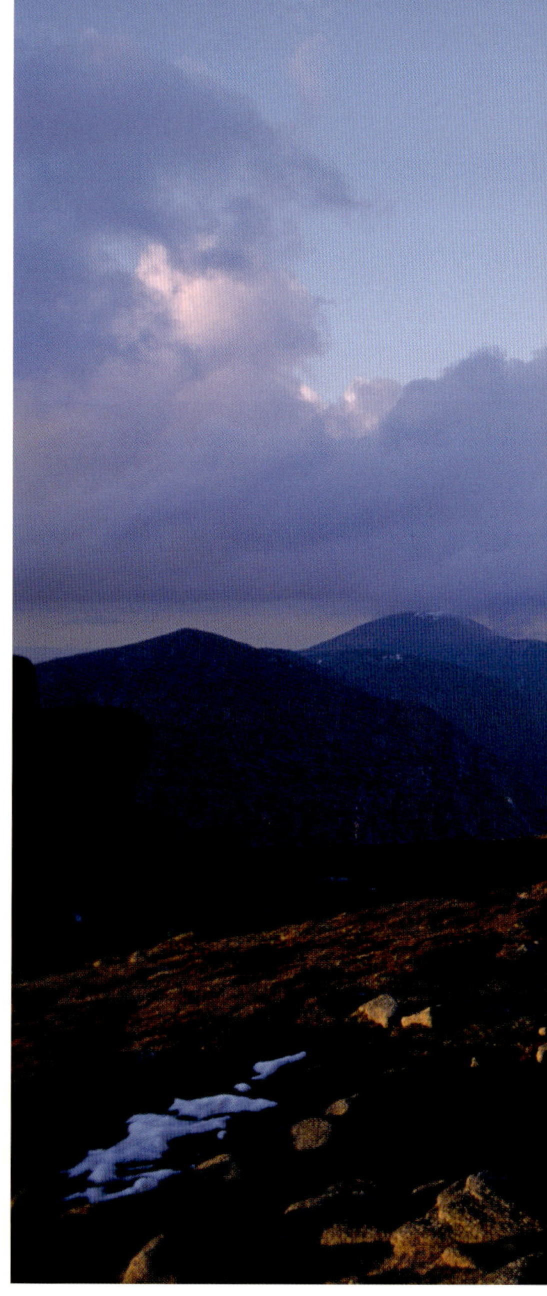

Above: This granite tor on the summit of Slieve Binnian shows the horizontal bedding typical of Mourne granite. It is still unclear exactly how the tors formed, but it is widely believed that they were caused by differential weathering over many thousands of years.

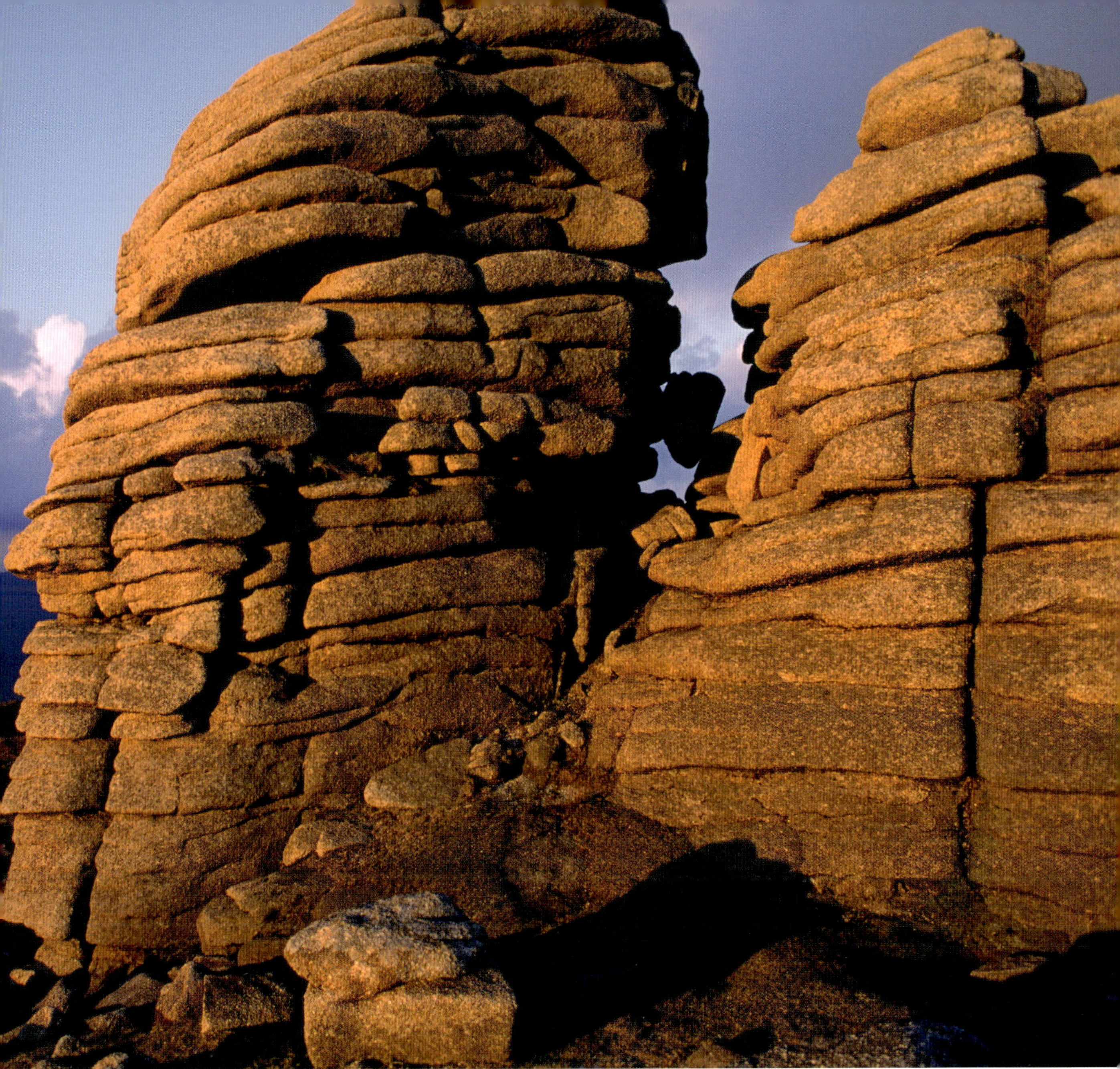

The landforms we see today are largely the result of such erosion – the characteristic profiles of the mountains including the tors of Slieve Binnian and Slieve Bearnagh, the U-shaped Trassey and Silent valleys and the ice-carved fjord of Carlingford Lough.

Even the surrounding lowlands are littered with glacial debris, especially south of the Mournes around Annalong and Kilkeel, where generations of local farmers have assembled through back-breaking labour countless millions of granite boulders into a network of characteristic stone walls.

SMUGGLING IN THE MOURNES

During the 18th and 19th centuries, the Mourne coastline was heavily used by smugglers bringing in tobacco, wine, spirits, leather, silk and spices. Using light and manoeuvrable schooner-rigged craft called 'wherries', they landed on isolated beaches and small bays, then off-loaded their illicit cargoes onto pack animals before transporting them inland via remote paths and tracks. Perhaps the most famous of these old smugglers' routes is the Brandy Pad, connecting the coast around Bloody Bridge via the heart of the Mournes with the Trassey Valley and the rural lowlands of County Down. In 1835, almost half of the houses in the nearby village of Hilltown were public houses.

Right: The Brandy Pad beneath Slieve Bearnagh.

Below: Walkers near the summit of Slievenaglogh with the Ben Crom Reservoir and Slieve Bearnagh prominent in the distance.

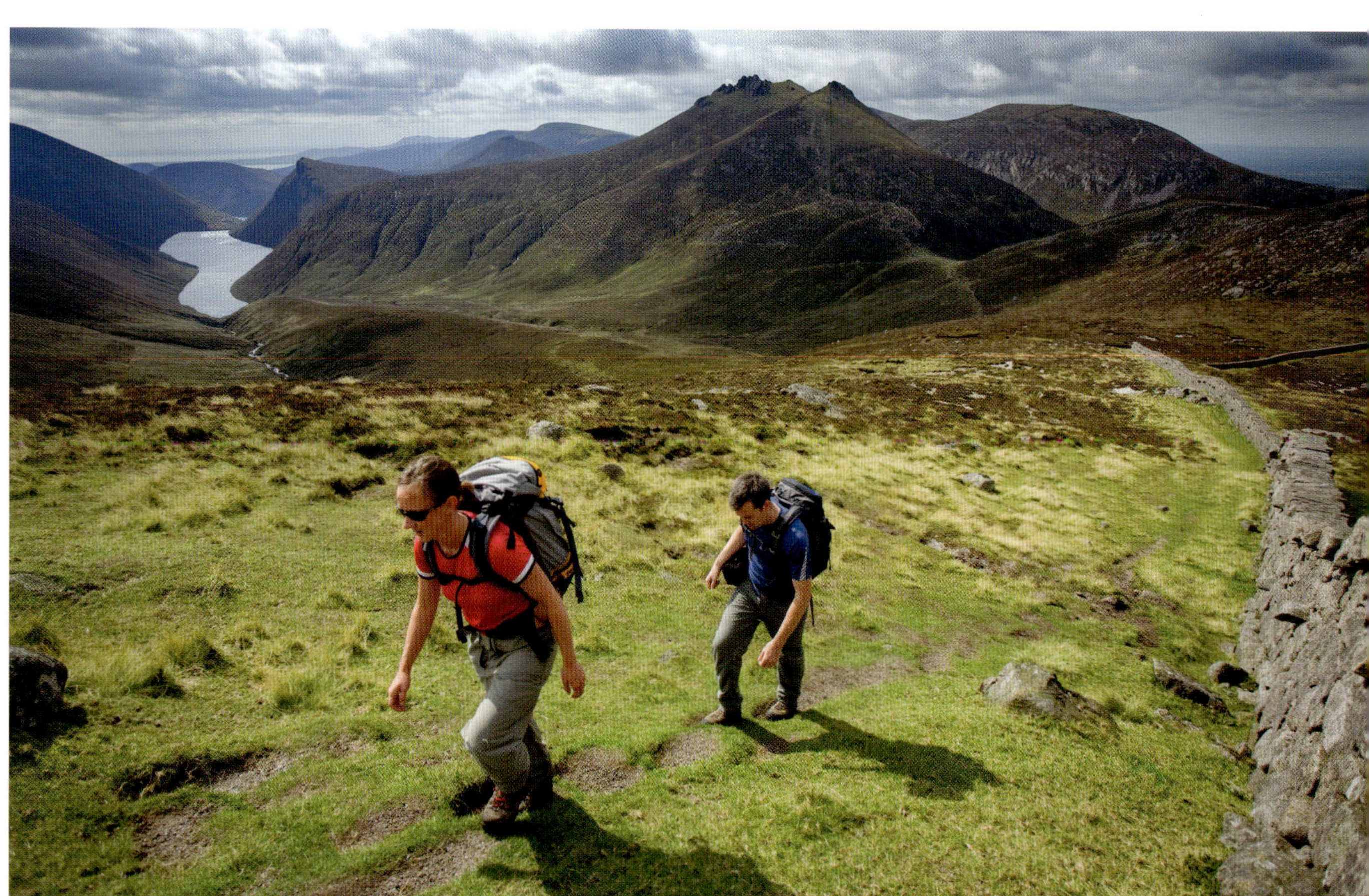

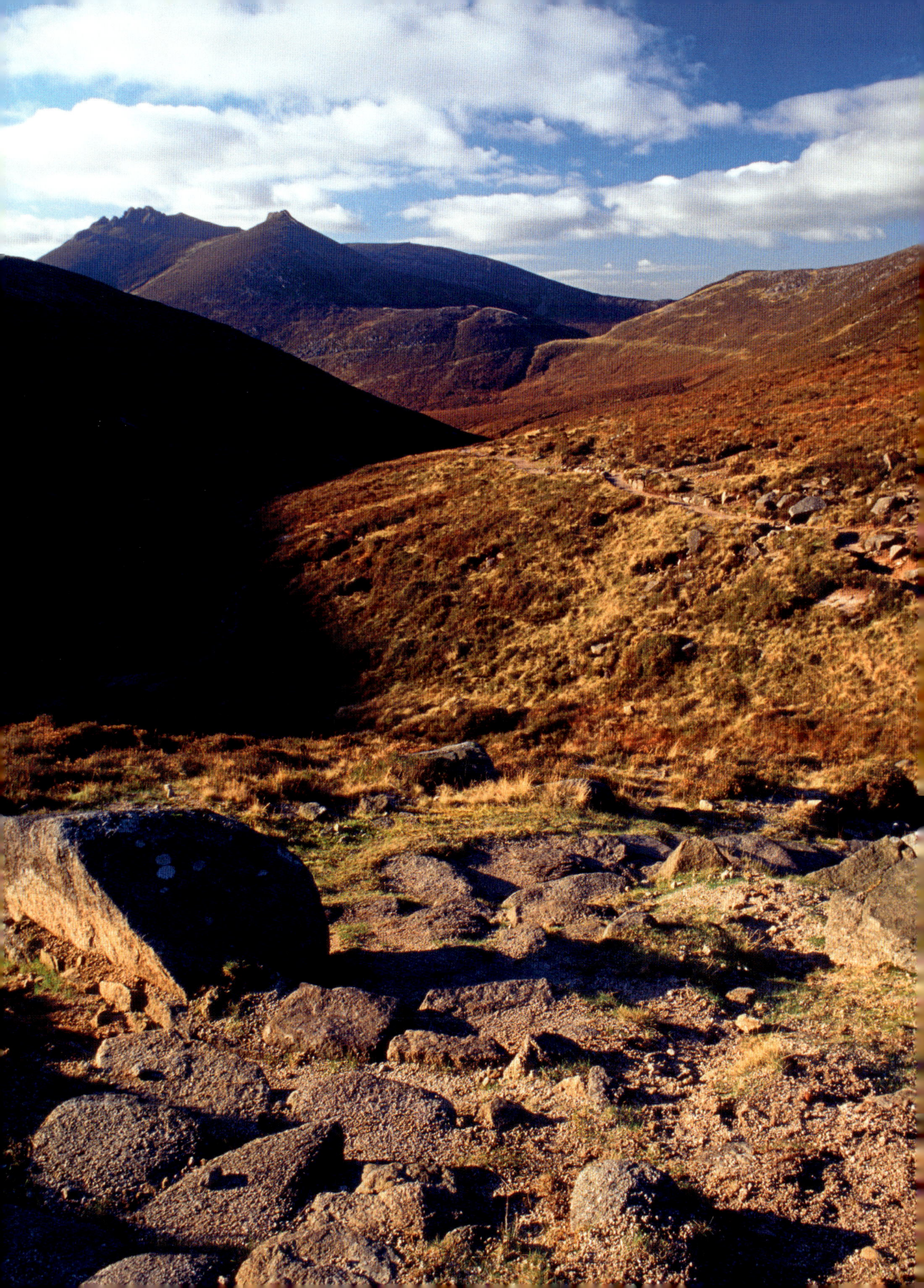

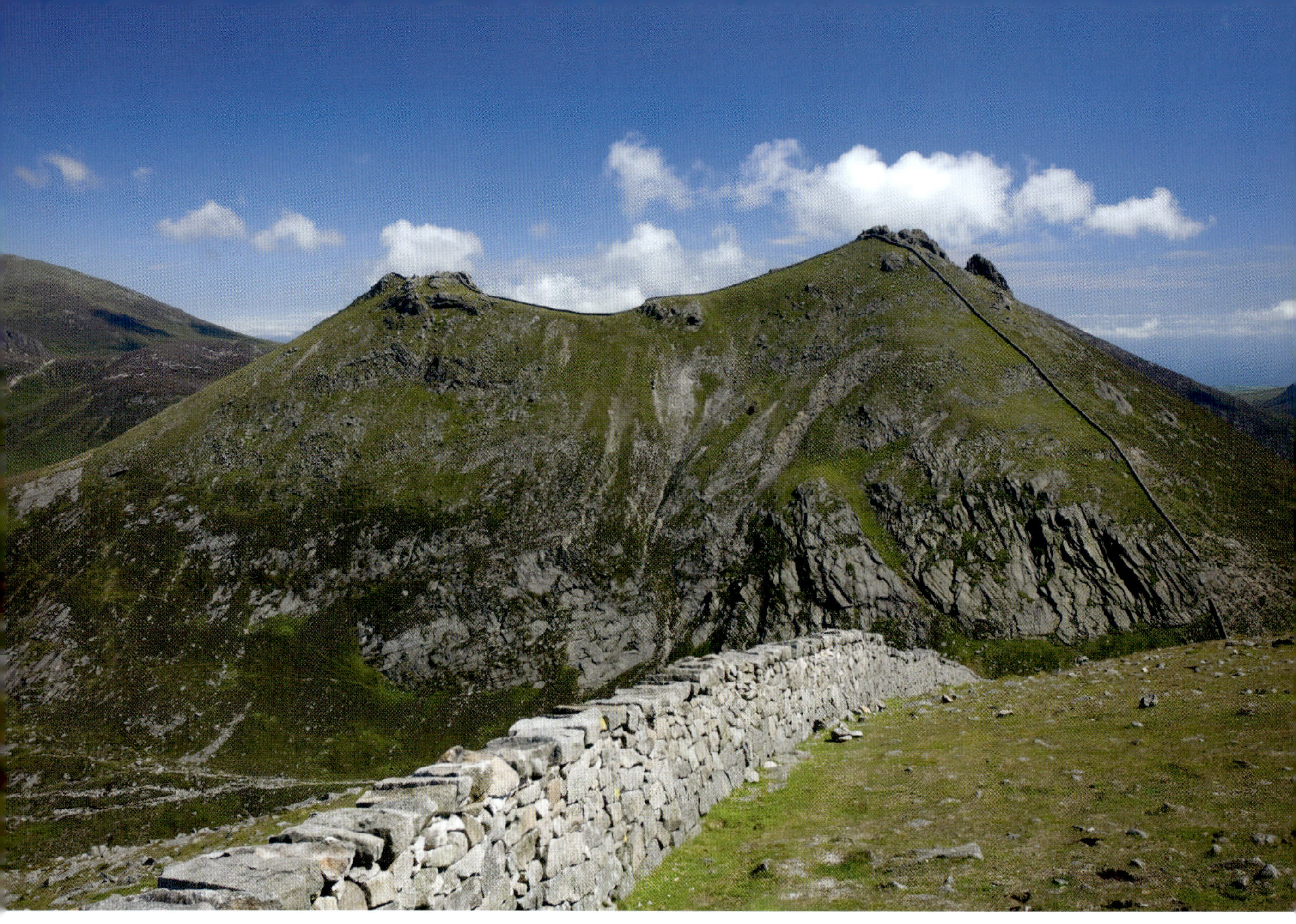

THE MOURNE WALL

Built between 1904 and 1922 by the Belfast City and District Water Commissioners, the Mourne Wall was designed to keep cattle and sheep out of the 9,000-acre catchment area of the Silent Valley Reservoir. Constructed entirely by hand, the wall is more than thirty kilometres long and on average almost two metres in height. It was built entirely from dressed granite blocks, and thousands of local men were involved in its building. It took eighteen years to complete, with work taking place only between April and October. In some of the higher and more remote areas, workers camped on the sides of the mountains for days at a time. Three stone towers were built into

Above: Looking southeast along the Mourne Wall from the shoulder of Slieve Meelmore towards Slieve Bearnagh.

Above right: The Mourne Wall is not the only wall of significance in the Mournes. This is Batts Wall on the summit of Eagle Mountain. The dry-stone wall is more than 8km long and was built decades before the Mourne Wall. It encloses the Leitrim Estate and was a famine relief project funded by the wealthy landowner Narcissus Batt, who at that time used the Leitrim Estate as a hunting lodge.

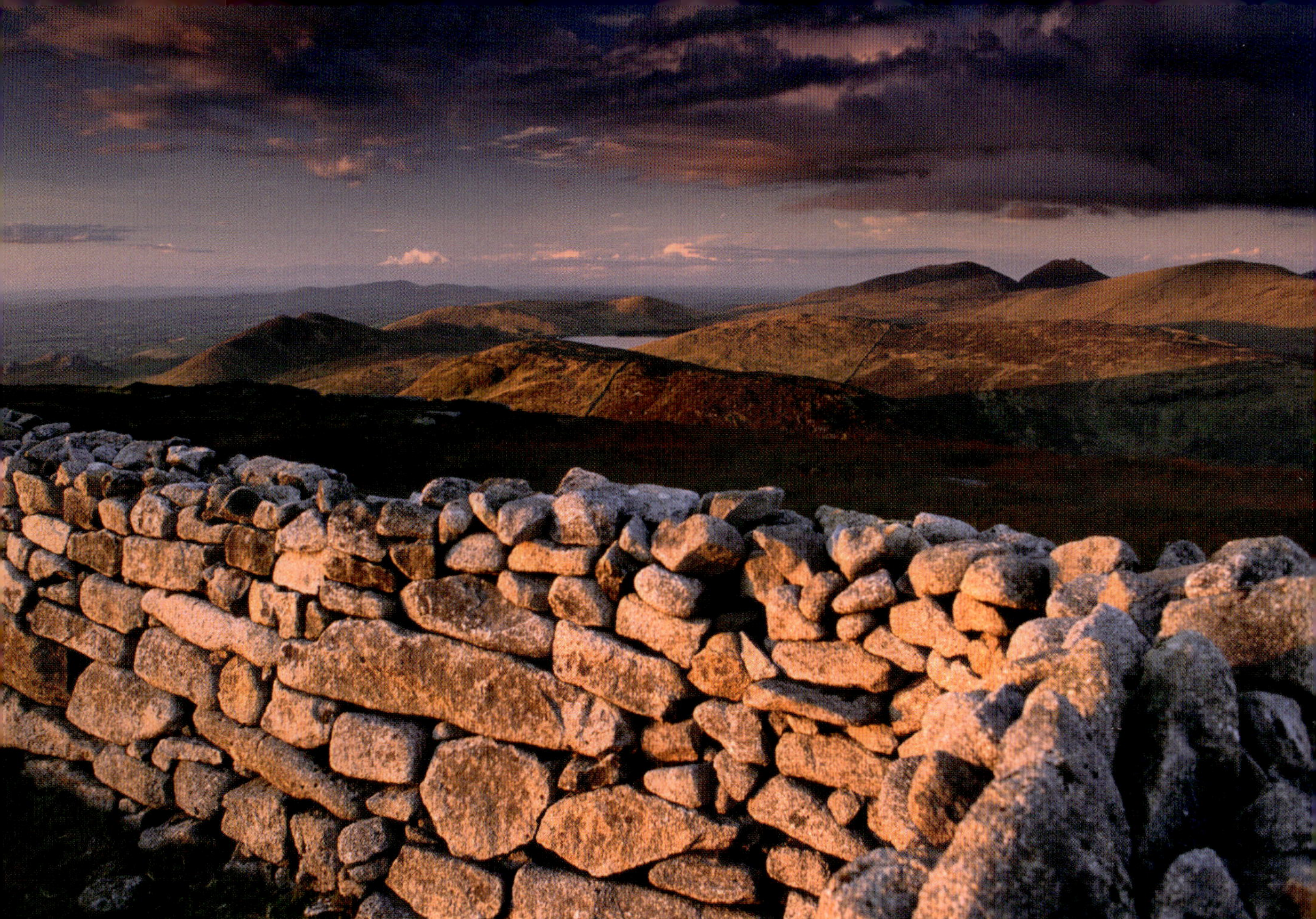

the wall on the summits of Slieve Donard, Slieve Commedagh and Slieve Meelmore to provide shelter for the workers on these especially exposed sections.

For generations of visitors, the Mourne Wall has acted variously as shelter from the wind and weather and a navigational guide in poor visibility. If the construction of the wall was a feat of will and endurance, it is in some small way still celebrated today by the walkers who follow its whole course in a single day, crossing no less than thirteen summits along the way. It is one of the great tests of stamina in Irish hill-walking.

Maintaining the wall into the future is an ongoing challenge. Severe weather, lightning strikes, subsidence, livestock and even people crossing and walking on top of the wall (which is strongly discouraged) have taken their toll over the decades. In 2017 and 2018, £1.6 million was spent on a major project to restore degraded sections of the wall using helicopters to ferry in loads of stone, but still using traditional stonemason skills to arrange and assemble the repaired sections.

THE SILENT VALLEY RESERVOIR

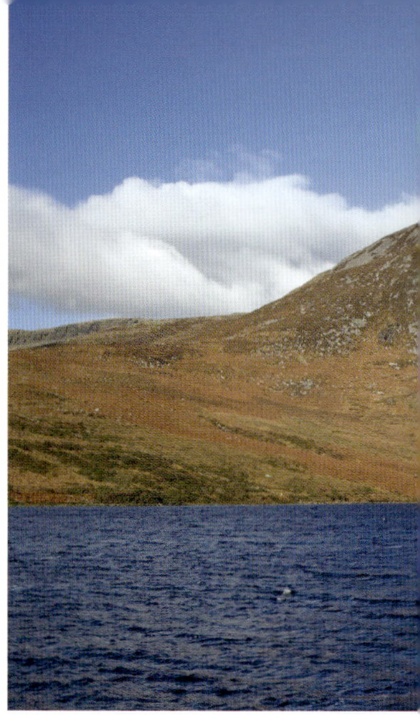

The modern topography of the High Mournes is dominated by the Silent Valley and Ben Crom reservoirs. They originated from the passing of the Belfast Water Act in 1893 in response to the rapidly increasing population of Belfast and the need to secure a reliable water supply; the Mourne mountains, with their high levels of rainfall and lack of human or agricultural settlement in the upland areas, were an obvious resource.

The building of the Silent Valley Reservoir, flooding the area previously known as Happy Valley, was the first stage in this project, but work did not begin until 1923. It still remains one of the greatest feats of civil engineering in Ireland. More than two thousand men worked on the ten-year build, many living in a temporary village known as Watertown, which had its own hospital, police station, shops, canteen, and even a cinema. There was a coal-fired power plant on-site, and as a result Watertown had the first electric street lighting in Ireland.

Before work could even begin on the dam itself, a

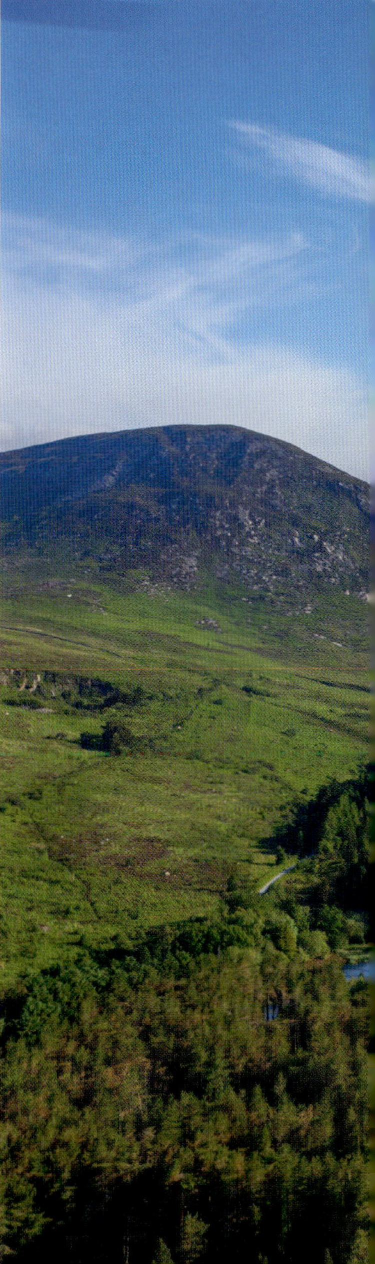

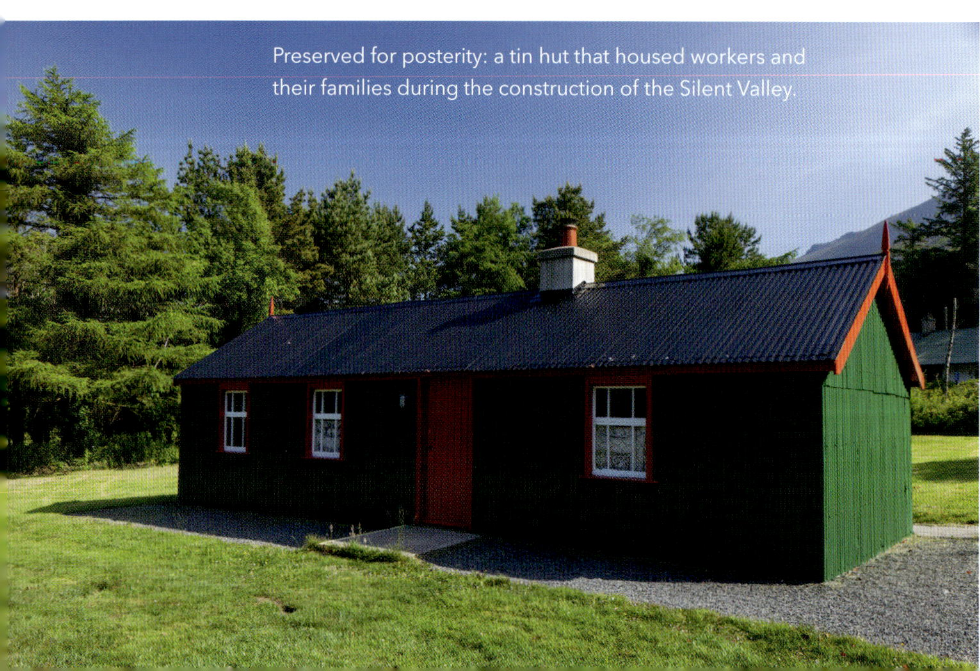
Preserved for posterity: a tin hut that housed workers and their families during the construction of the Silent Valley.

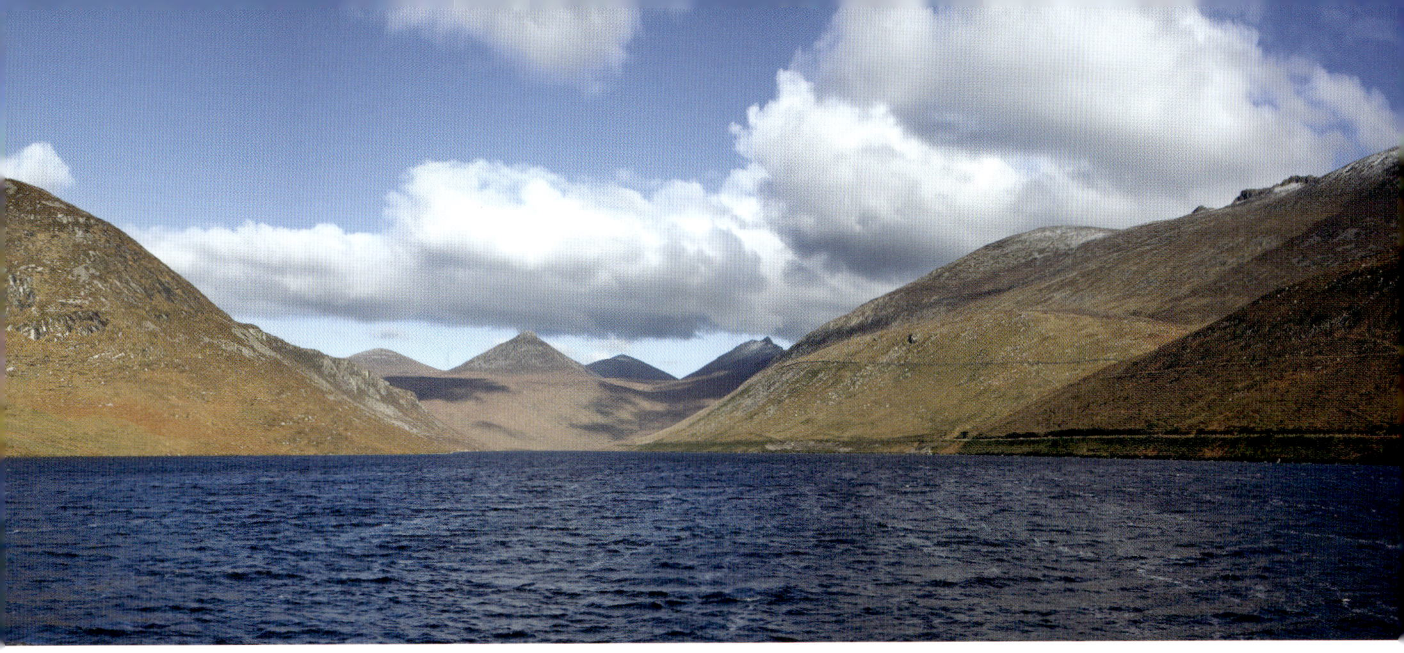

Above: Looking north up the Silent Valley Reservoir.

Here: Aerial view of the Silent Valley Dam and Reservoir. The craggy mountain to the right of picture is Slieve Binnian.

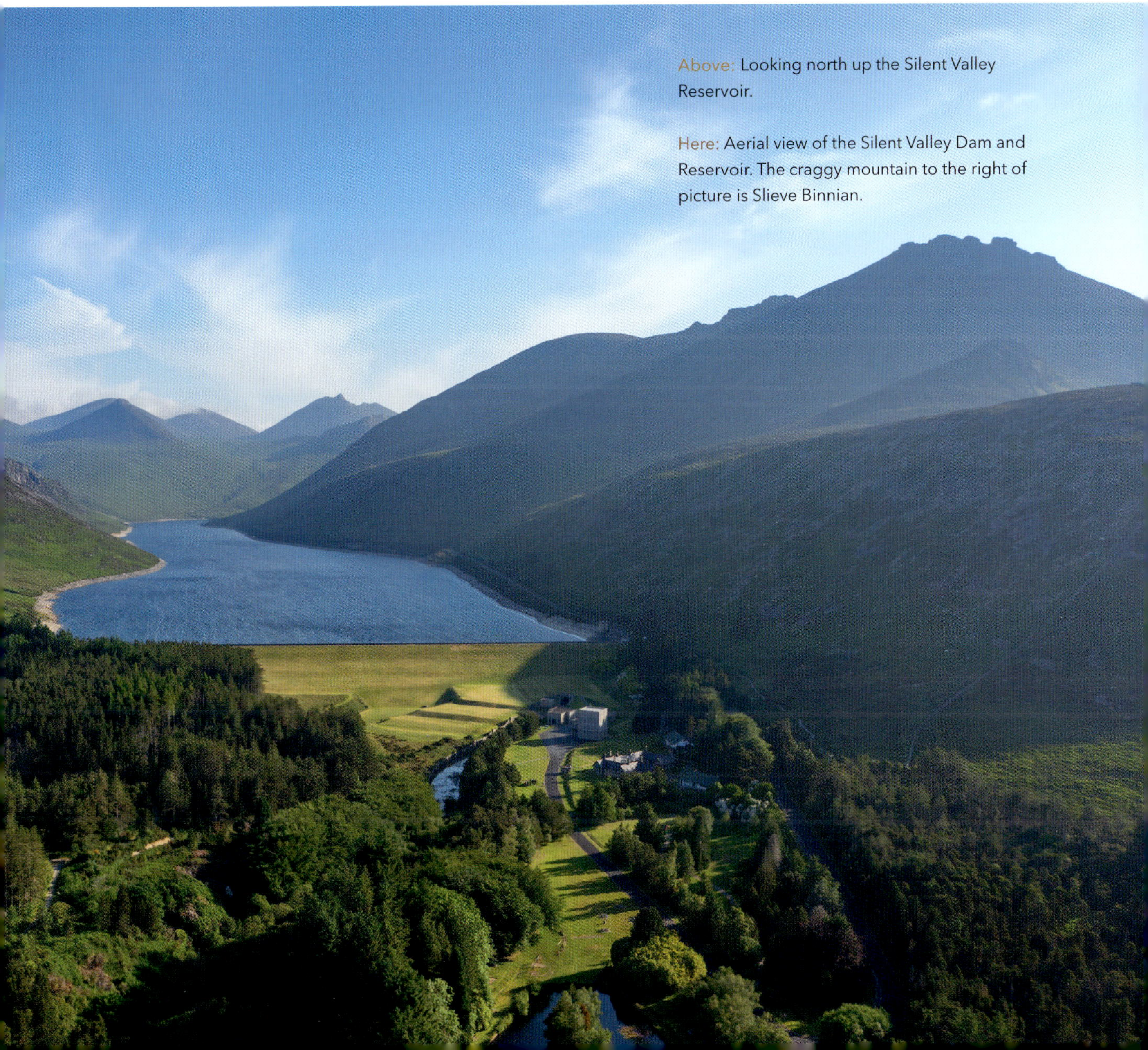

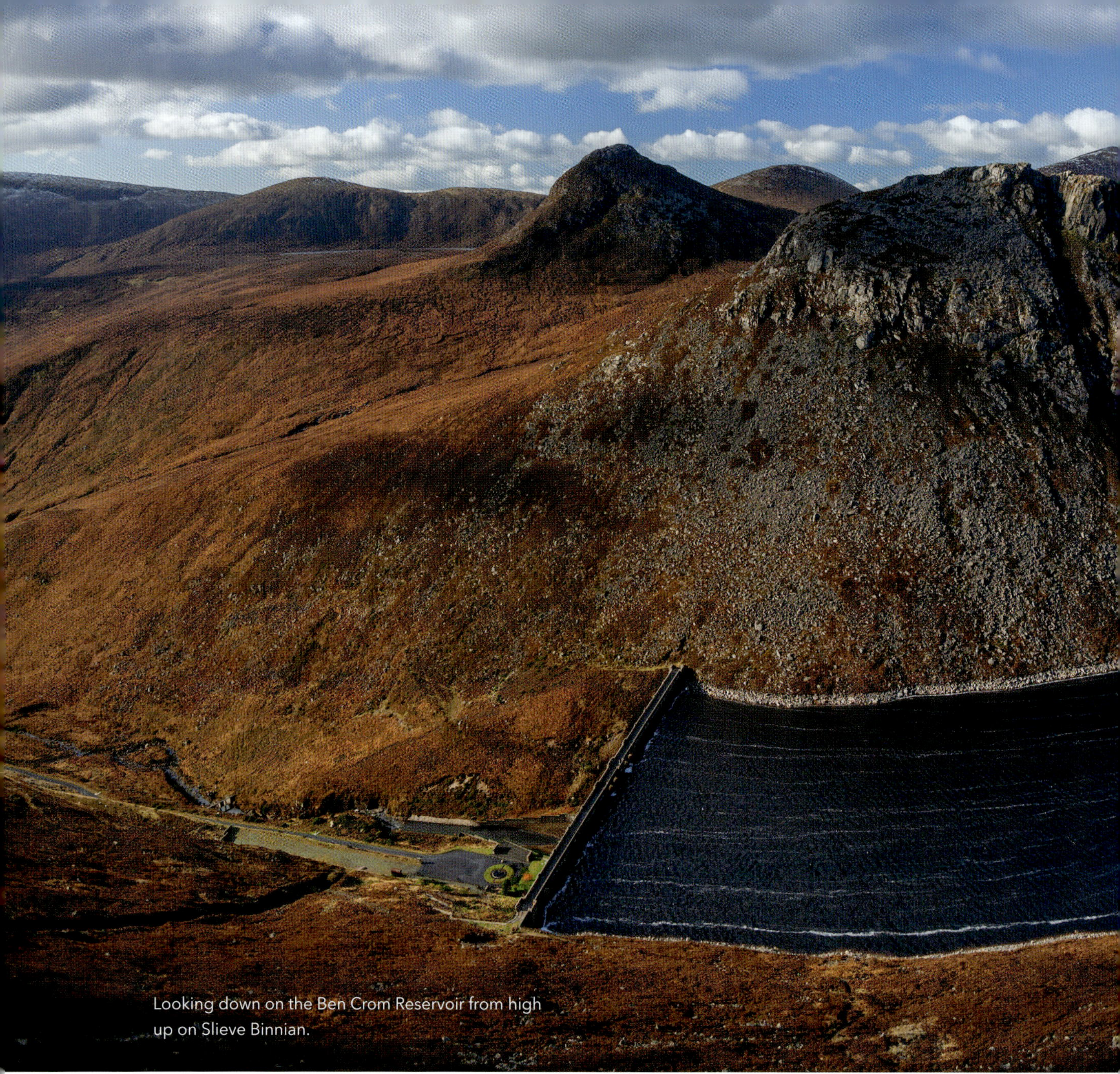

Looking down on the Ben Crom Reservoir from high up on Slieve Binnian.

steam railway had to be built to carry materials between the construction site and Annalong Harbour, some seven kilometres away. During the construction of the dam, many challenging engineering difficulties were overcome, in particular the excavation of a 60m trench to reach bedrock and secure the foundations, which required men to work in specially pressurised shafts. Workers returning to the surface had to, like divers, use decompression chambers to avoid getting the bends.

Such were the difficulties that plans to dam the adjacent Annalong Valley were

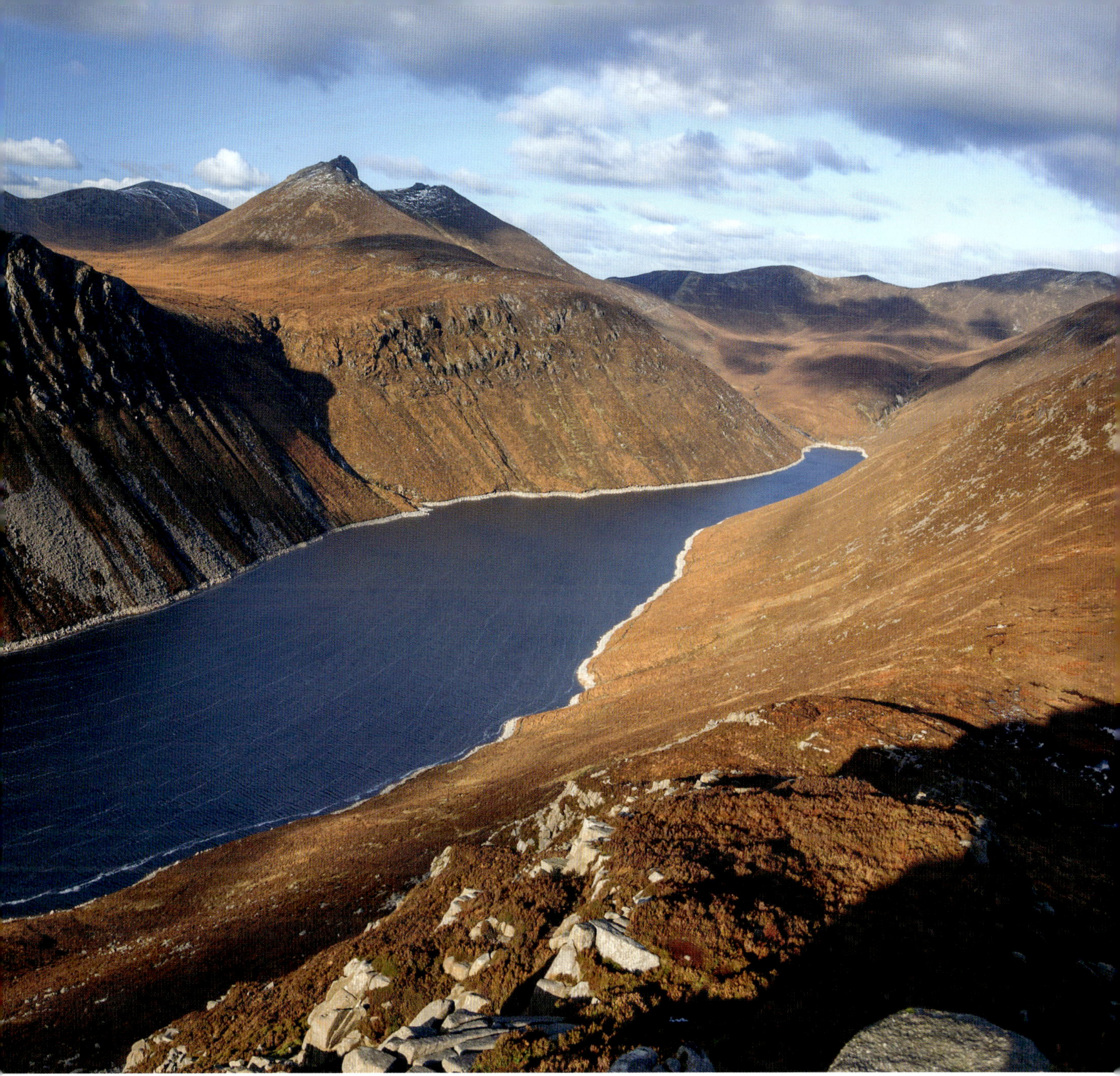

scrapped. It was decided instead to pipe water from this valley under Slieve Binnian and into the reservoir. The Binnian Tunnel was another great engineering accomplishment and was finished in 1951. It is almost four kilometres long and was bored using rudimentary equipment by today's standards. Despite this, the teams working from either end were just inches off when they met deep under Slieve Binnian. It is no longer in use today, however in 1957 the Ben Crom Reservoir was completed, adding a further 1.7 billion litres' capacity to the Mourne water supply.

QUARRYING IN THE MOURNES

Since Neolithic times, Mourne granite has been prized as a construction material; blocks have been found as far away as the 5,000-year old Newgrange passage tomb in County Meath. In the medieval period, it was used to manufacture millstones and crosses such as the 9th century Downpatrick High Cross. During the 18th and 19th centuries, large-scale quarrying of the granite began in earnest. Not only was the rock used locally, both in great estates such as Tollymore and Castlewellan and engineering projects such as the Mourne Wall and Silent Valley Reservoir, but it was also shipped out from the harbours at Newcastle, Annalong and Kilkeel to supply demand for kerbstones, monuments and grand Victorian buildings in the rapidly growing cities of Britain and Ireland.

In most quarries, the massive slabs were carried down from the mountains by horse and cart, but above Newcastle a funicular railway was constructed to bring rock down the slopes of Slieve Donard directly to the harbour in small carts known as 'bogies'. In time, Mourne granite could be found gracing buildings and kerbstones all across Britain and Ireland, and more recently it was used in the Queen Elizabeth II September 11th Garden in New York.

Above right: The rock pinnacles of the Pot of Legawherry near the summit of Slieve Commedagh.

Right: A walker beside the glacial erratic of Cloghmore in Rostrevor Forest Park. This fifty-tonne granite boulder was deposited by retreating glaciers and is known locally as 'the big stone'. Local legend asserts that the boulder was thrown here from the Cooley Mountains by the giant Fionn mac Cumhaill.

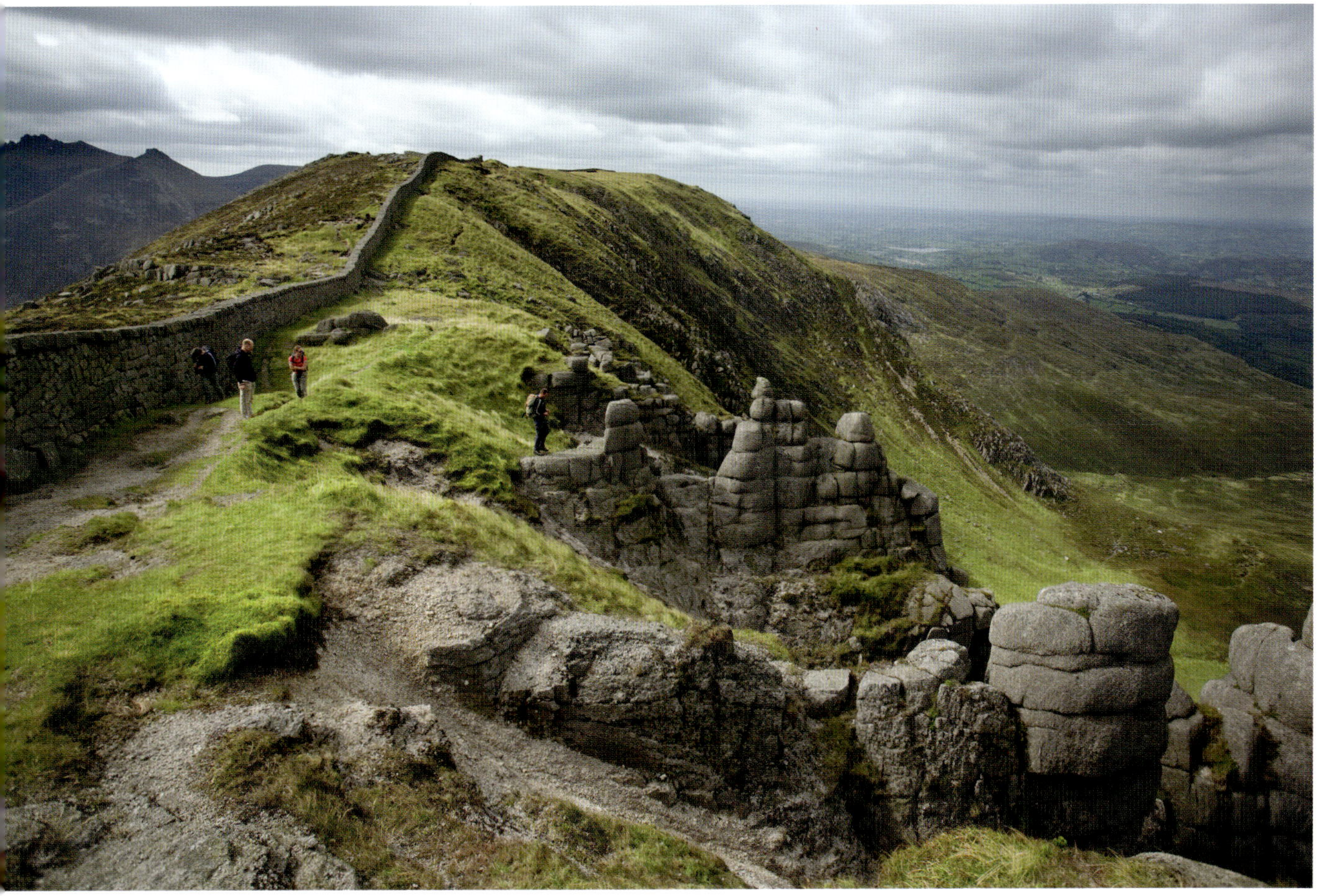

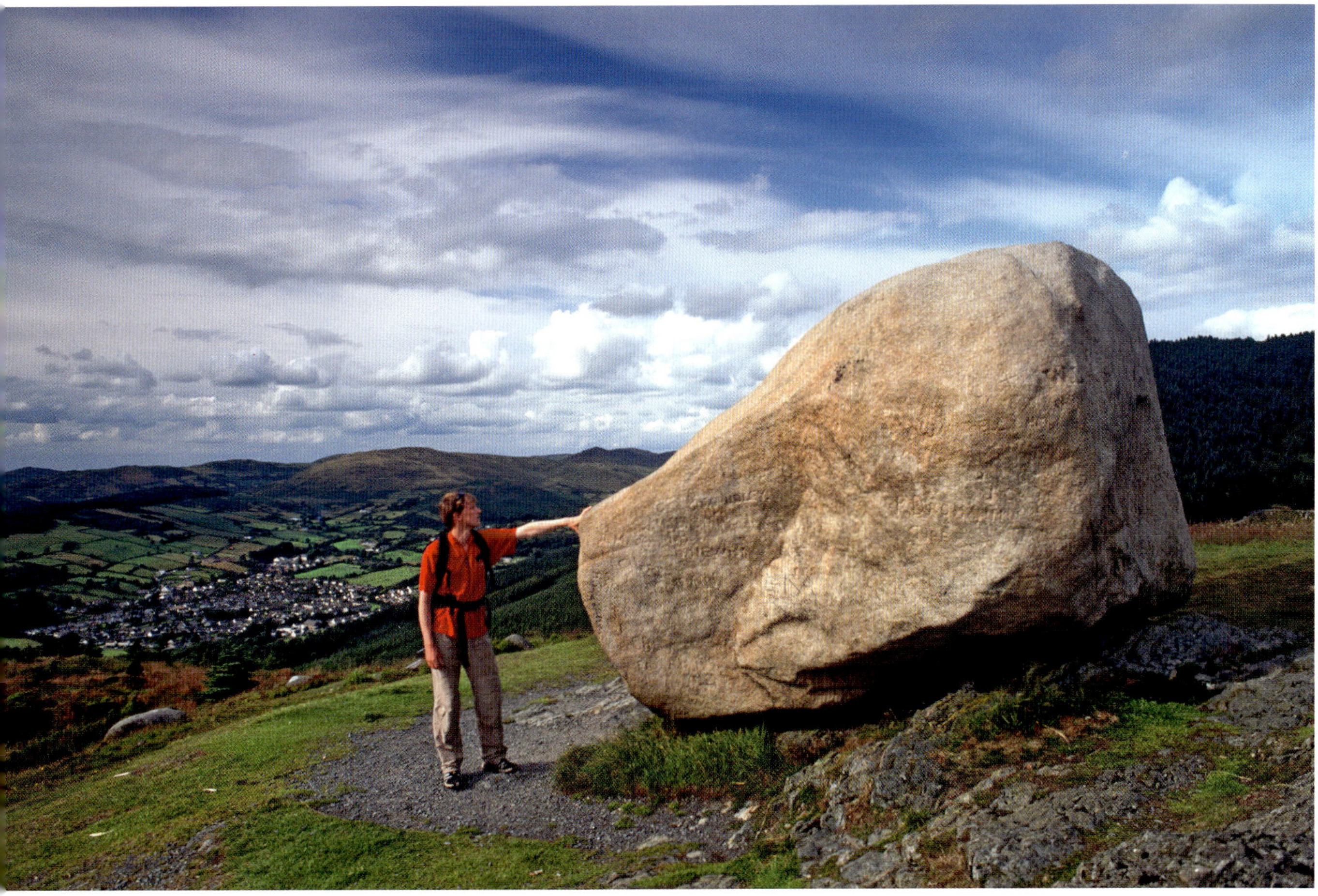

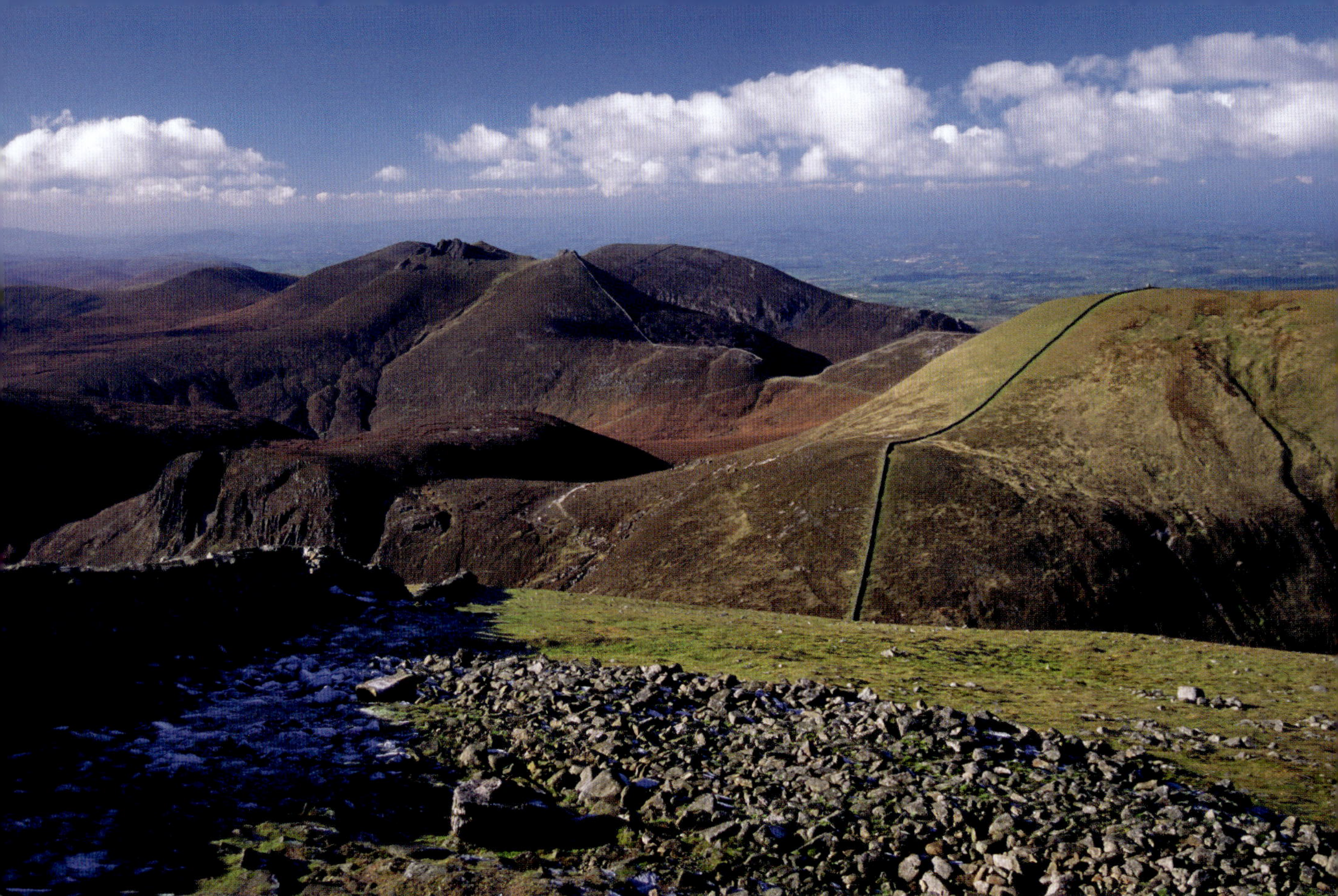

SLIEVE DONARD

Slieve Donard – or simply 'Donard', as it is often called – is the mountain most synonymous with the Mournes, not just because it is the highest, but also because of its position overlooking the seaside town of Newcastle. There is relatively easy access for walkers. The most popular route of ascent begins in the heart of Newcastle and follows the rocky Glen River Path up to the Mourne Wall at the saddle between Donard and its neighbour Slieve Commedagh. From there, you simply turn left and follow the wall all the way up the east shoulder to the top.

In recent years, much work has been carried out on upgrading and improving the path, with flagstone sections built right onto the upper slopes of the mountain. Despite these improvements, the ascent of Donard is a significant physical challenge and in bad weather conditions can rapidly become life-threatening. There have been many fatalities on the mountain, and the local mountain rescue team respond to dozens of call-outs every year – often to poorly equipped and inexperienced parties.

There is a great deal of history and folklore attached to Slieve Donard, and it has undoubtedly been a landform of significant cultural and spiritual importance since the Neolithic period. The summit is marked by two large and ancient burial cairns, both of which unfortunately have been badly damaged and degraded over the years. The Great Cairn, which is right on the summit, dates from 3300–3000 BC, while the Lesser Cairn, a short distance to the northeast, has been dated to 2300–1950 BC.

The mountain is referred to in Irish mythology as one of the twelve chief mountains of Ireland, and an earlier name, Sliabh Slángha, is attached to the mythical figure of Slángha, who is said to be buried in the Great Cairn. During the 9th century, Irish monks compiling The Triads of Ireland described it as one of the 'three great heights' of Ireland. Slieve Donard became the mountain's dominant name from around the 12th century and comes from the Irish *Sliabh Dónairt*, meaning 'Dónairt's Mountain'. The name refers to St Donard or Domhanghart, a follower of St Patrick who founded a monastery at Maghera, within sight of the mountain, and then used the Great Cairn as a hermit's cell and the Lesser Cairn as an oratory.

Below left: The Glen River tumbles down over many waterfalls from its source high on Slieve Donard. On the lower slopes it rushes through Donard Wood, photographed here in early spring.

Left: View of the Mournes from Slieve Donard.

Below right: A walker takes a break in the shelter of the Mourne Wall near the summit of Slieve Donard.

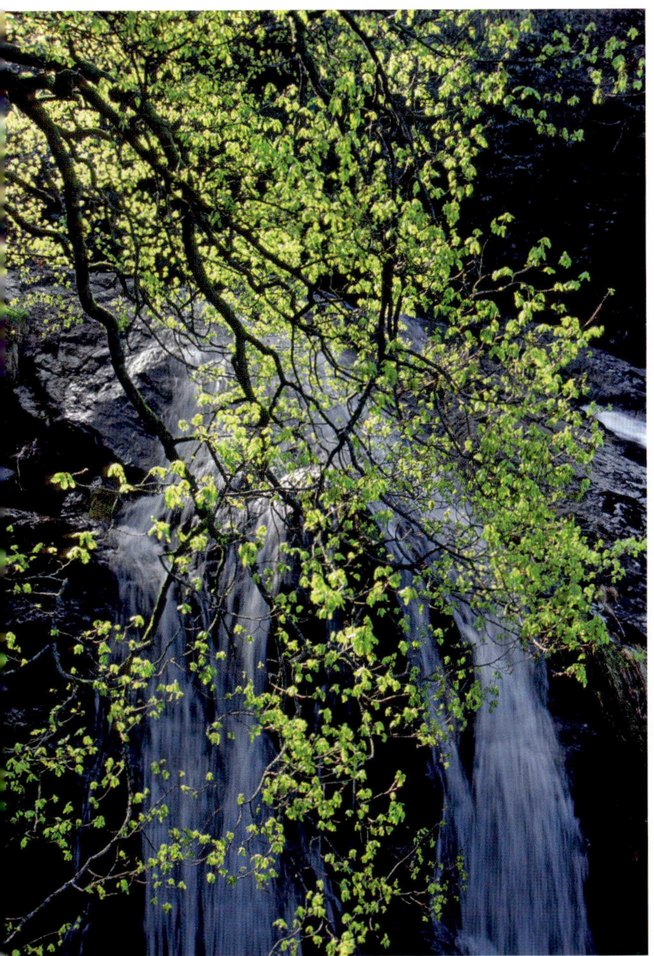

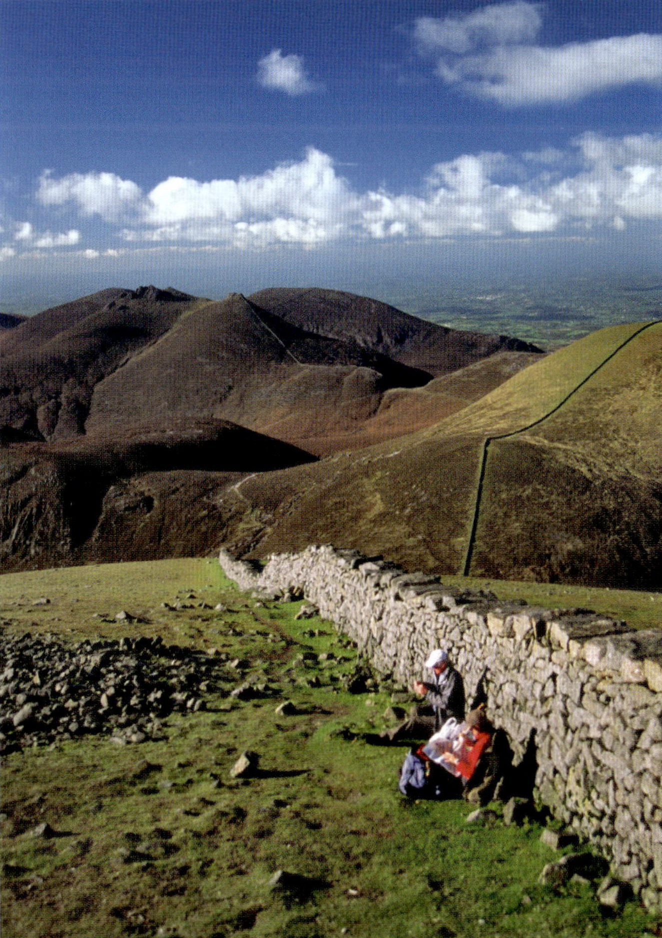

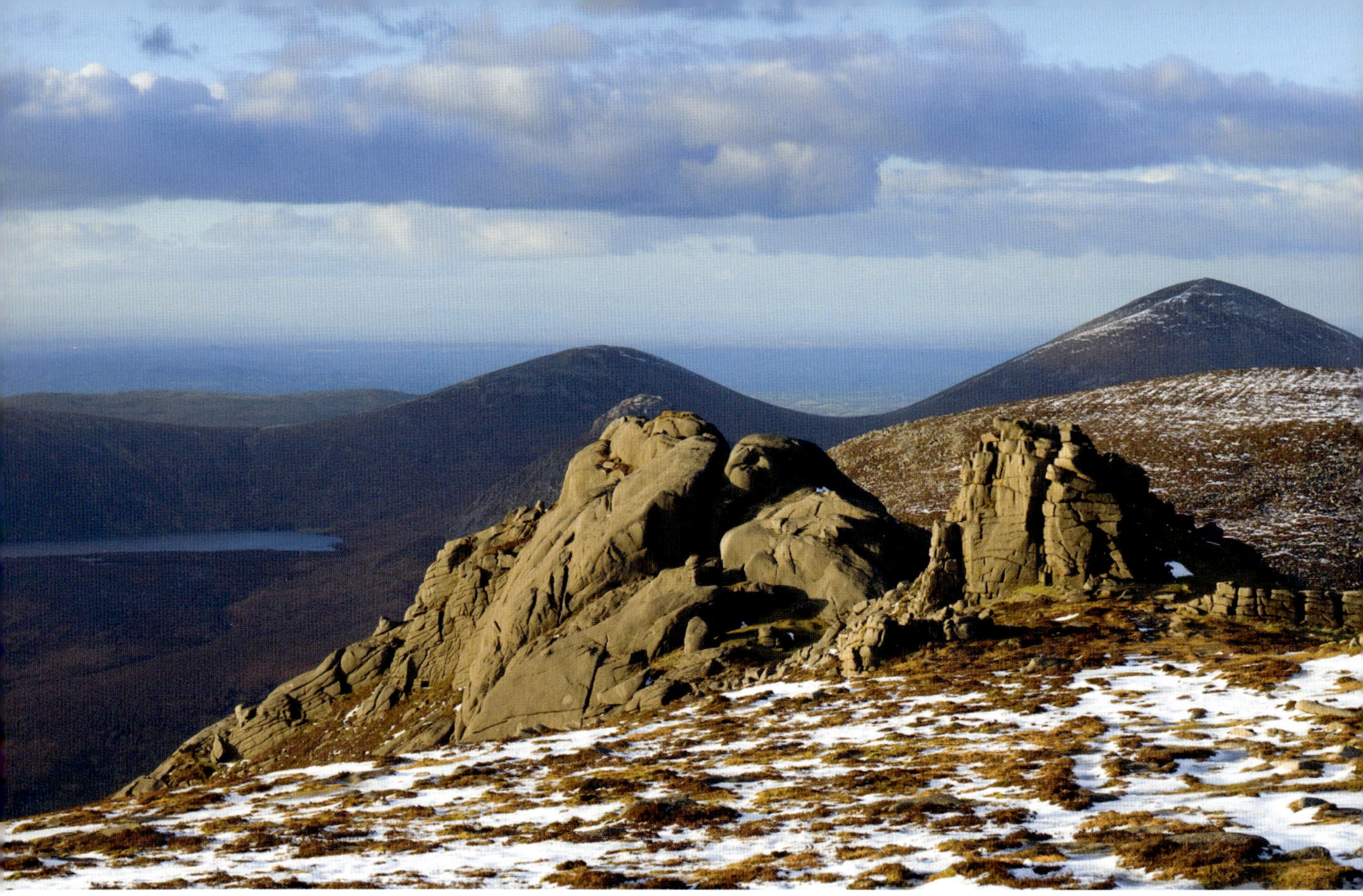

SLIEVE BINNIAN

Slieve Binnian may be the third highest summit in the Mournes, but it is probably the most interesting to climb and explore. The name derives from the Irish *Sliabh Binneáin*, or 'mountain of the little peak', which is probably a reference to the unusual and very distinctive granite tors that erupt in several places along the 2km-long summit ridge. It gives the mountain a crenelated profile shared only by Slieve Bearnagh, and it is quite easy to spot from the surrounding countryside. The origin of these tors is not entirely clear but is thought to lie in a long process of differential weathering.

The easiest ascent of Slieve Binnian is by following the Mourne Wall from Carrick Little all the way up the mountain's eastern slopes. In fine weather, though, it is well worth traversing the whole summit ridge taking in the summit tors, the Black Castles and the North Tor before descending on a path to the Annalong Valley and back to Carrick Little.

Seen from the south, Slieve Binnian takes on a more classic pyramidal profile, looming over its much smaller sibling, Wee Binnian. This is a classic view of the Mournes and it is easy to pick out the stunningly direct line of the Mourne Wall up the steep southwest ridge of the mountain.

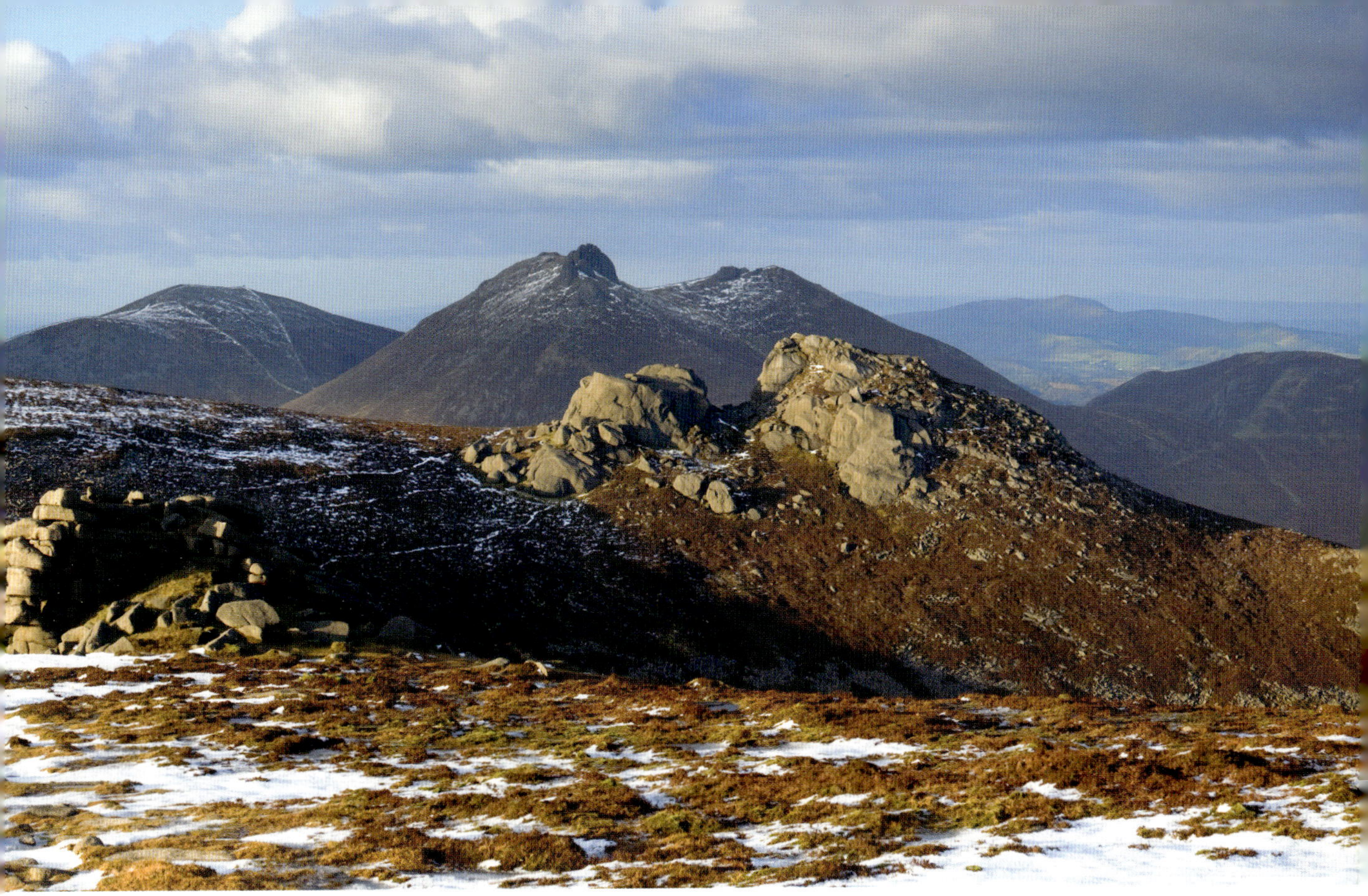

Above: Looking north across the summit tors of Slieve Binnian towards Slieve Bearnagh and the Meelmores.

Below: A rainbow follows a clearing shower, as seen from Slieve Binnian.

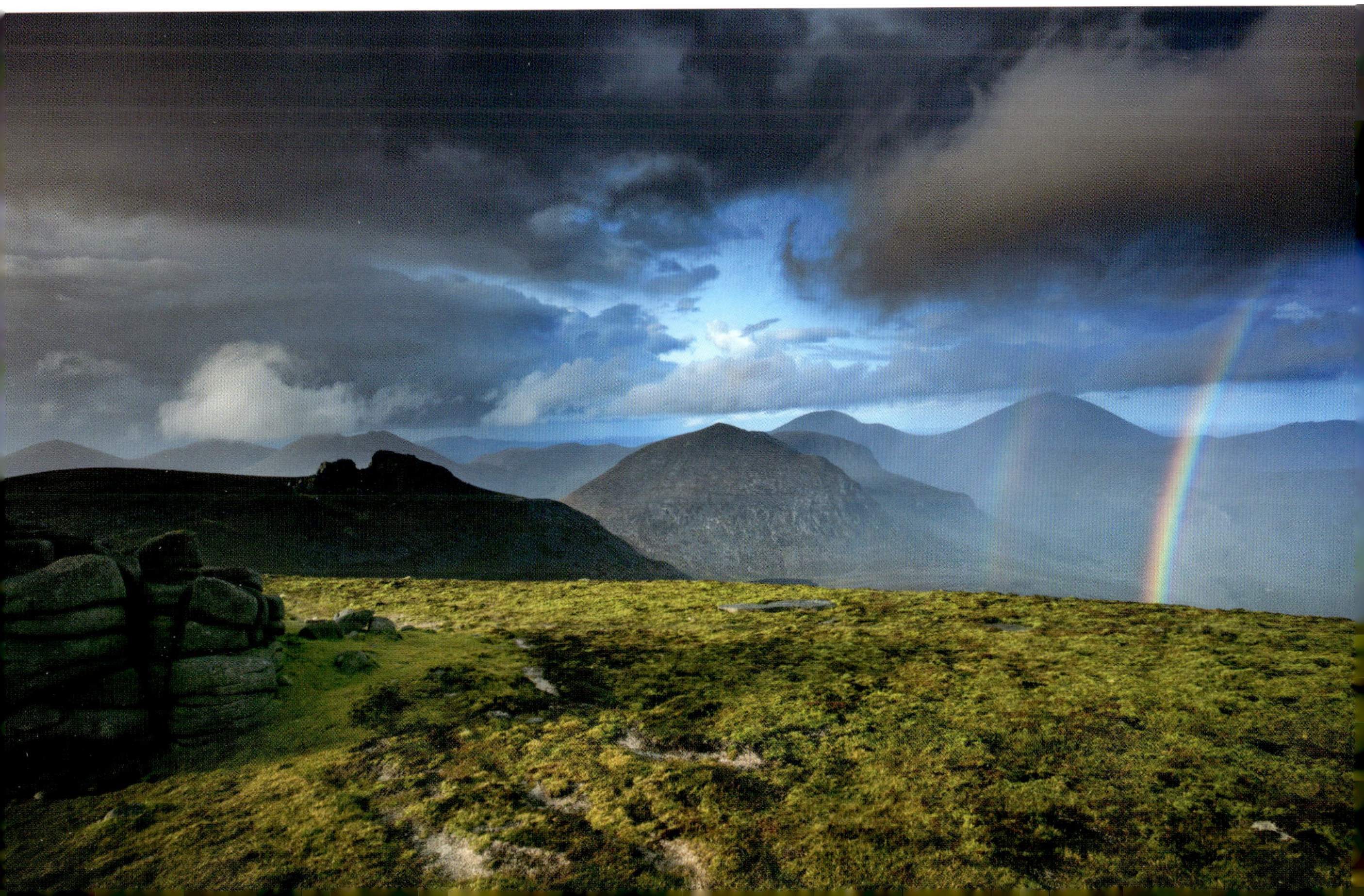

SLIEVE BEARNAGH

At a height of 739m, Slieve Bearnagh is the fourth highest summit in the Mournes and derives its name from the Irish *Sliabh Bearnach* or 'gapped mountain'. There is an undeniably conspicuous gap between the two enormous granite tors which crown the summit. This is seen to best effect from the north, from where the top of the mountain resembles the crater of a volcano. Slieve Bearnagh is most easily climbed from the Trassey Valley, following a good track to the col at Hare's Gap, from where the Mourne Wall can be followed up the steep upper slopes to the summit.

Below: An early winter's morning near the summit of Slieve Bearnagh.

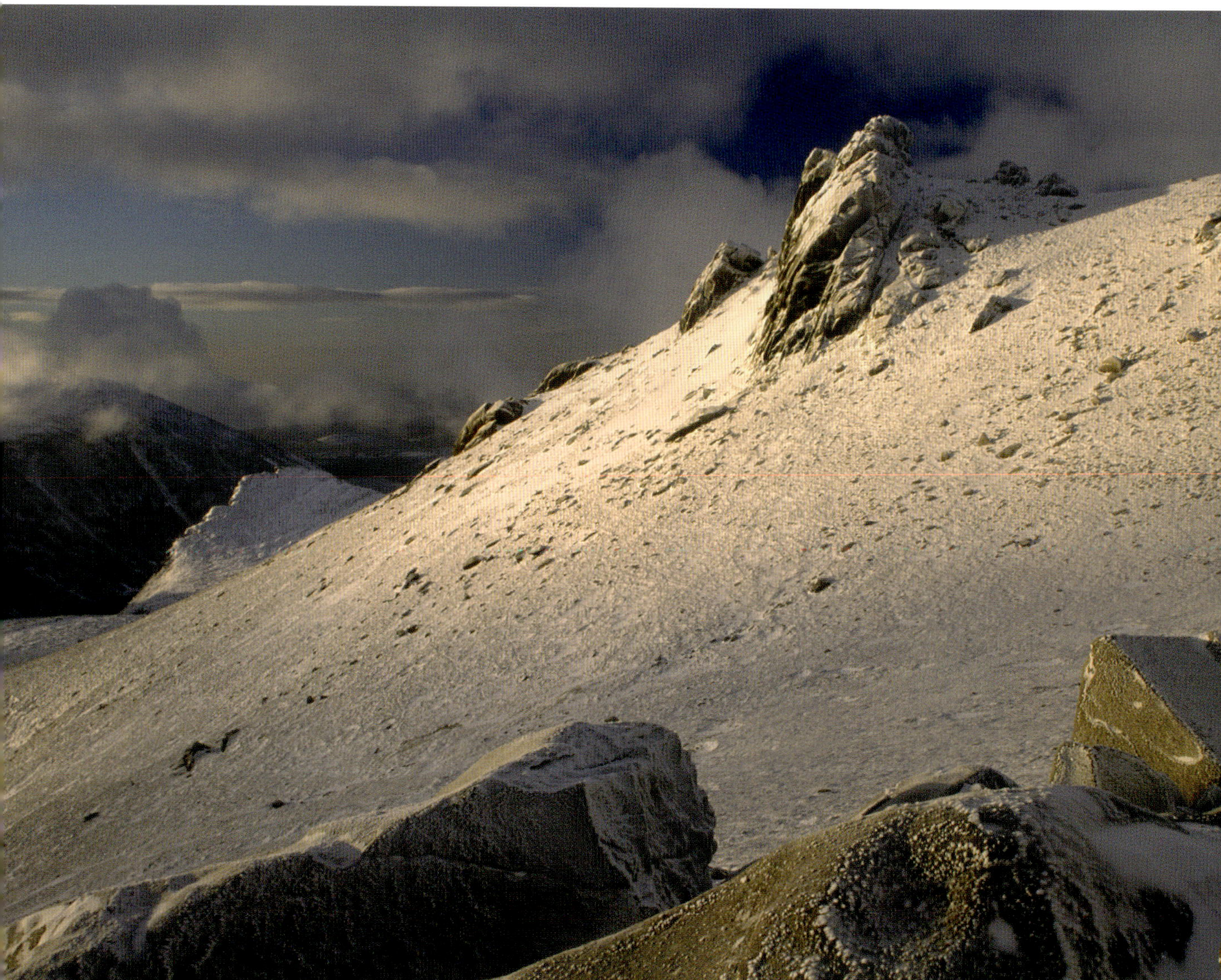

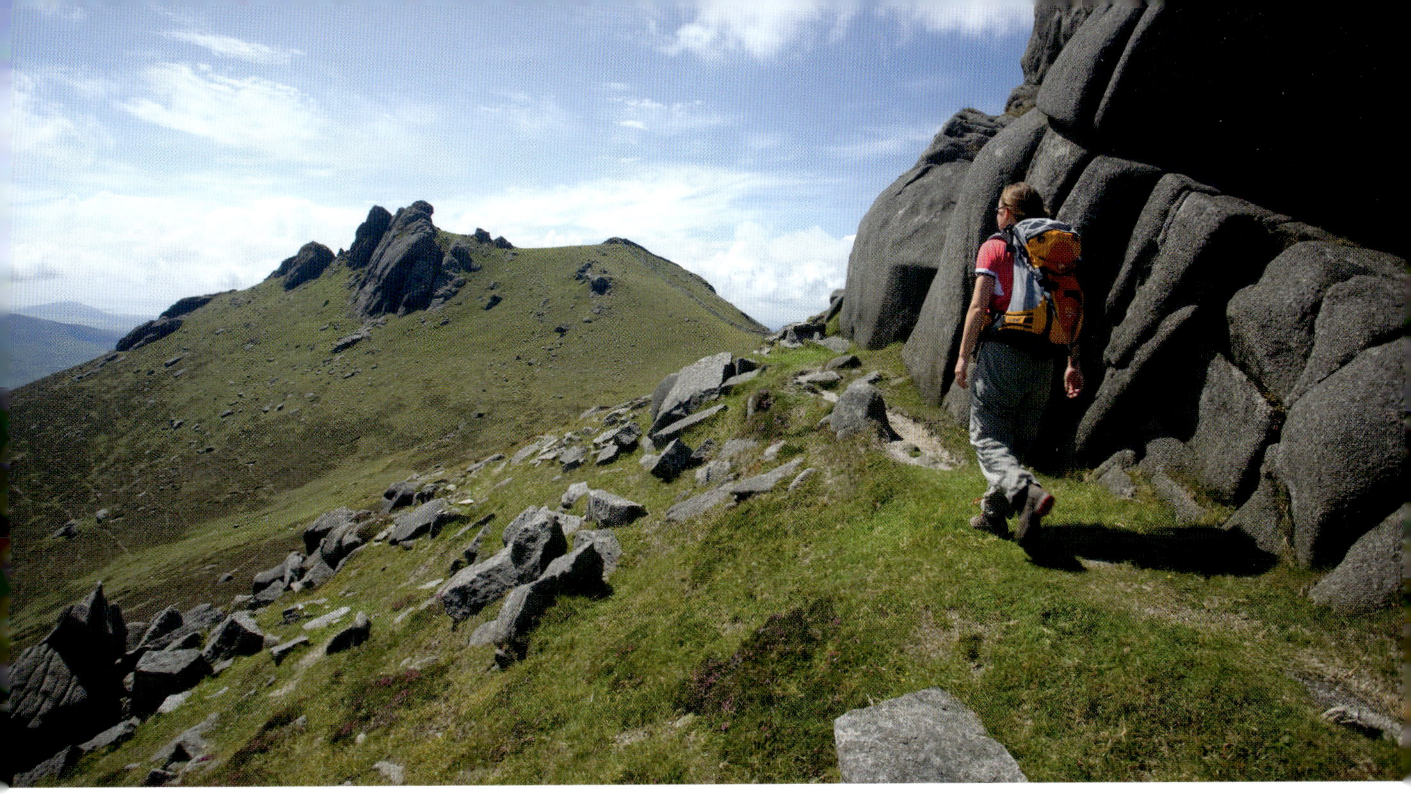

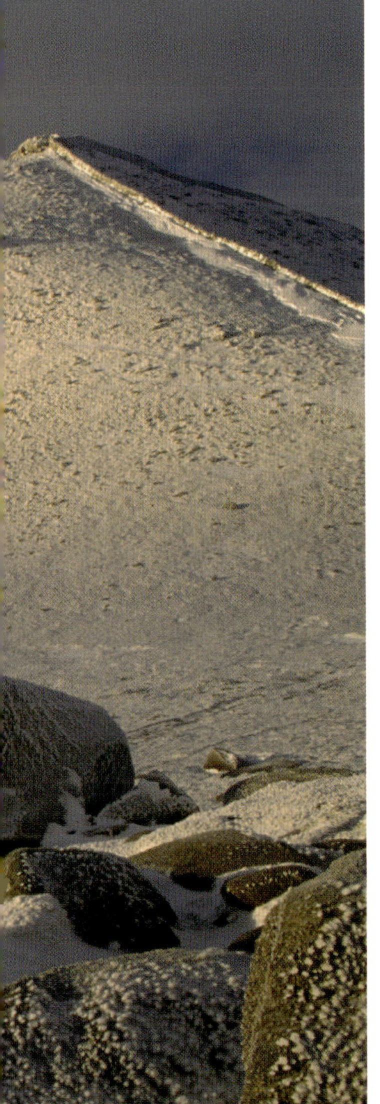

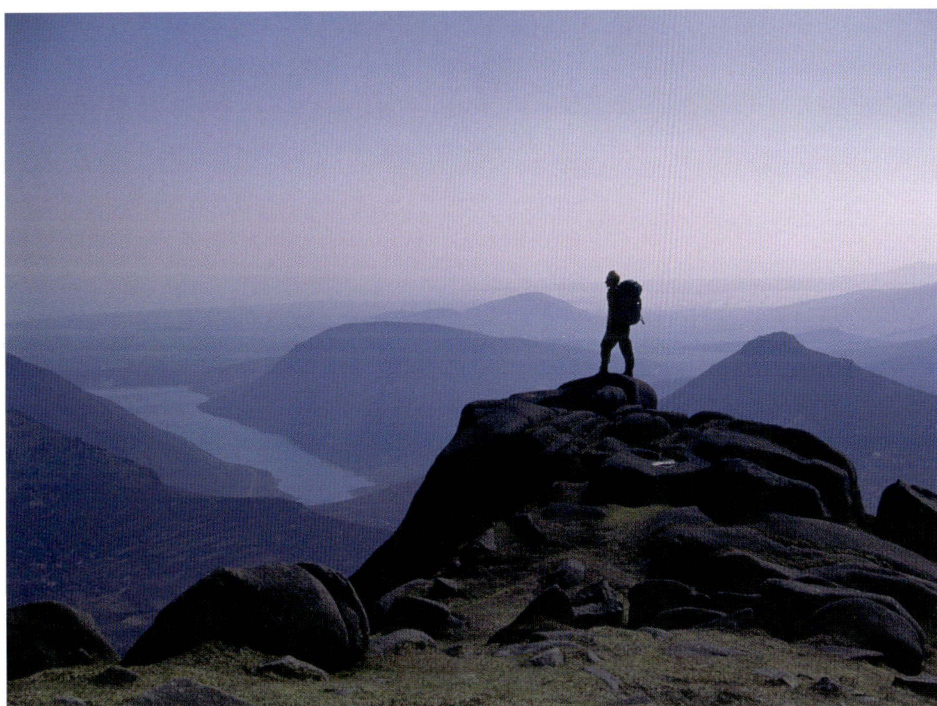

 Walking on the summit of Slieve Bearnagh, in summer and winter.

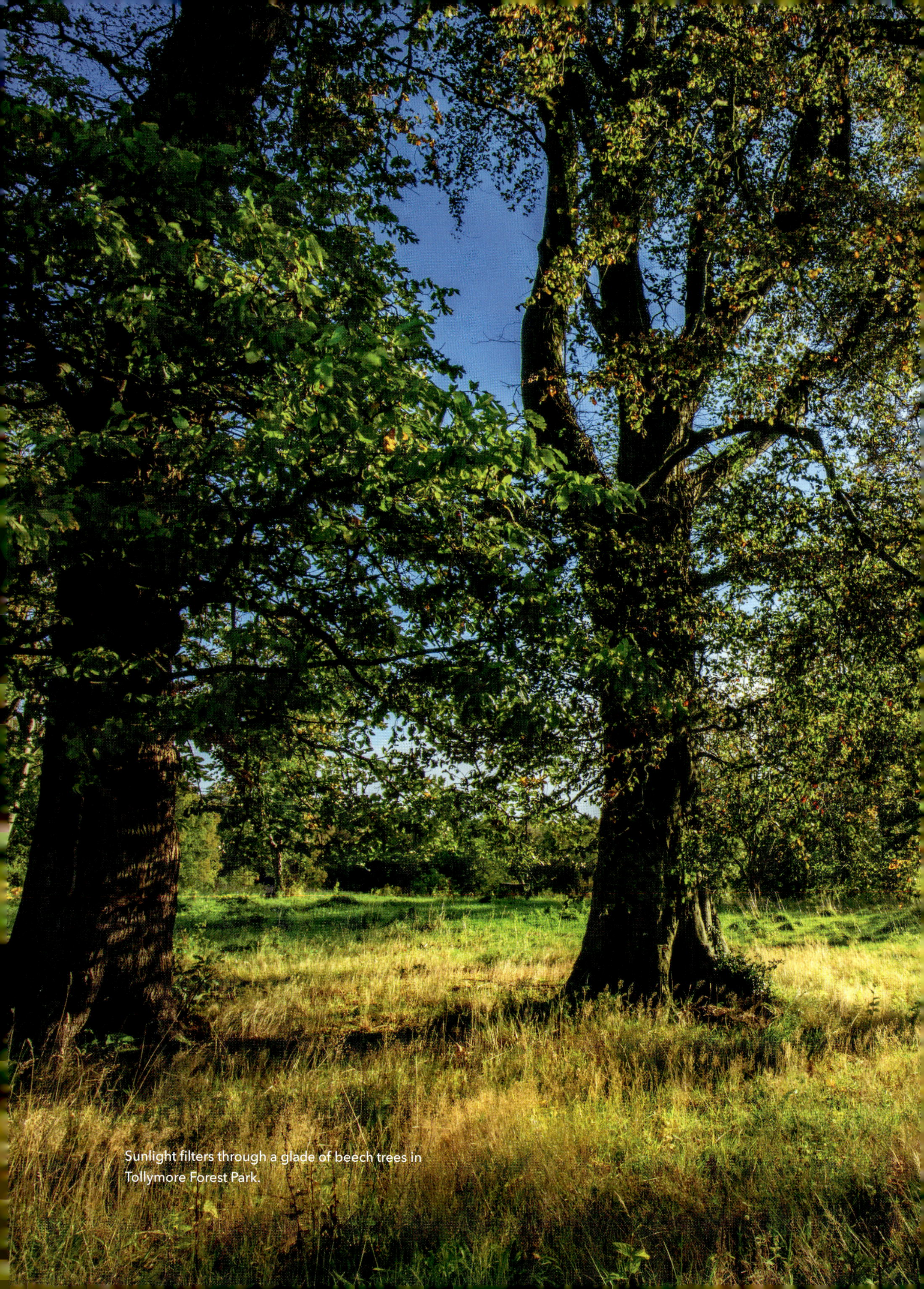

Sunlight filters through a glade of beech trees in Tollymore Forest Park.

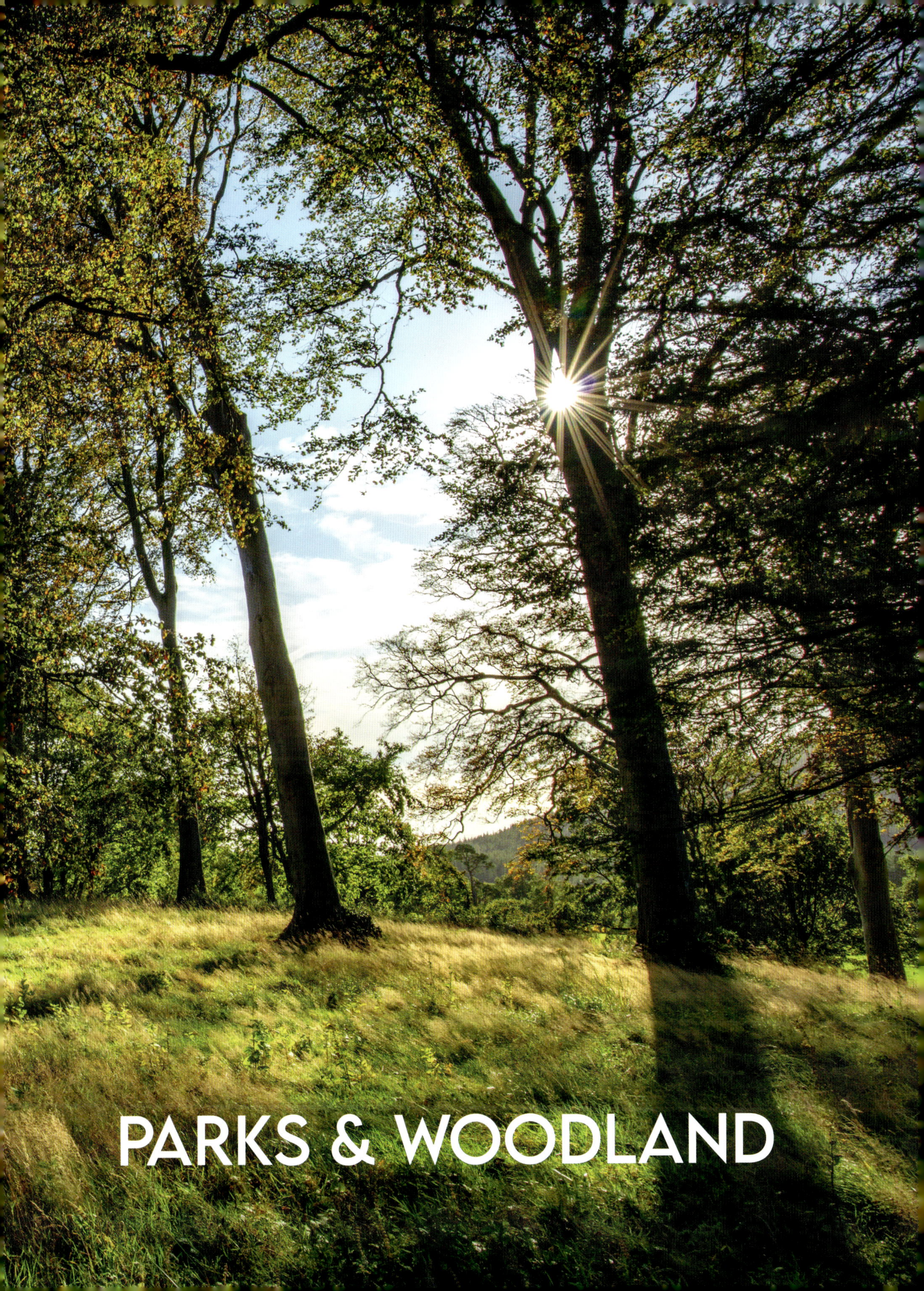
PARKS & WOODLAND

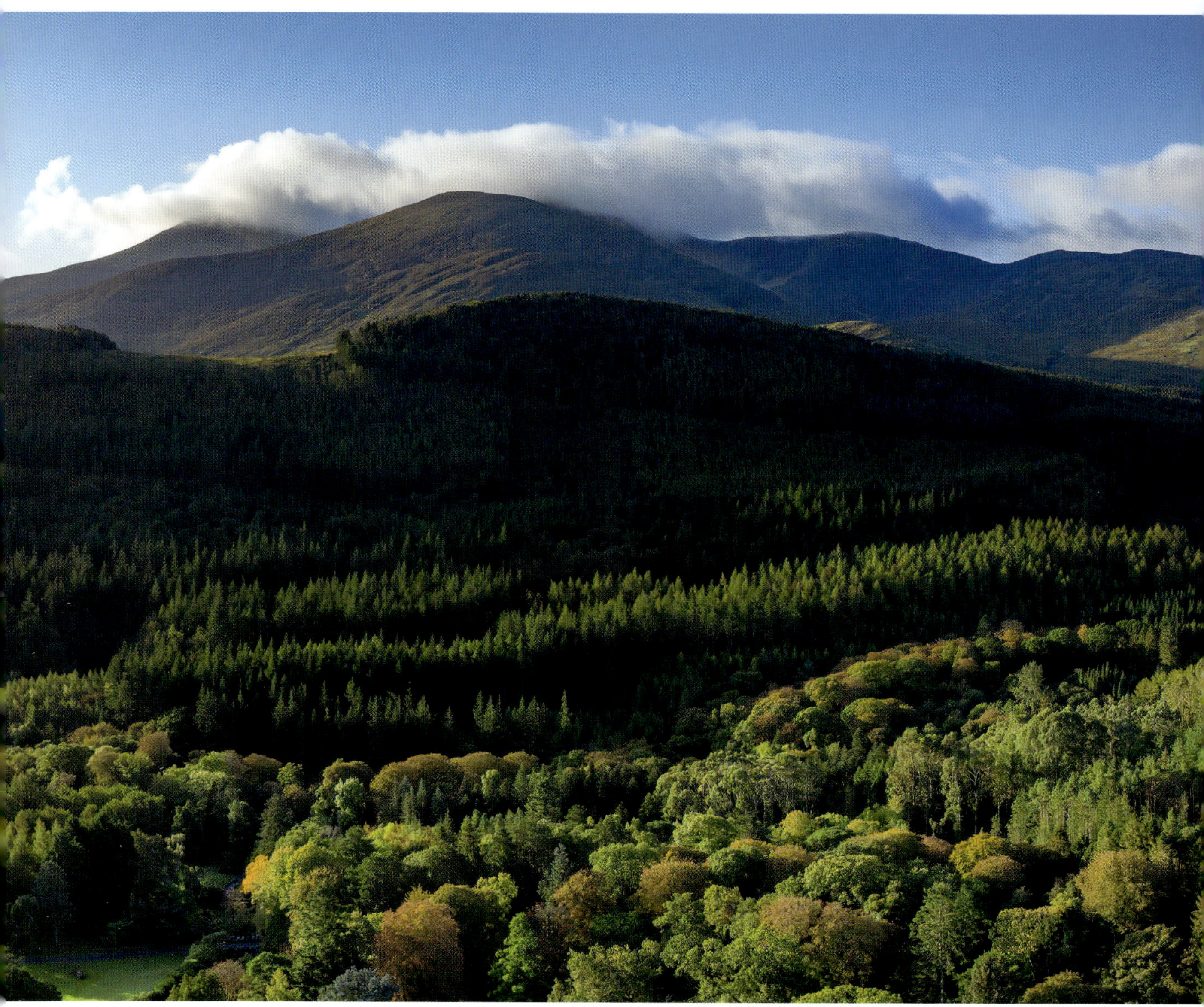

The Mourne area contains arguably the finest collection of formal parkland and recreational forestry in Northern Ireland. Two great estates to the north of the High Mournes are foremost amongst these: Tollymore, which nestles right on the lower slopes of Slieve Commedagh, and Castlewellan, just a few kilometres further north. The third great forest park is Rostrevor, to the southwest of the Mournes. All three were originally private estates of local aristocracy but were acquired by the Forest Service and local councils by the 1970s. Today they are important havens for nature and also major recreational hubs, featuring excellent campsites and many miles of walking, riding and biking trails.

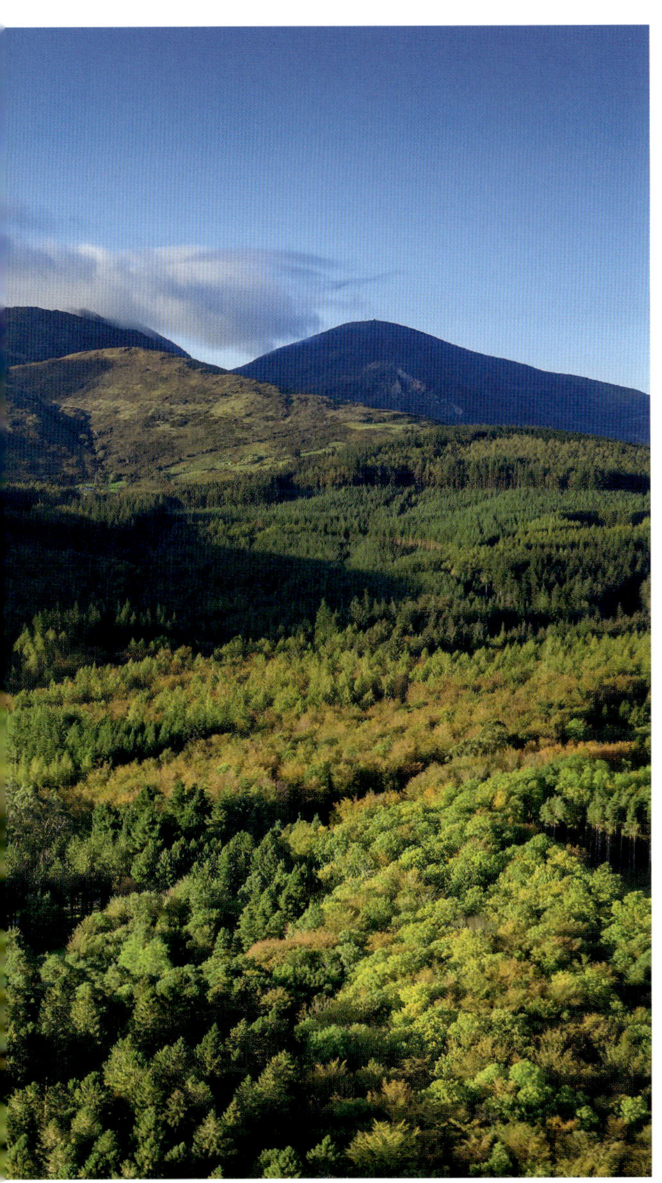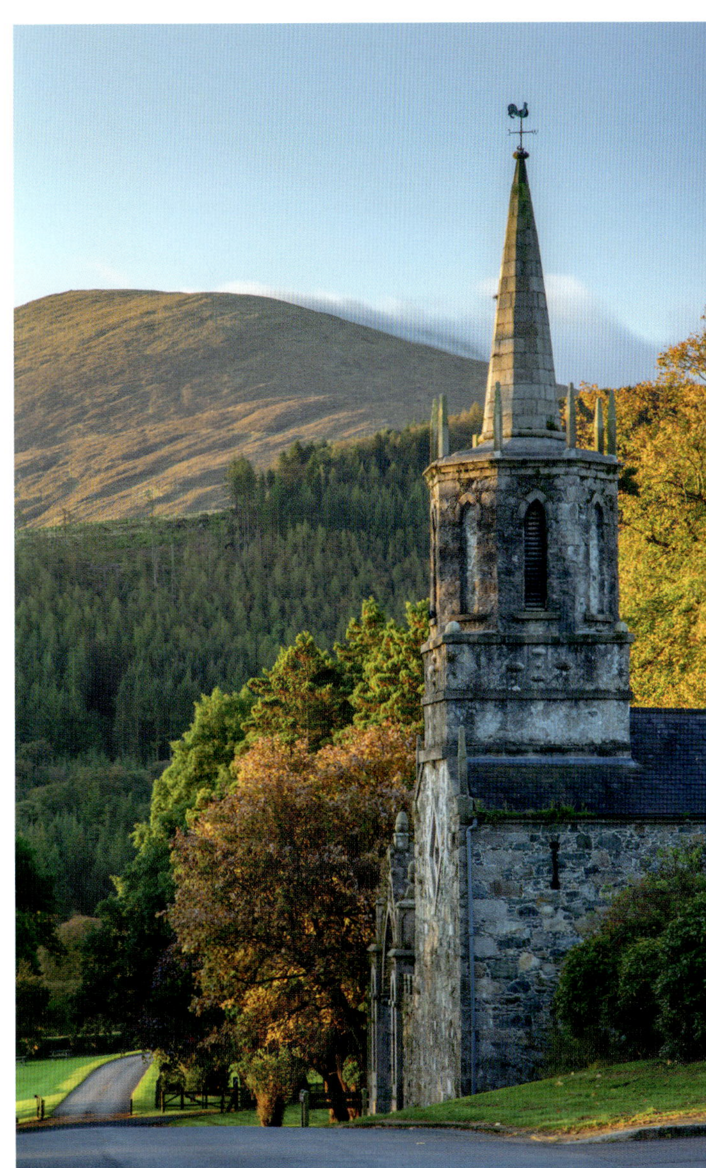

TOLLYMORE

The name Tollymore derives from the Irish *Tulaigh Mhór*, which means 'large hill or mound'. Given the mountainous backdrop, this could refer to any one of several Mourne summits which overlook the Tollymore estate. In fact, the name is thought to invoke the much lower, yet conspicuous, tree-covered hills within the park boundaries: The Drinns and Curraghhard. The area now known as Tollymore came under the control of the Magennis family following the Anglo-Norman invasion of Ulster, but by the late 1600s, it had passed to the Hamilton family.

The formal parkland and many fine follies and structures of Tollymore Forest Park have their origins in the mid-1700s through the efforts of James Hamilton, the 1st Earl of Clanbrassil, and under the influence of his friend, the famed astronomer and architect Thomas Wright. This work was continued by the 2nd Earl of Clanbrassil. There are two enormous Gothic entrance arches, the Barbican and Bryansford gates, built from local granite; a faux-church complete with a convincing steeple, known as Clanbrassil Barn; and also numerous beautiful stone bridges that crisscross the Shimna River.

In the 1770s, the 2nd Earl of Clanbrassil built a stone shelter set into the side of a small gorge on the Shimna. Known as The Hermitage, it was conceived

Right: The granite obelix in Tollymore, which was erected by the Earl of Roden in memory of his son Robert Bligh Jocelyn.

Below right: The Shimna River is crossed by sixteen bridges as it flows through Tollymore Forest Park. Foley's Bridge, built in 1787, is one of the finest.

Below: Autumn colours in Tollymore Forest Park.

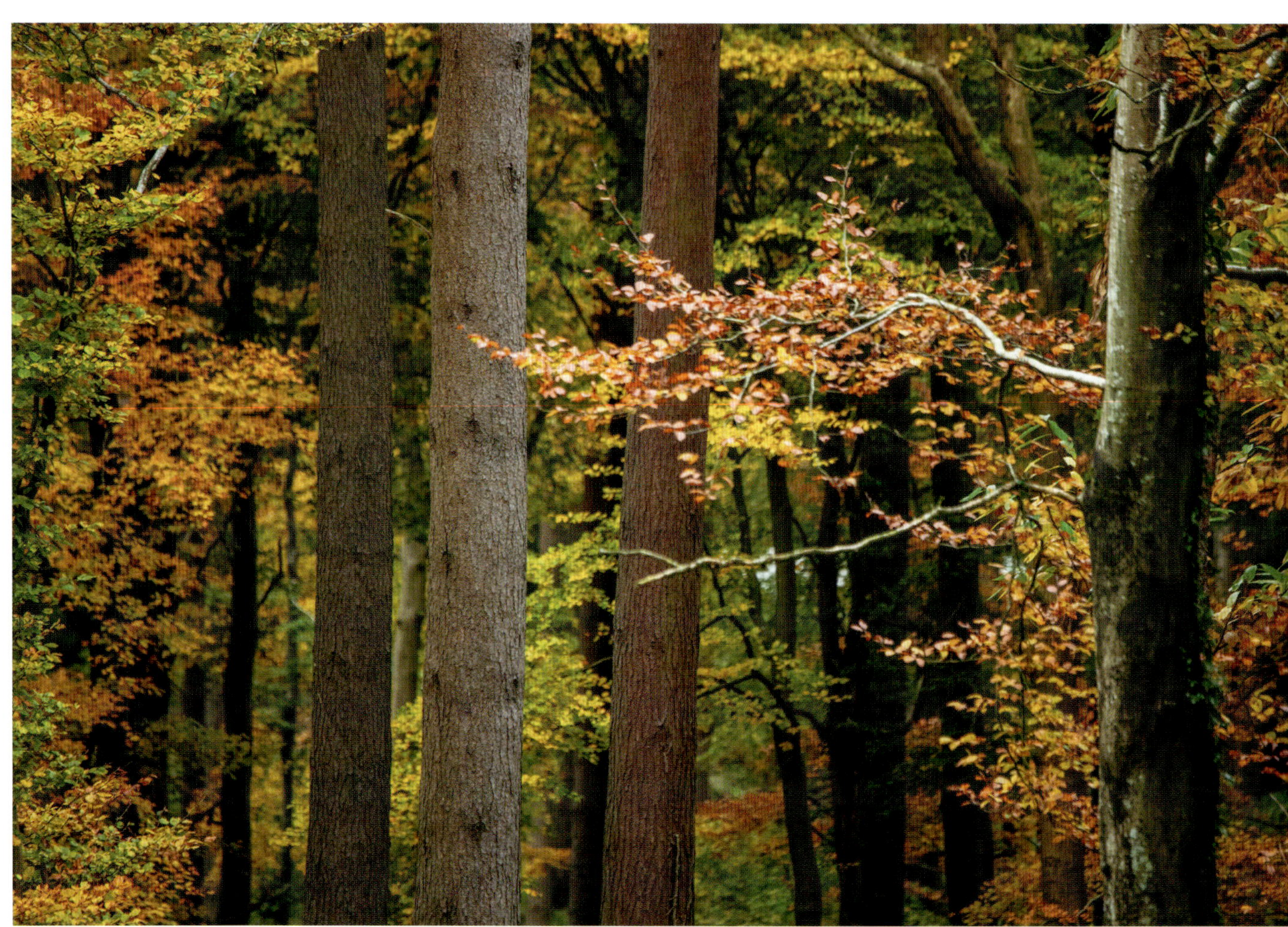

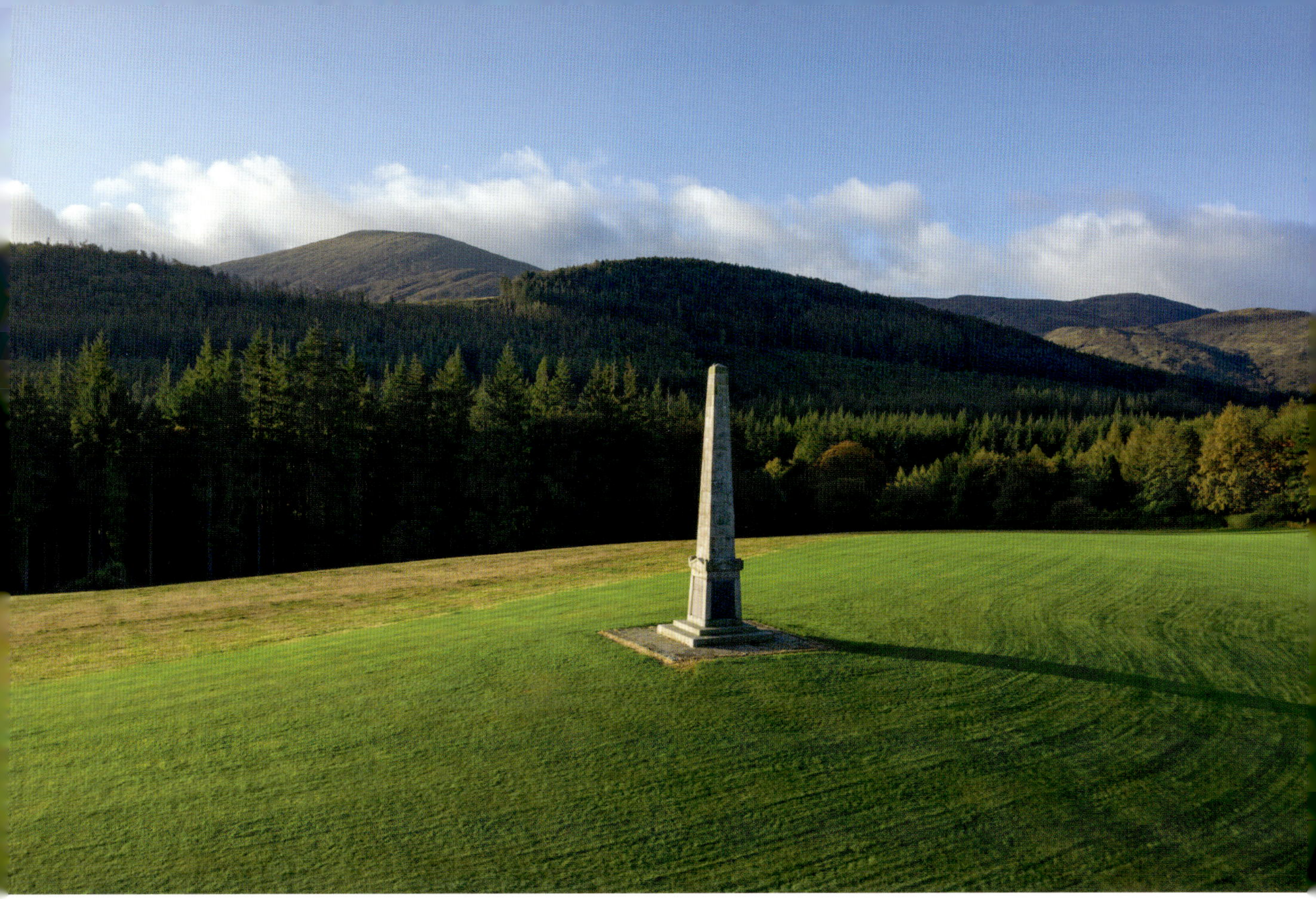

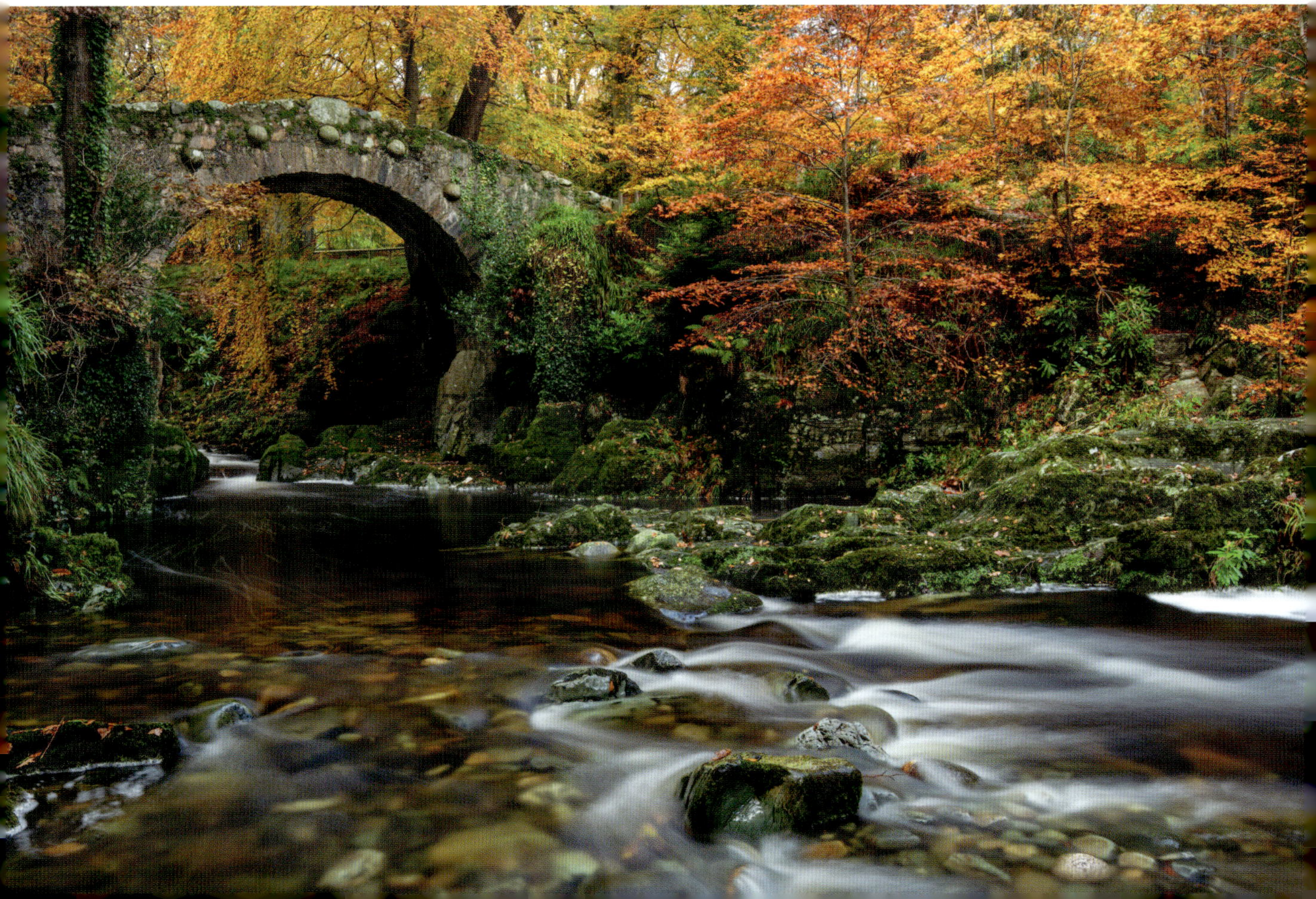

as a memorial to his friend John Montagu but was traditionally used as a place for ladies to sit out of the elements while the men fished the nearby river.

The combination of Tollymore's beautiful natural setting and aged stone-built curiosities has made it a popular filming location. It was used extensively for the TV series *Game of Thrones*, as well as the 2014 film *Dracula Untold*. At the end of the 18th century, the estate passed to the Jocelyn family, who held the earldom of Roden, and was eventually sold by them in 1941 to the Forest Service, who have managed it ever since. Surprisingly the main house of the estate, Bryansford House, was demolished in 1952.

The 630 hectares of Tollymore Forest Park contain a wide variety of trees. Along with the native deciduous species like oak, willow, birch and ash, there are large stands of beech, as well as coniferous species such as larch and spruce. Oak harvested from Tollymore was used by Belfast shipyard Harland & Wolff to fit out the interior of the *Titanic*. There are plenty of exotic varieties in the park including yew, Douglas fir, Monterey pine and some enormous Himalayan cedar along the main drive. There are even experimental

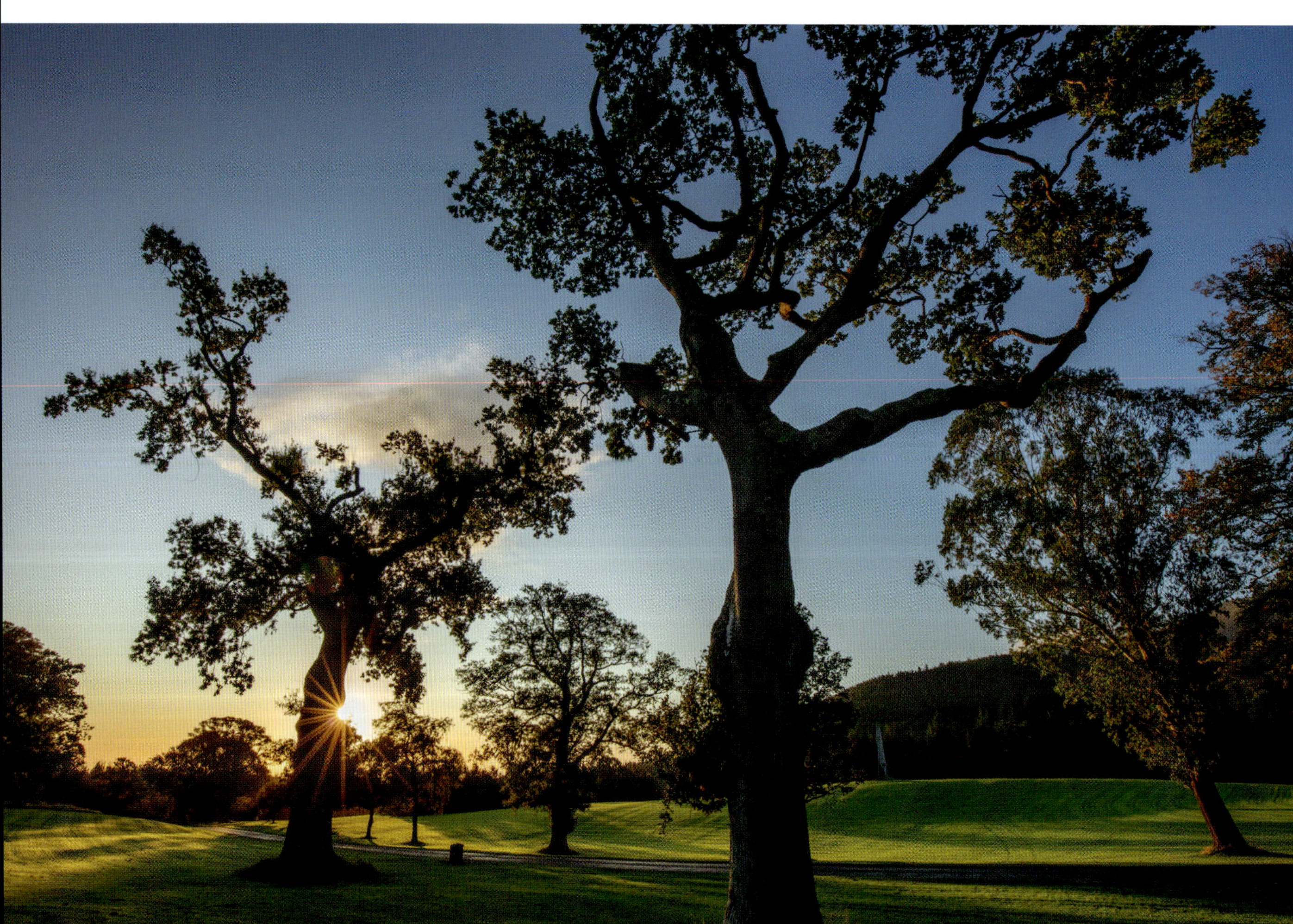

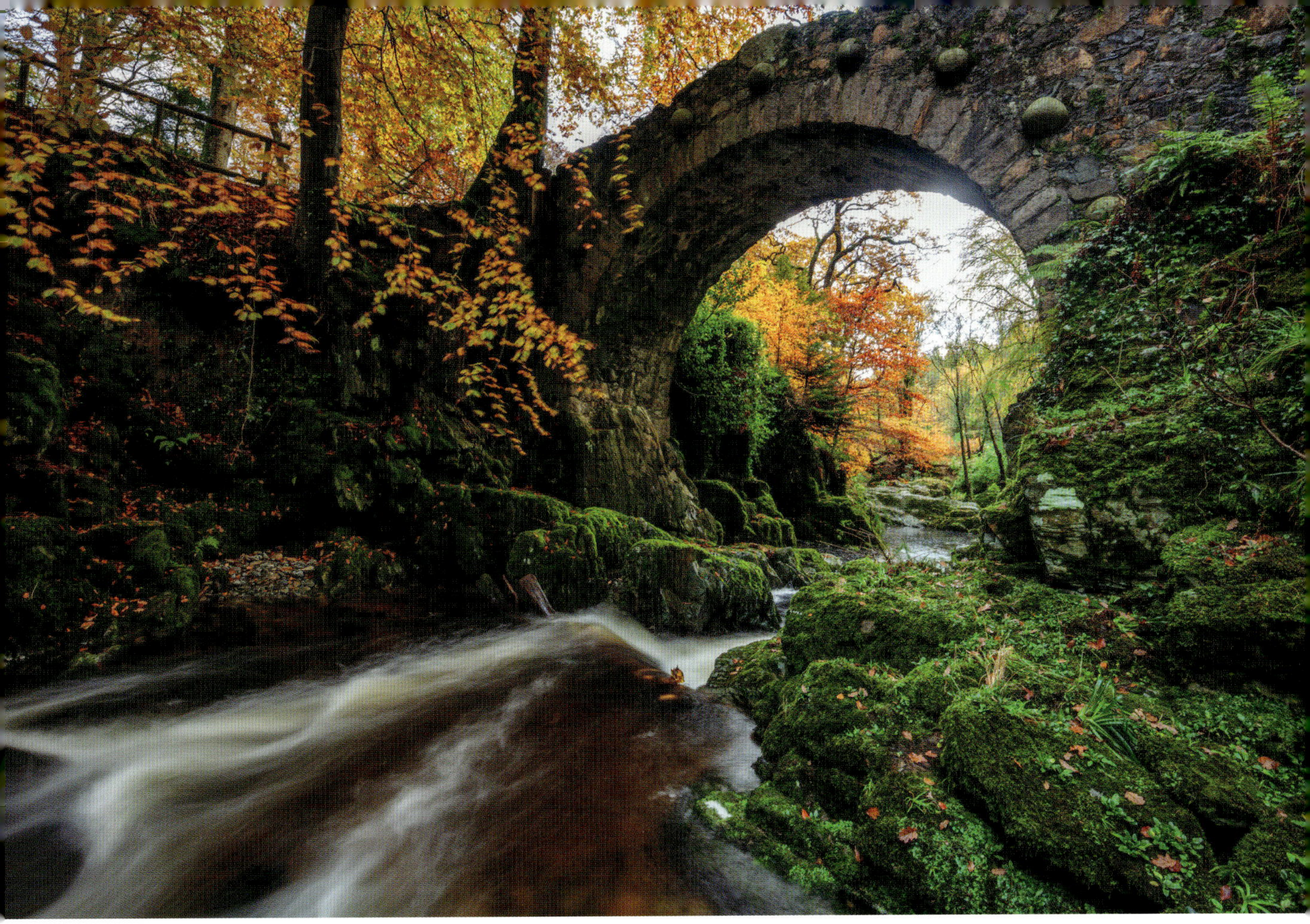

Above: The Shimna River flows under Foley's Bridge in late autumn. Built in 1787, it is one of the finest of the sixteen bridges that span the Shimna in Tollymore Forest Park.

Left: Sessile oaks along an avenue in Tollymore.

Right: Fly agaric toadstool in Tollymore Forest Park.

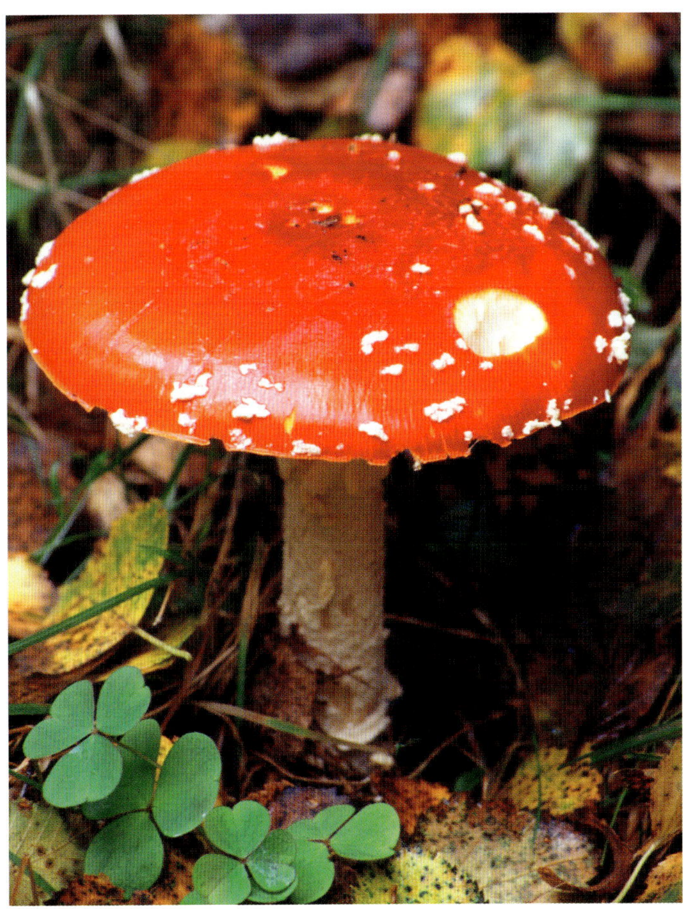

stands of eucalyptus and monkey puzzle. Tollymore's arboretum, created in 1752, is one of the oldest in Ireland.

Tollymore is a haven for wildlife, and the Shimna River has been designated as an Area of Special Scientific Interest. The red squirrel has found a home here, as have foxes, badgers, otters and the rare pine marten. Hidden away in the quieter reaches of Tollymore are herds of fallow deer. Among the many bird species are dippers and kingfishers along the river, and in the woodland, occasional breeding pairs of great spotted woodpecker.

This vast estate is one of the most popular recreational spots in the Mournes, with a beautifully situated campsite and more than twenty kilometres of signposted walking trails. Even outside the summer months, it provides an excellent low-level option for walkers when the weather is too bad to venture into the High Mournes.

Below: Built in 1856 in the Scottish baronial style, Castlewellan Castle is now run as a privately owned Christian conference centre.

Above right: Autumn reflections on Castlewellan Lake.

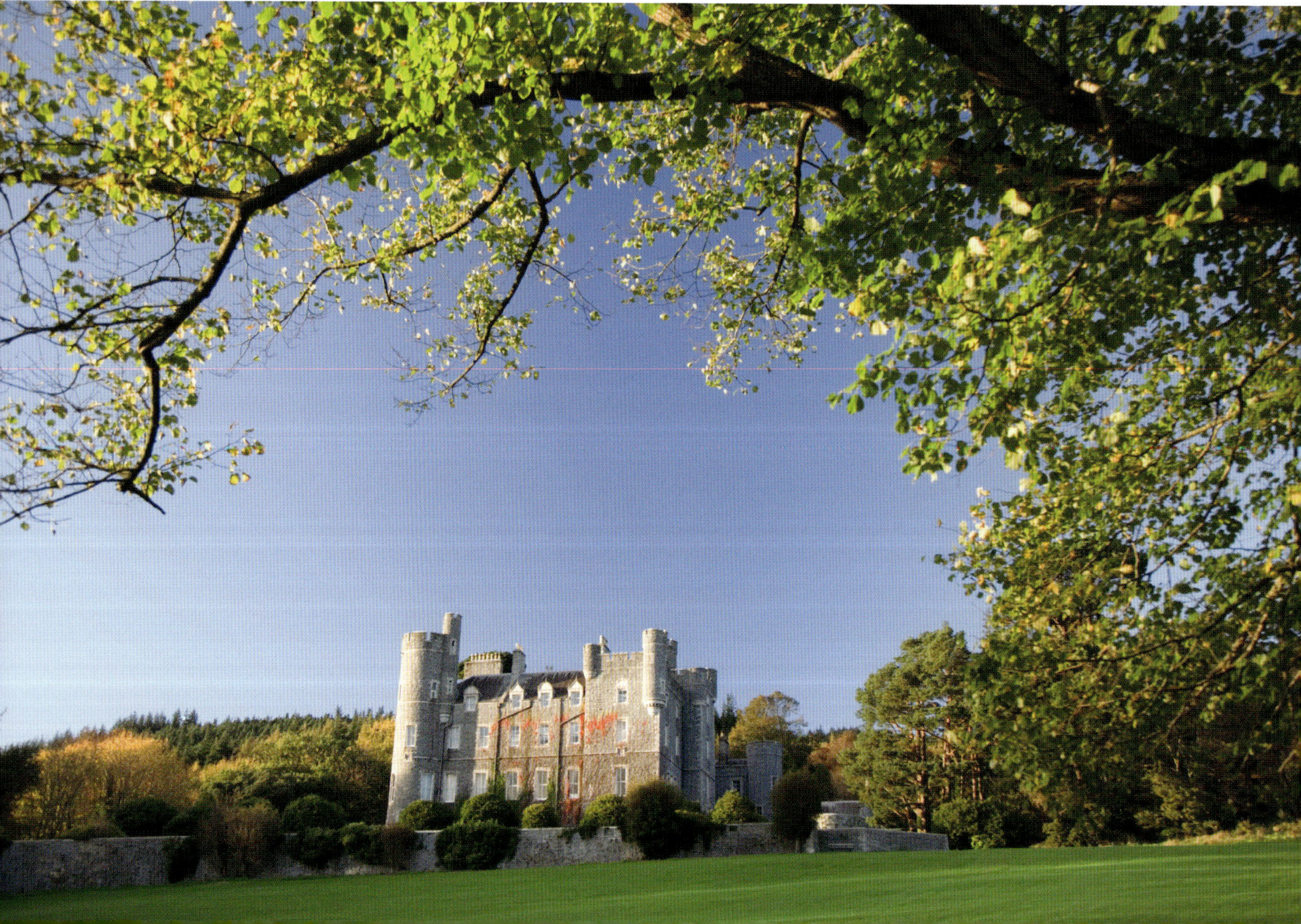

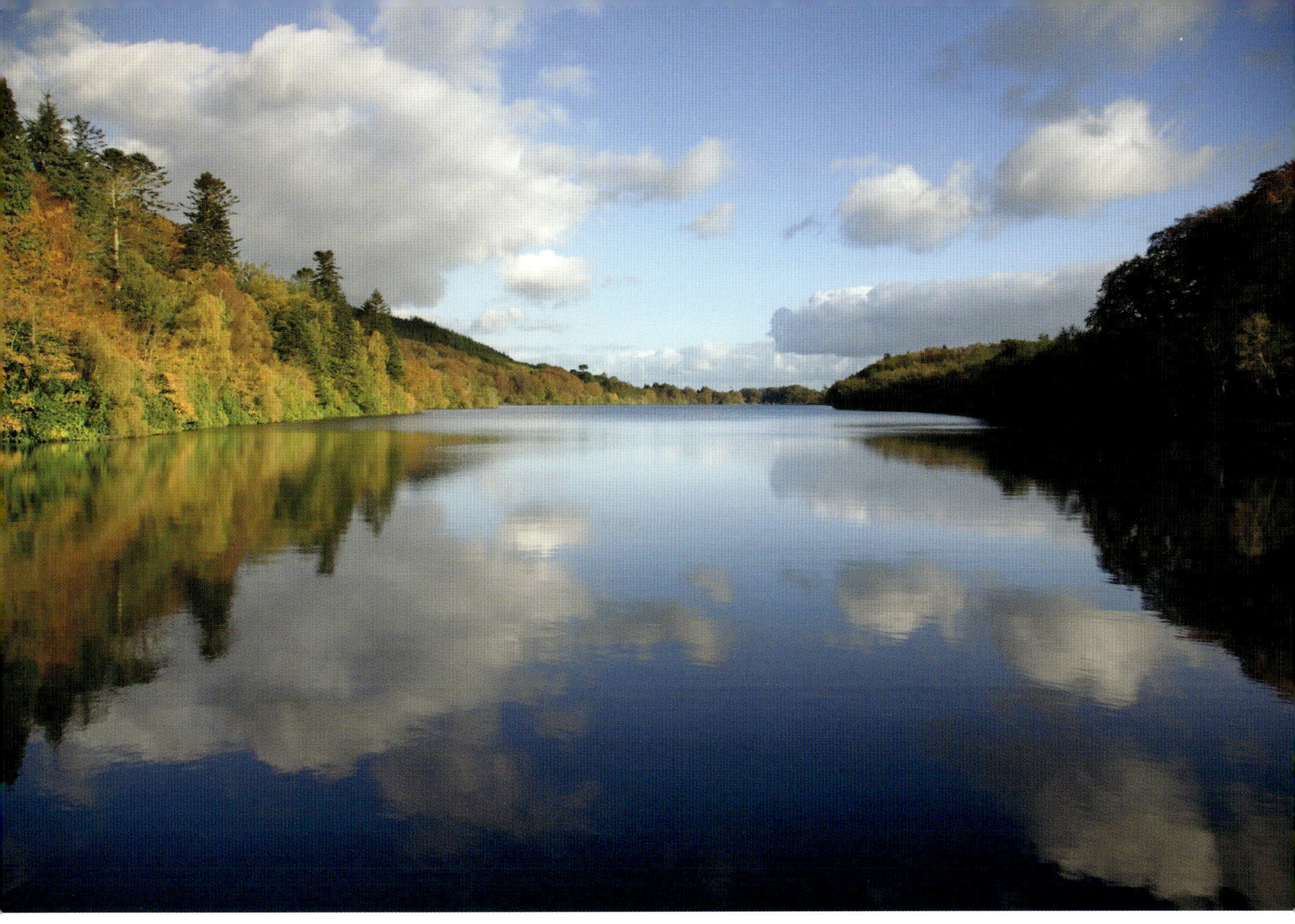

CASTLEWELLAN

Only a few kilometres north of Tollymore, set into a natural bowl on the southern slopes of Slievenaslat, is a 460-hectare swathe of mixed woodland. The estate of Castlewellan was developed by the Annesley family in the 19th century – they also designed and built the nearby town of the same name – and was sold to the Forest Service in 1967. The estate is dominated by Castlewellan Castle, built in 1856 by William Richard Annesley, 4th Earl Annesley. It is constructed in the Scottish baronial style from dressed Mourne granite and is now a Christian conference centre.

Just like Tollymore, Castlewellan has a fine arboretum, started in 1740, which hosts hundreds of species of tree from Asia, Oceania, and North and South America. It boasts approximately thirty 'champion' trees and has some excellent examples of cypress, Japanese Maple and Giant sequoia.

Where Tollymore has the rapids of the Shimna River flowing through its heart, Castlewel-lan is focused around the quiet waters of the forty-hectare Castlewellan Lake, a popular spot for kayaking, sailing and stand-up paddle boarding. North of the lakeshore, woodland and forestry rise across the lower slopes of Slievenaslat, with several clearings affording beautiful views of the Mournes. To take full advantage of these views, there are around twenty kilometres of walking trails and roughly the same length of purpose-built mountain bike trails exploring all corners of the estate. In 2001, a peace maze was constructed in the southeast corner of Castlewellan, which at the time was the largest maze of its kind in the world. These excellent recreational amenities are supported by tea rooms and a fully serviced campground.

Below: Looking across the woods and lake of Castlewellan Forest Park towards the High Mournes.

Above right: An aerial view of Rostrevor, with Rostrevor Forest Park in the background.

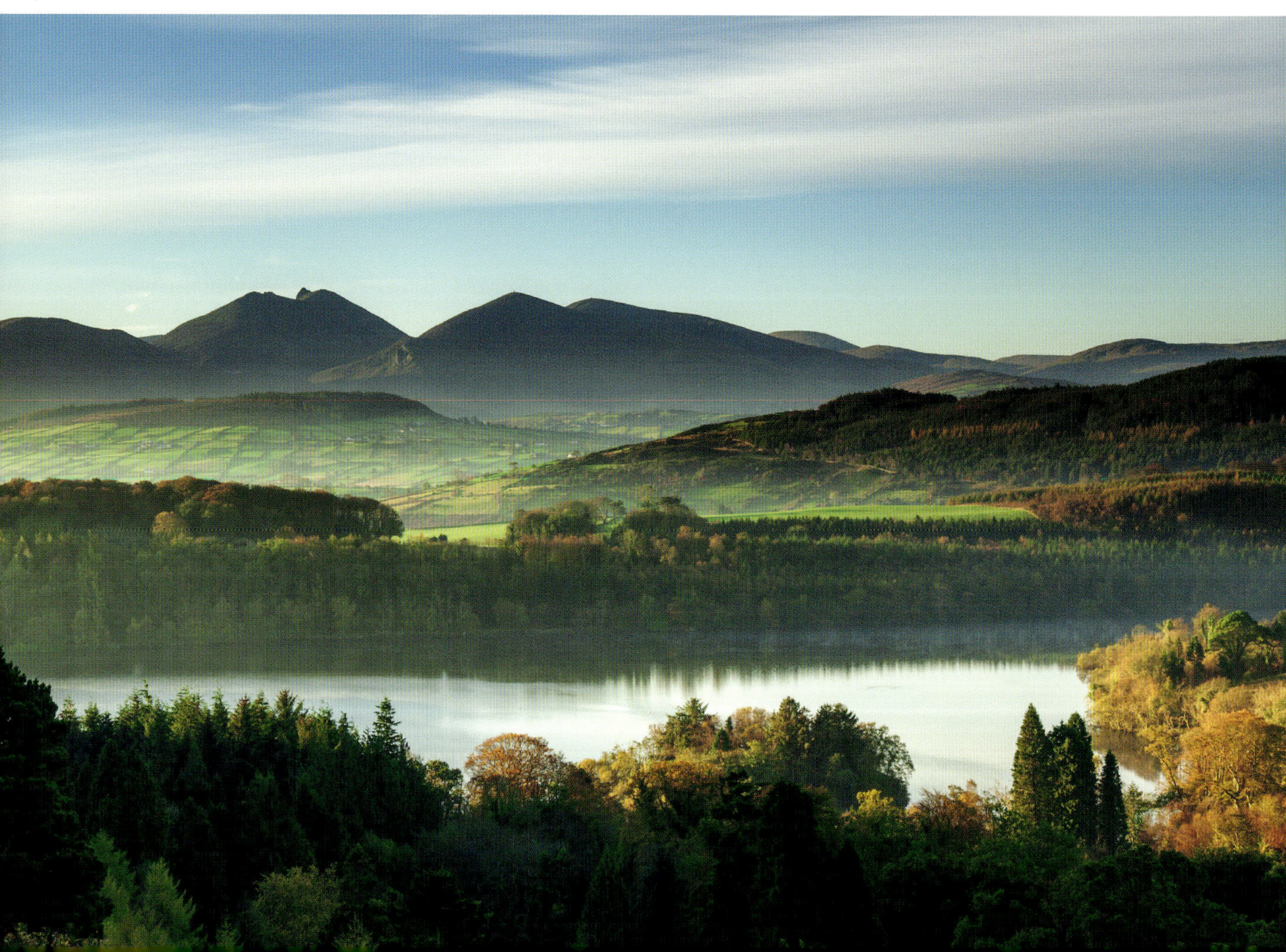

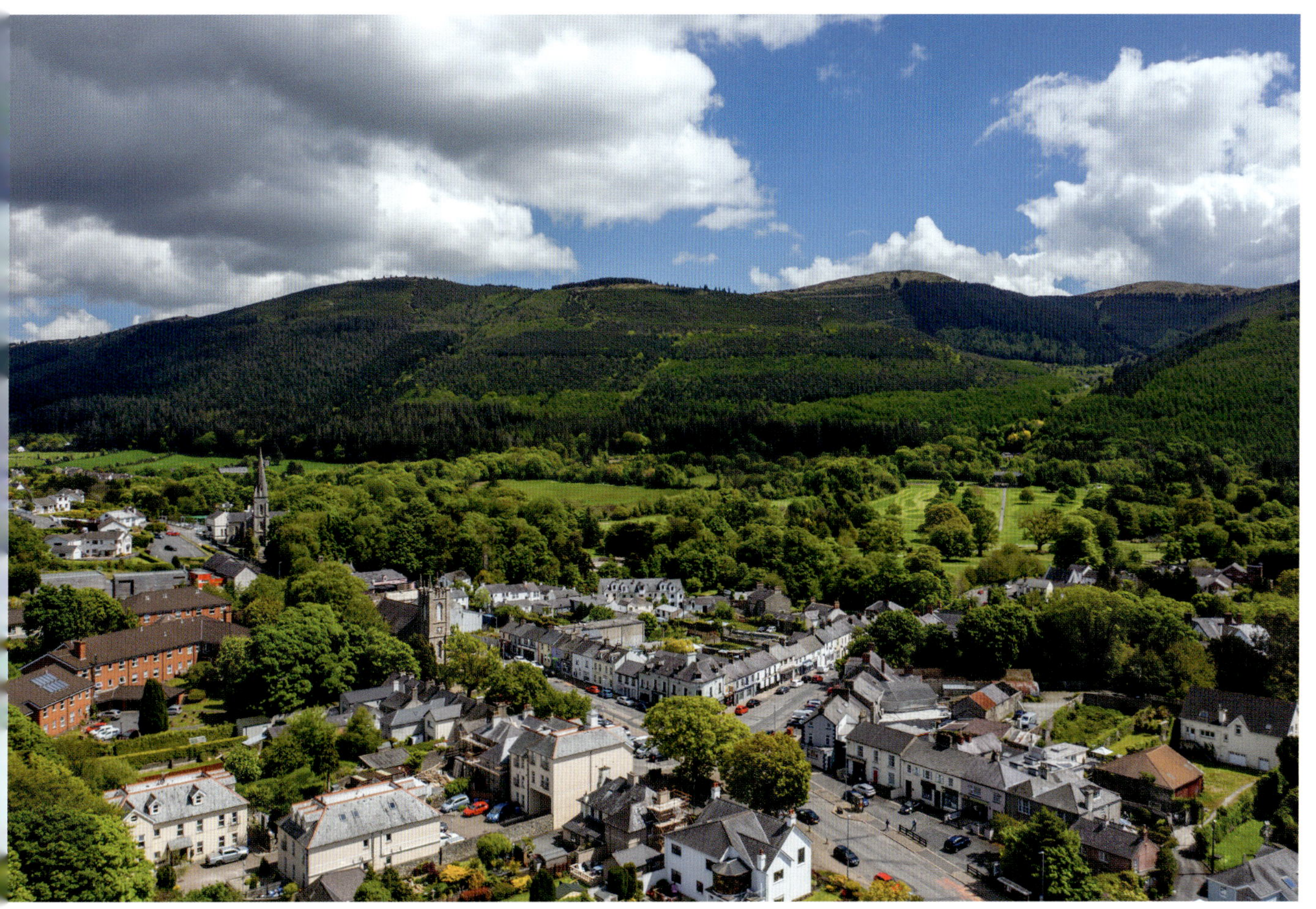

ROSTREVOR

Rostrevor is the largest of the three forest parks in the Mourne region. It dominates the northern shores of Carlingford Lough and the nearby village of Rostrevor, with extensive forestry covering a large section of the southern slopes of Slievemartin. Most of this is coniferous forest, which extends almost all the way to its 485-metre-high summit. Lower down there are good stands of deciduous species, including forty-one acres of beautiful and ancient oak woodland, which is a designated nature reserve and Special Area of Conservation. The red squirrel has found a home here, along with several rare species of woodland flora.

Rostrevor forest incorporates the formal parkland

and arboretum of Kilbroney Park, which was the estate of the Ross family from the 1700s. The estate was inherited by a second cousin of the Queen Mother, Lady Elizabeth Bowes-Lyon, in 1919, and in 1937 the future Queen Elizabeth II holidayed there. Other notable visitors over the years included the writers Charles Dickens, William Makepeace Thackeray, Seamus Heaney and C.S. Lewis. It is thought that the Narnia books were at least in part inspired by Lewis's stay here. The estate was sold to the local council in 1977.

Recreation is now at the heart of Rostrevor. There is excellent camping in the summer months and an extensive network of walking paths and tracks. In recent years, it has become an internationally renowned centre for downhill mountain-biking, with more than thirty kilometres of purpose-built trails to be ridden.

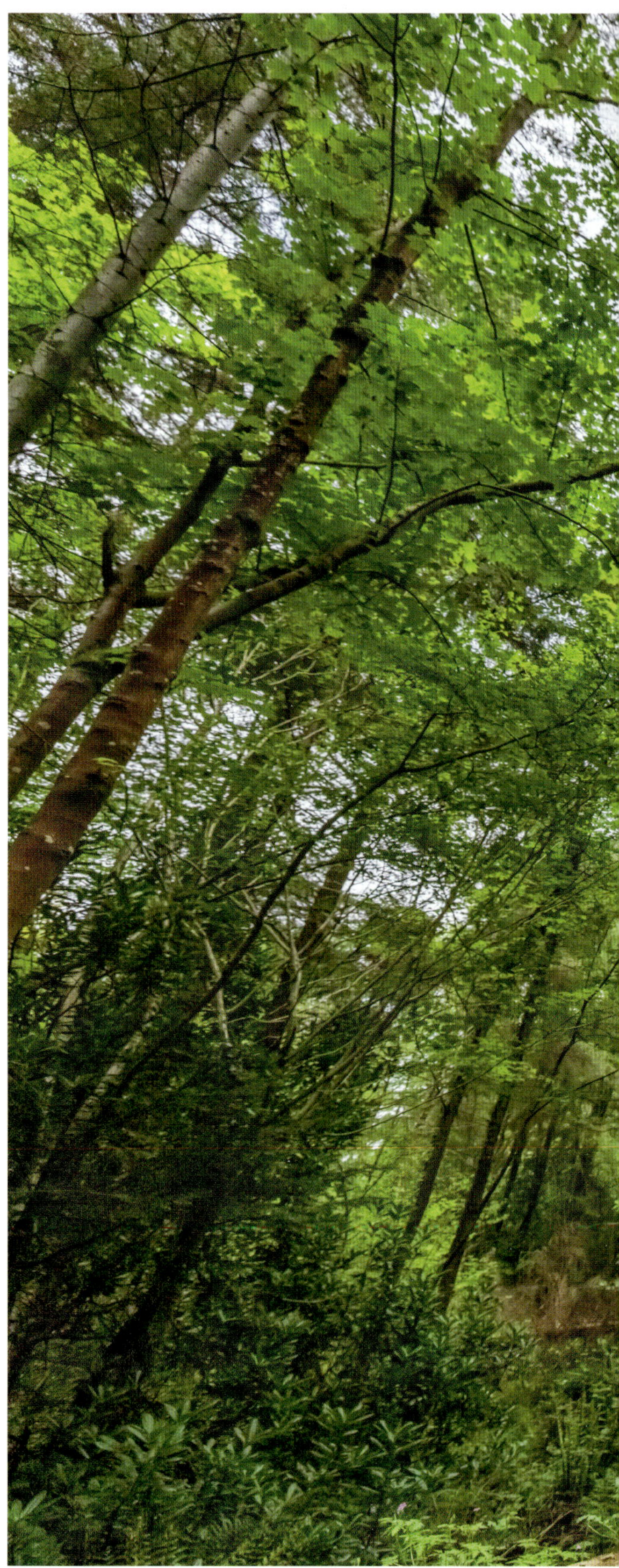

Right: Twelve-year old Geordan McCormack takes flight on one of Rostrevor's renowned mountain bike trails.

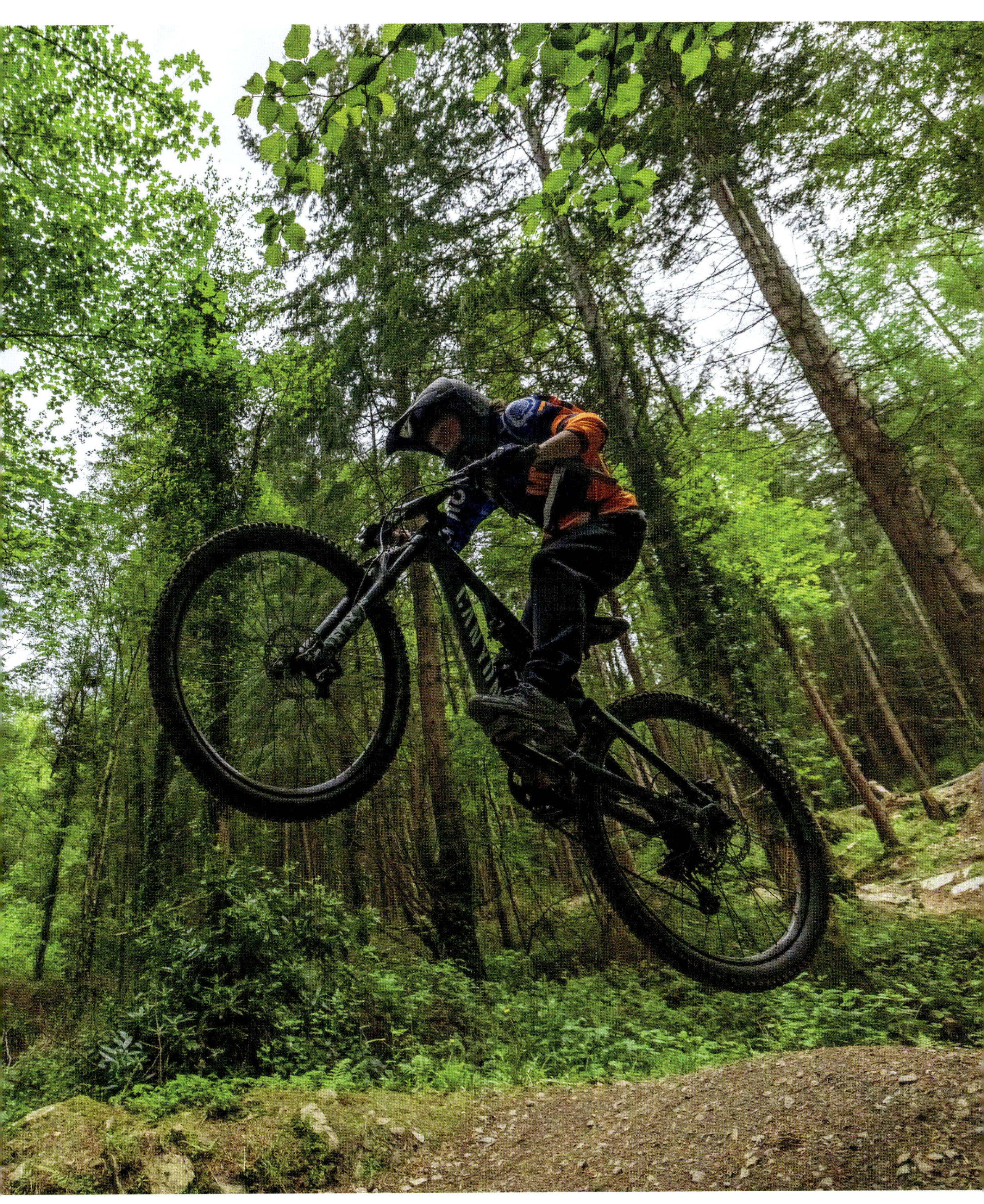

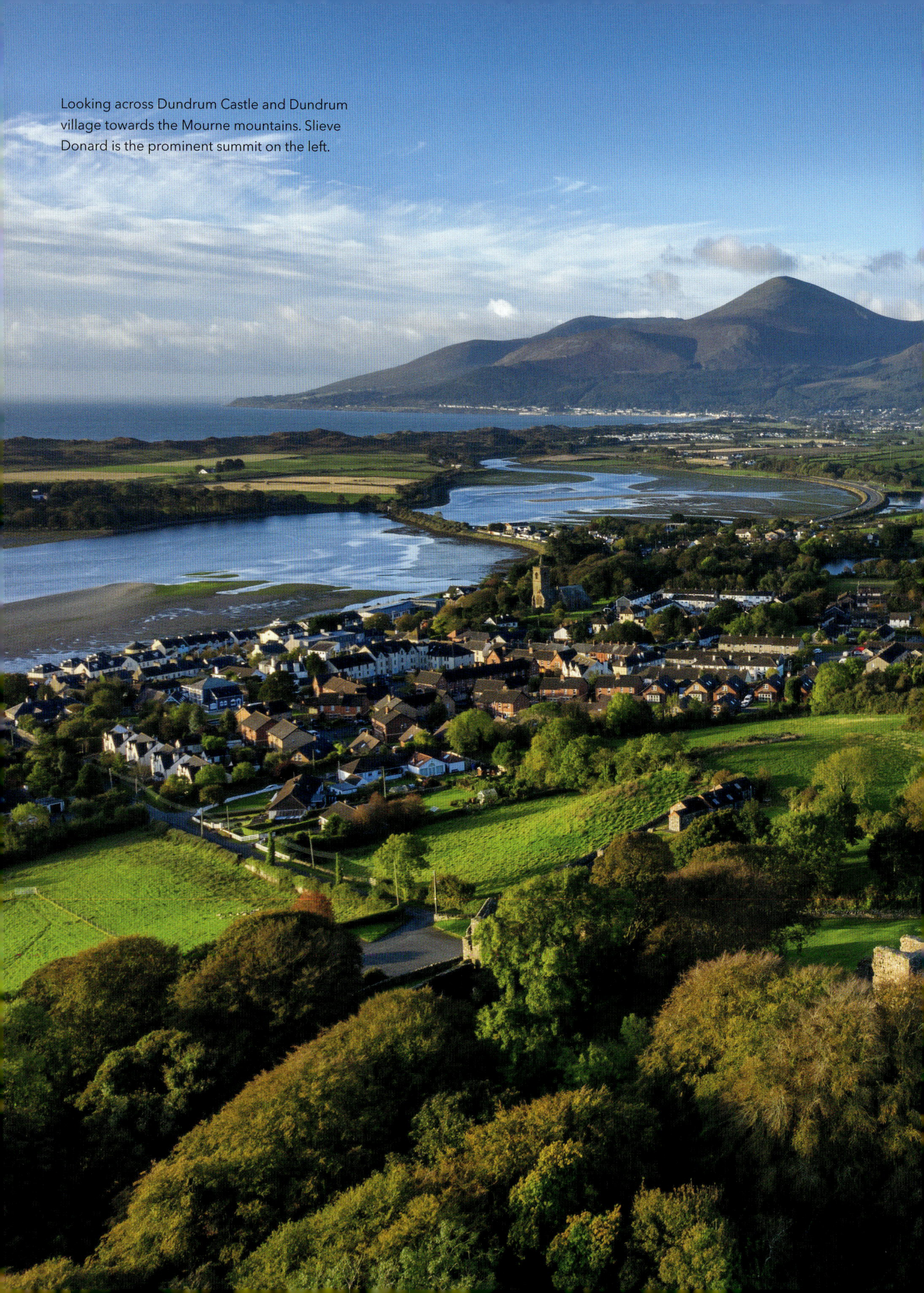

Looking across Dundrum Castle and Dundrum village towards the Mourne mountains. Slieve Donard is the prominent summit on the left.

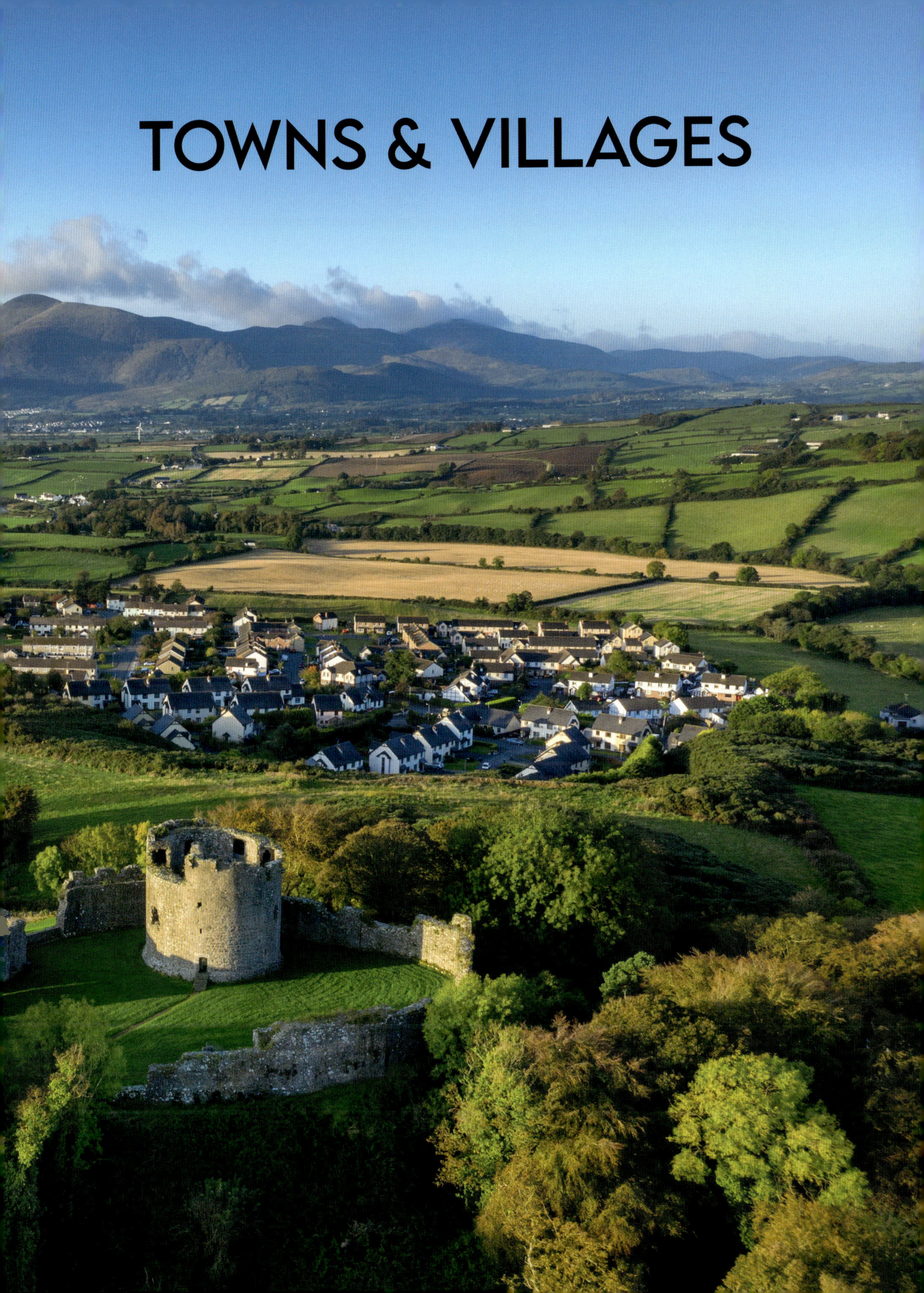
TOWNS & VILLAGES

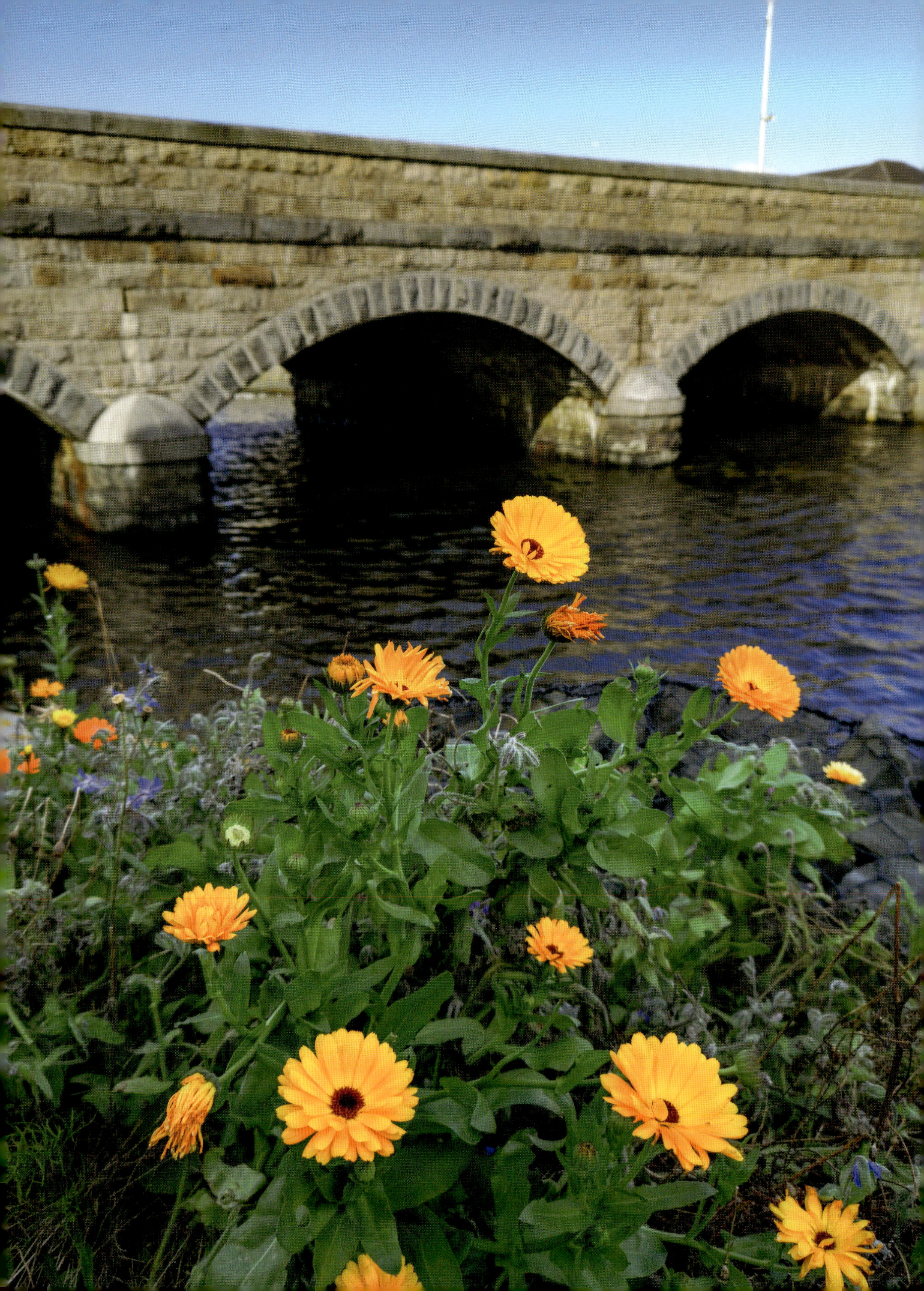

NEWCASTLE

No other town is as synonymous with the Mournes as Newcastle. Even by Irish standards, it is not large, but it casts a bigger shadow on the region than its population of around eight thousand would suggest. Its location, at the southern end of Dundrum Bay and the foot of Slieve Donard, lends it an iconic, picture-postcard backdrop. Today it is one of Northern Ireland's most popular seaside resorts and arguably its number-one location for outdoor pursuits.

The town grew up around the site of New Castle, an Anglo-Norman castle built by the Magennises at the mouth of the Shimna River. The remains of the castle were demolished in the 19th century and replaced by the Annesley Arms Hotel. In fact, it was the Annesley family who were responsible for much of the early development of Newcastle as a

Left: Flowers growing on the banks of the Shimna River in the centre of Newcastle.

Below: Newcastle Beach at low tide in winter, looking towards Newcastle seafront and the Mournes.

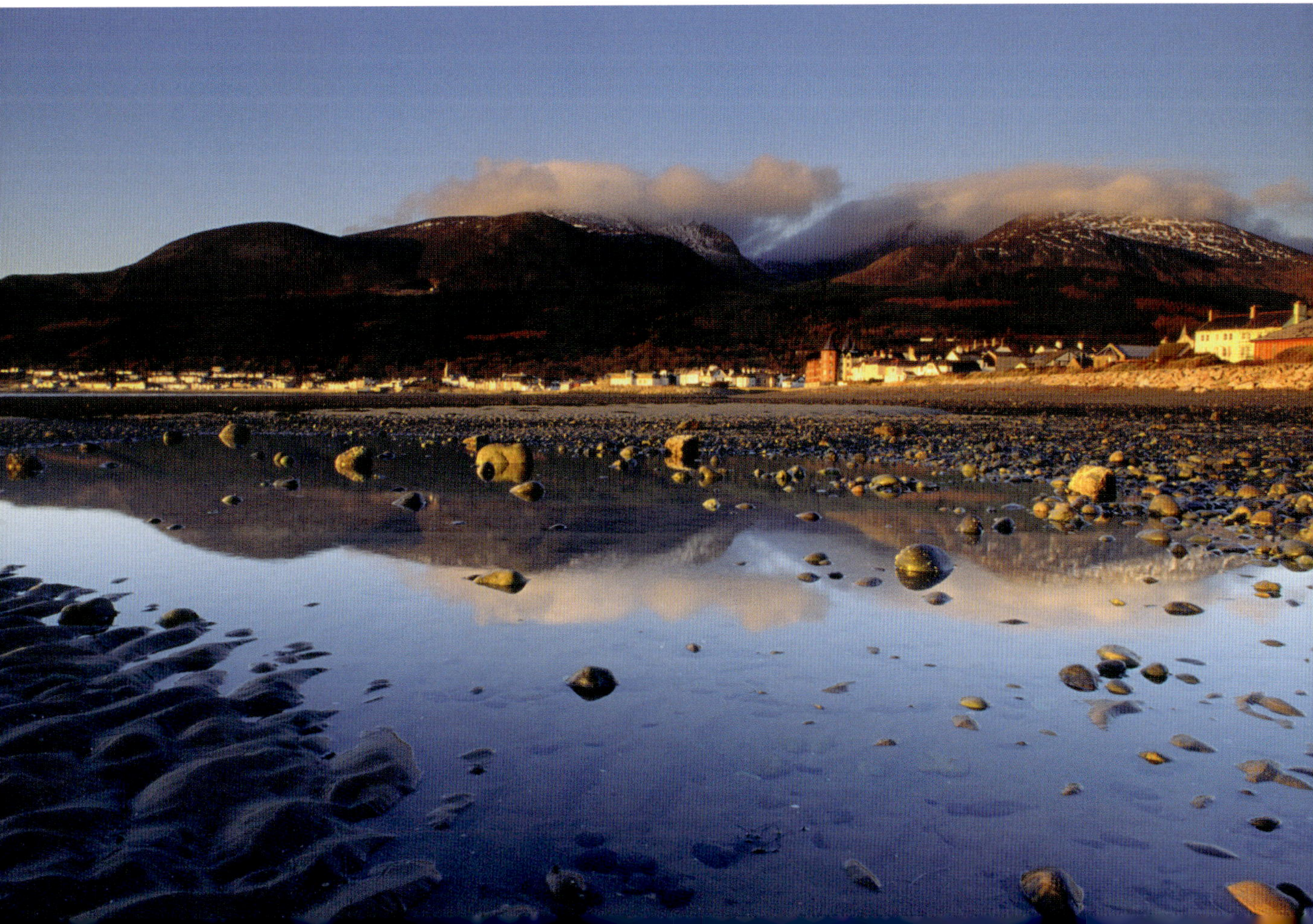

Victorian seaside resort. The opening of a railway line between Belfast and Newcastle in 1869 accelerated this growth, and in 1897 the Victorian splendour of the Slieve Donard Hotel became its centrepiece, an establishment which still dominates the town and whose guestbook includes the names of King Leopold of Belgium, Charlie Chaplin, Tiger Woods and the Miami Dolphins.

This period of the late 19th century also saw the development of the world-famous Royal County Down links golf course, which occupies a vast swathe of the dune and heath north of Newcastle and south of the National Trust's Murlough Nature Reserve. It has two eighteen-hole courses, of which the championship course was ranked the best in the world by *Golf Digest*.

Below: An aerial view of Newcastle, looking south along the seafront to Donard Wood and the summit of Slieve Donard at top left.

Above right: Fishing boats in Newcastle harbour.

Below right: Mosaic artwork by Maeve King at Newcastle harbour commemorating the grounding of the SS *Great Britain*.

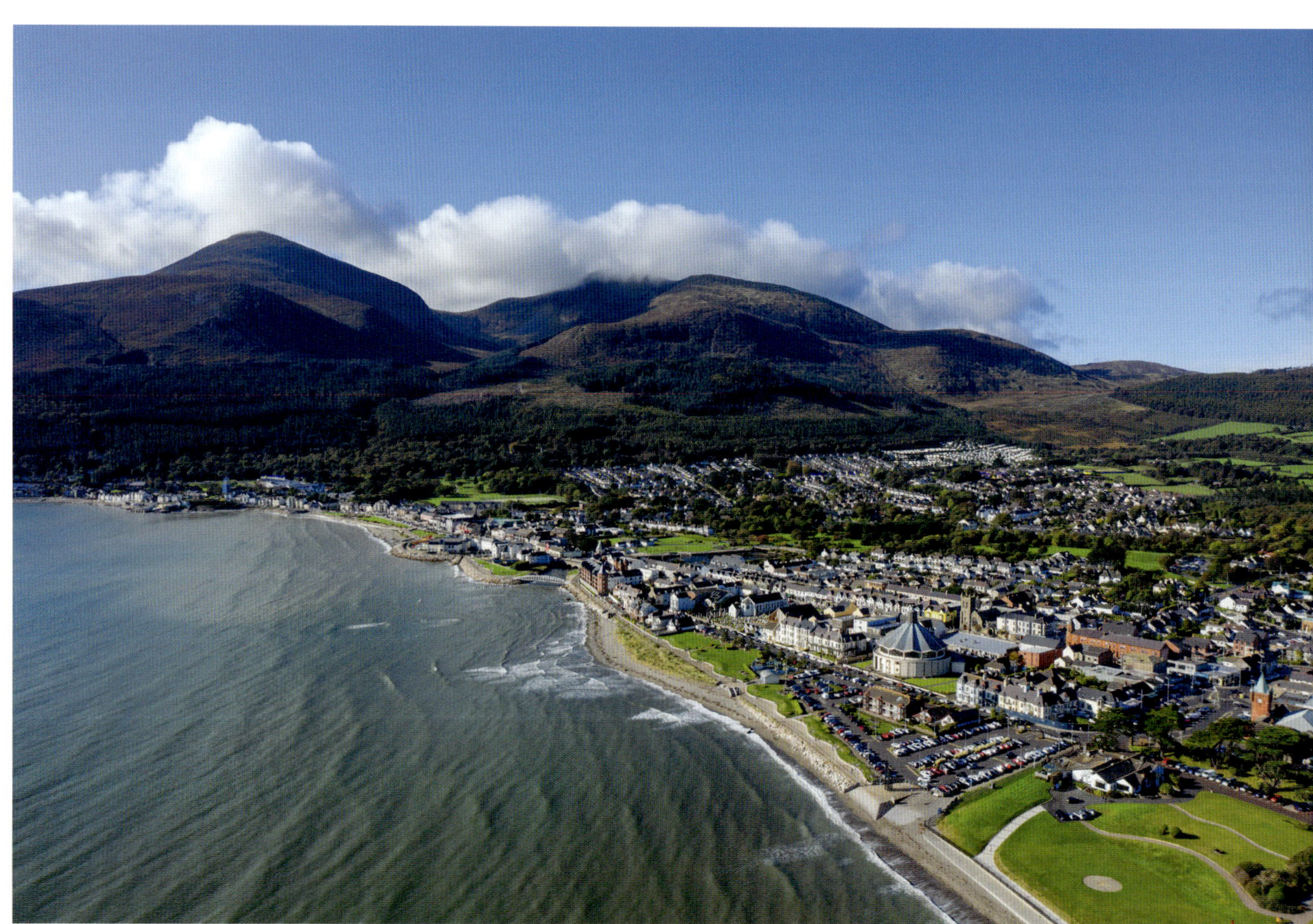

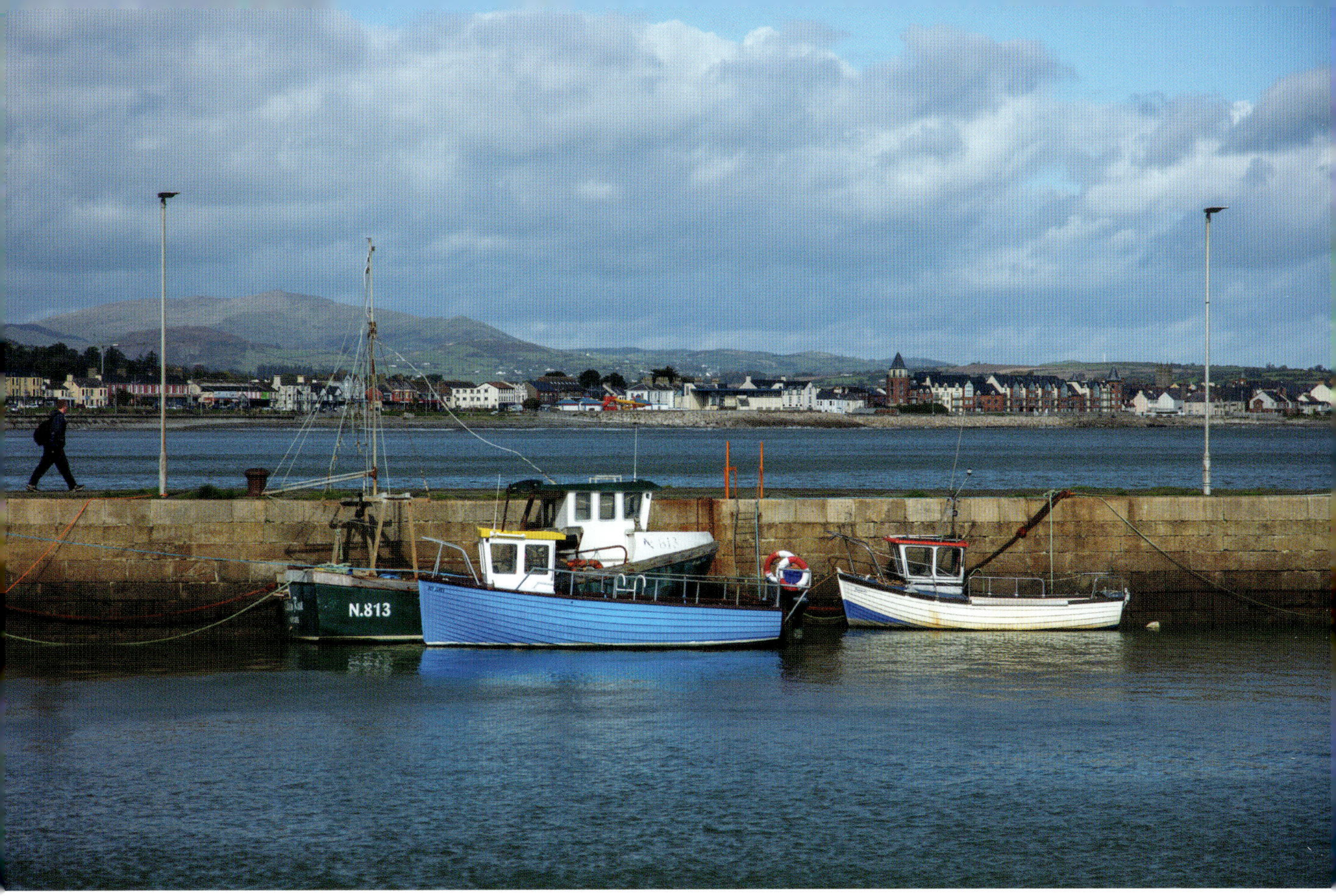

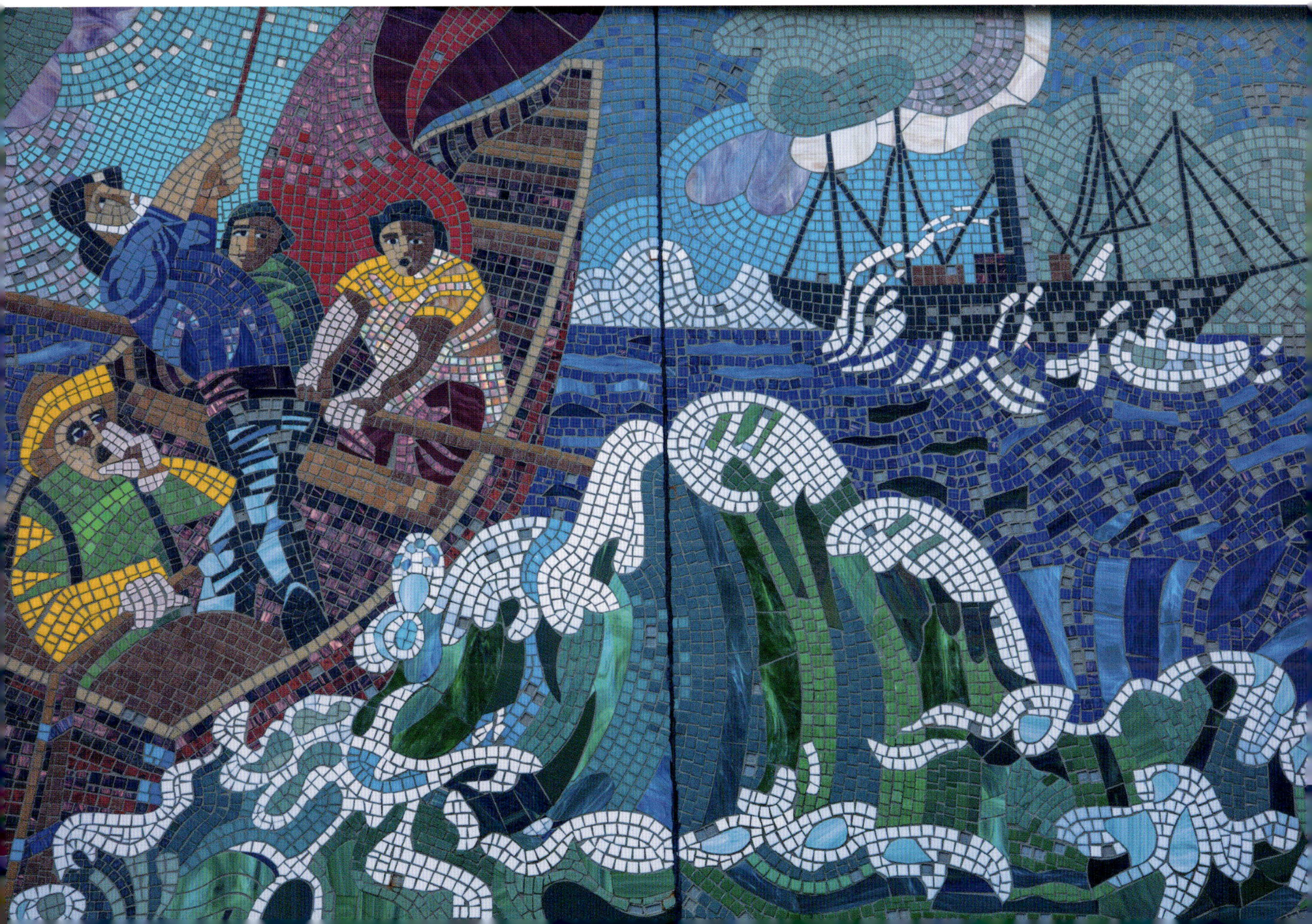

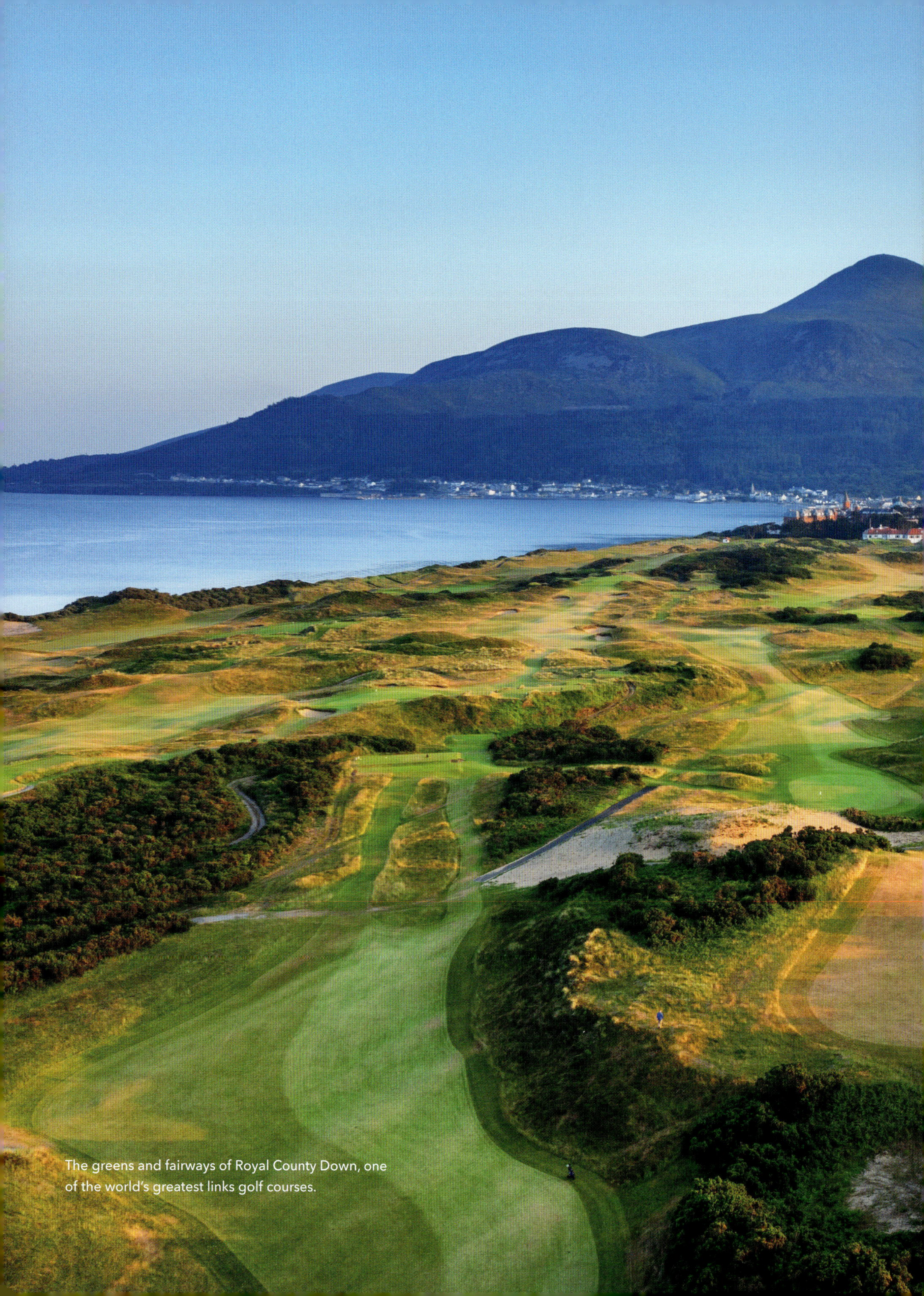

The greens and fairways of Royal County Down, one of the world's greatest links golf courses.

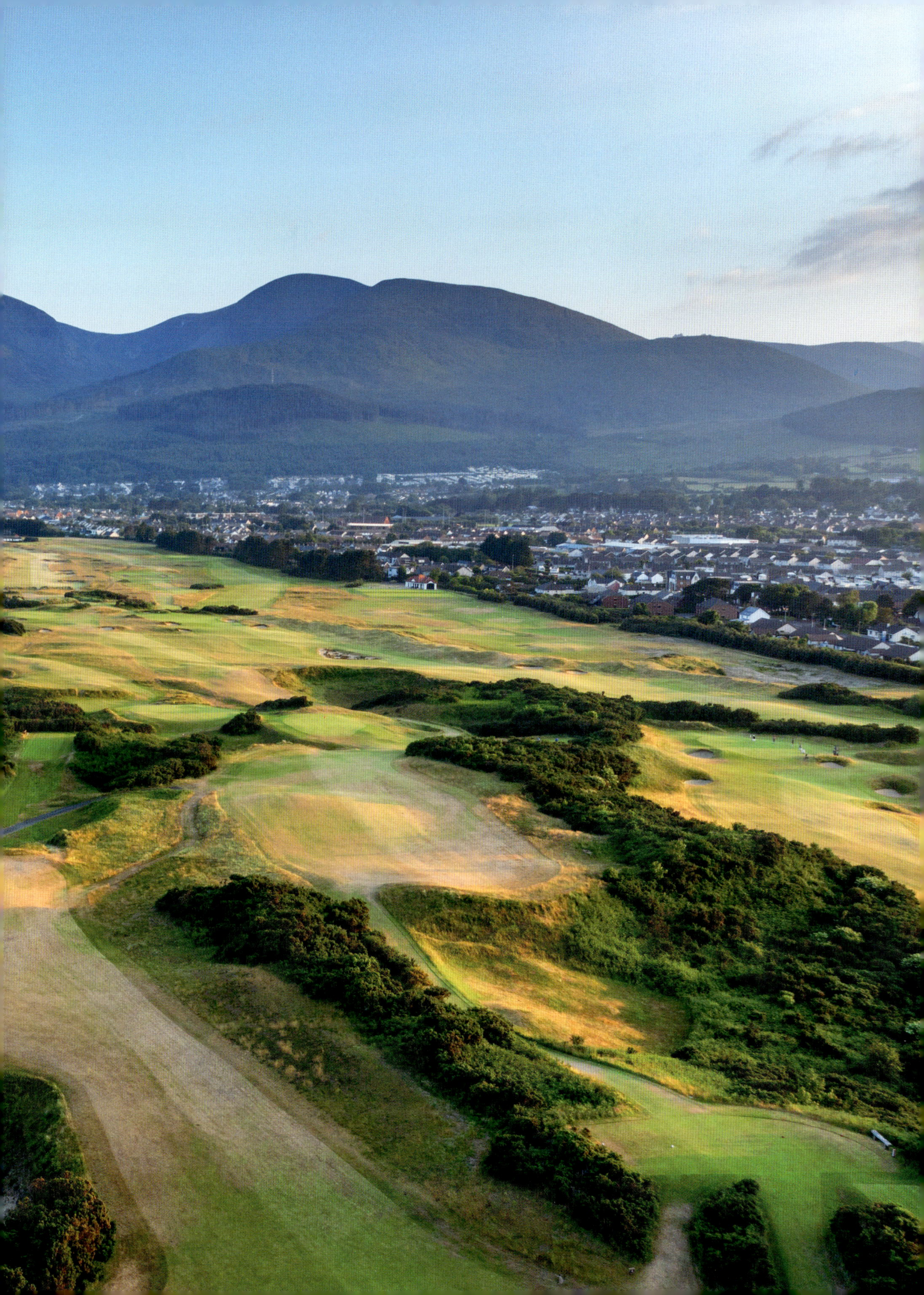

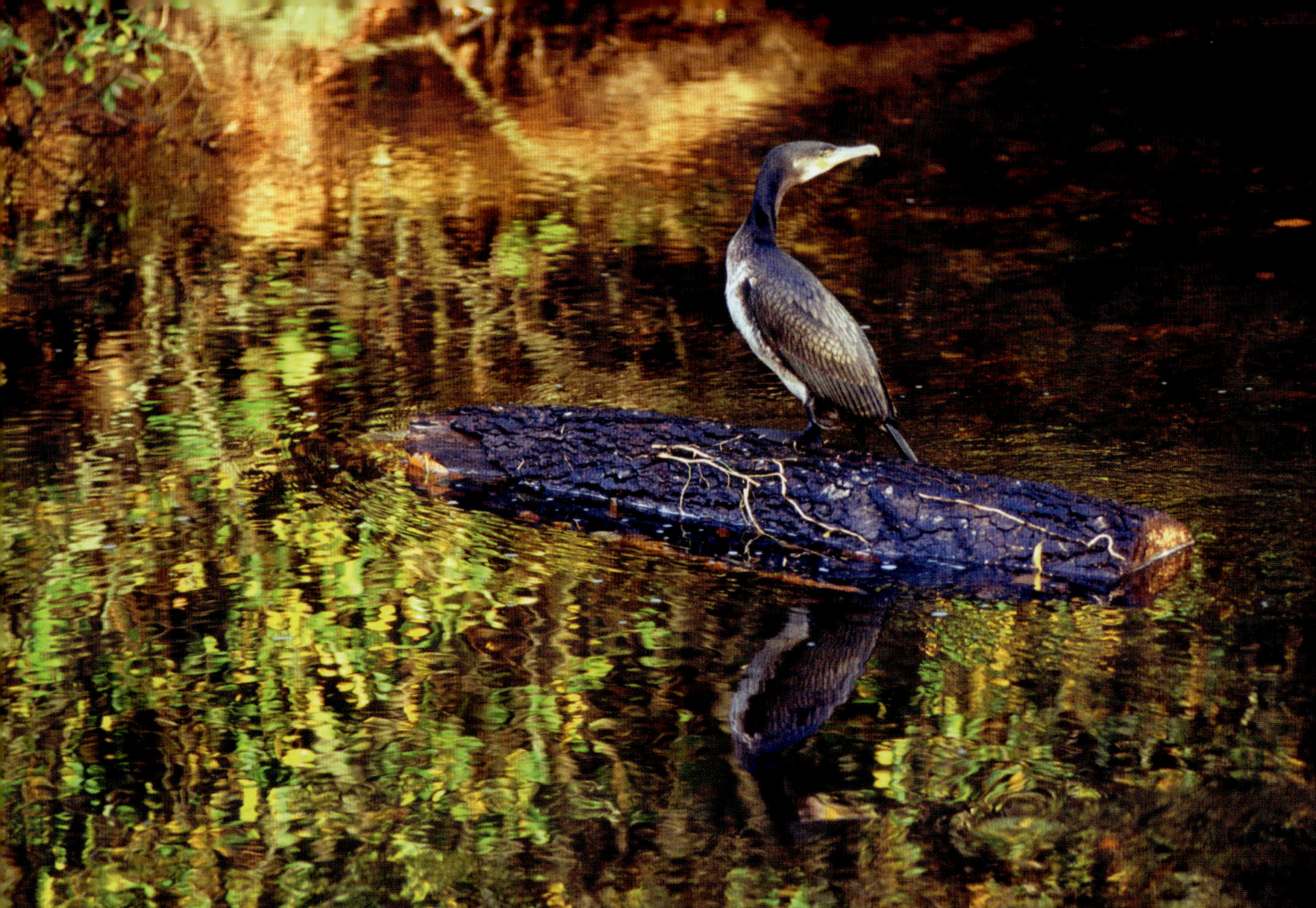

Newcastle's growth was not based solely on tourism. The burgeoning granite-quarrying industry saw the development of a significant operation on the slopes of Slieve Donard, and the harbour grew to accommodate the larger vessels that were used to export stone. Fishing was also a big part of the local economy, although commercial fishing has now largely moved to the town of Kilkeel. In January 1843, forty-six men from Newcastle lost their lives when their boats were caught out by a winter storm. Widow's Row, a line of small, terraced cottages above the harbour, was built to house the twenty-seven widows and 118 children left behind by the deceased men.

Above: A cormorant takes five on the Shimna River just outside Newcastle.

Above right: Heather and marram grass are the characteristic flora of Murlough National Nature Reserve, a 6,000-year-old dune system located just north of Newcastle town on the shores of Dundrum Bay.

Below right: Splashes of colourful paint and flowers brighten Widow's Row.

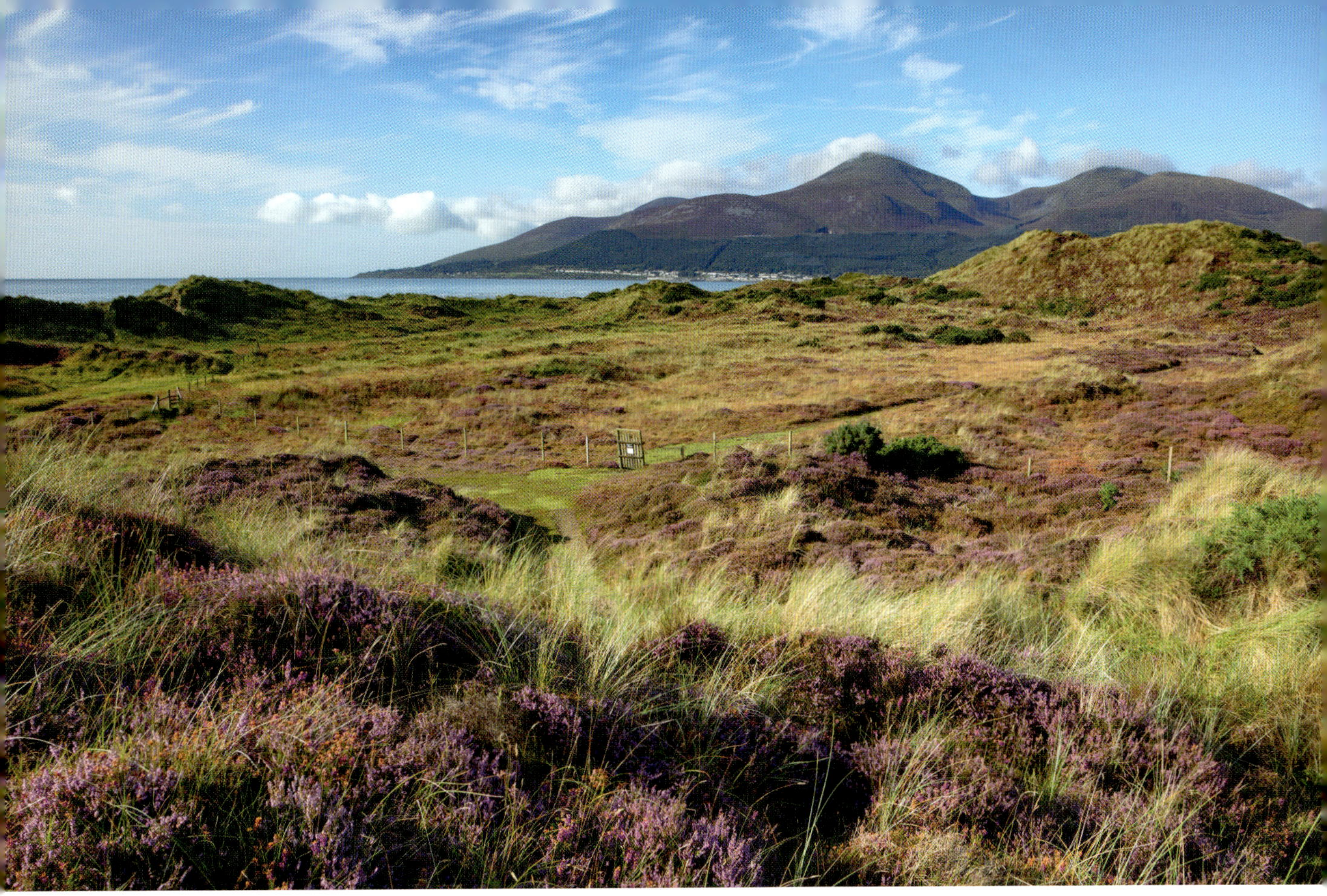

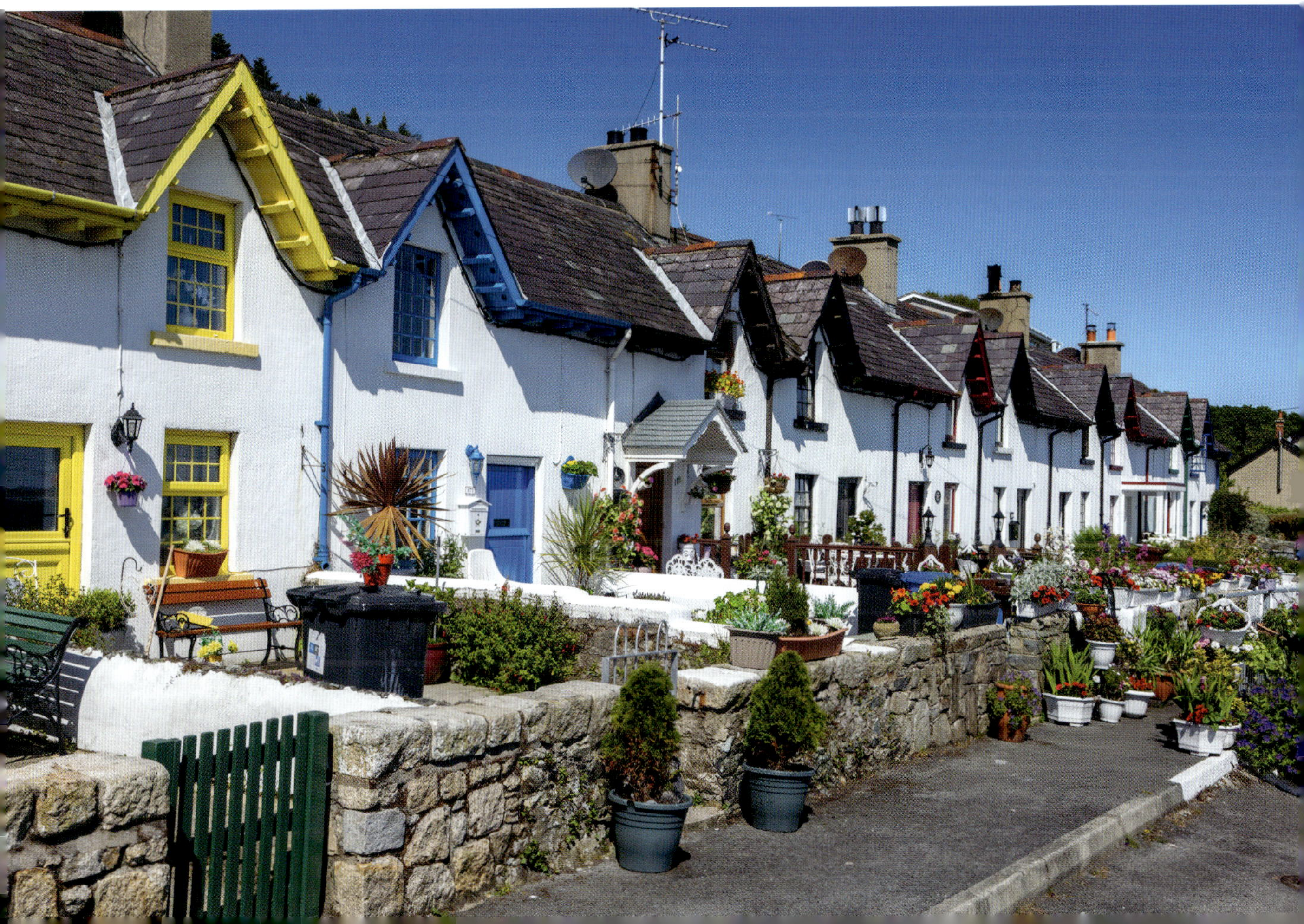

DUNDRUM

A few kilometres north of Newcastle, along the main A2 road to Belfast, is the village of Dundrum. The name is an anglicisation of the Irish *Dún Droma*, meaning 'The Fort of the Ridge', a reference to the prominent hill overlooking the town. Originally the site of a fort built by the Celtic Uladh clans, it was later used by the Anglo-Norman John de Courcy as the location for one of the most important castles in Ulster. That a village grew up around this castle is not surprising; not only was it strategically important, but it was also situated on the sheltered shores of Dundrum Inner Bay. From the 17th century onwards, Dundrum became an important port and was in use as recently as 1984. Today it is home to more than 1,500 people.

Below: The Twelve Arches Bridge just outside Dundrum village.

Above right: St Donard's Church of Ireland church, Dundrum village.

Below right: Looking across the rooftops of Dundrum village and Dundrum Bay to the slopes of Slieve Donard.

Overleaf below left: The Rostrevor River flowing down out of the Fairy Glen and into Rostrevor itself.

Overleaf above right: The main avenue of Kilbroney Park, Rostrevor.

Overleaf below right: A colourful trawler pulled ashore at Greencastle.

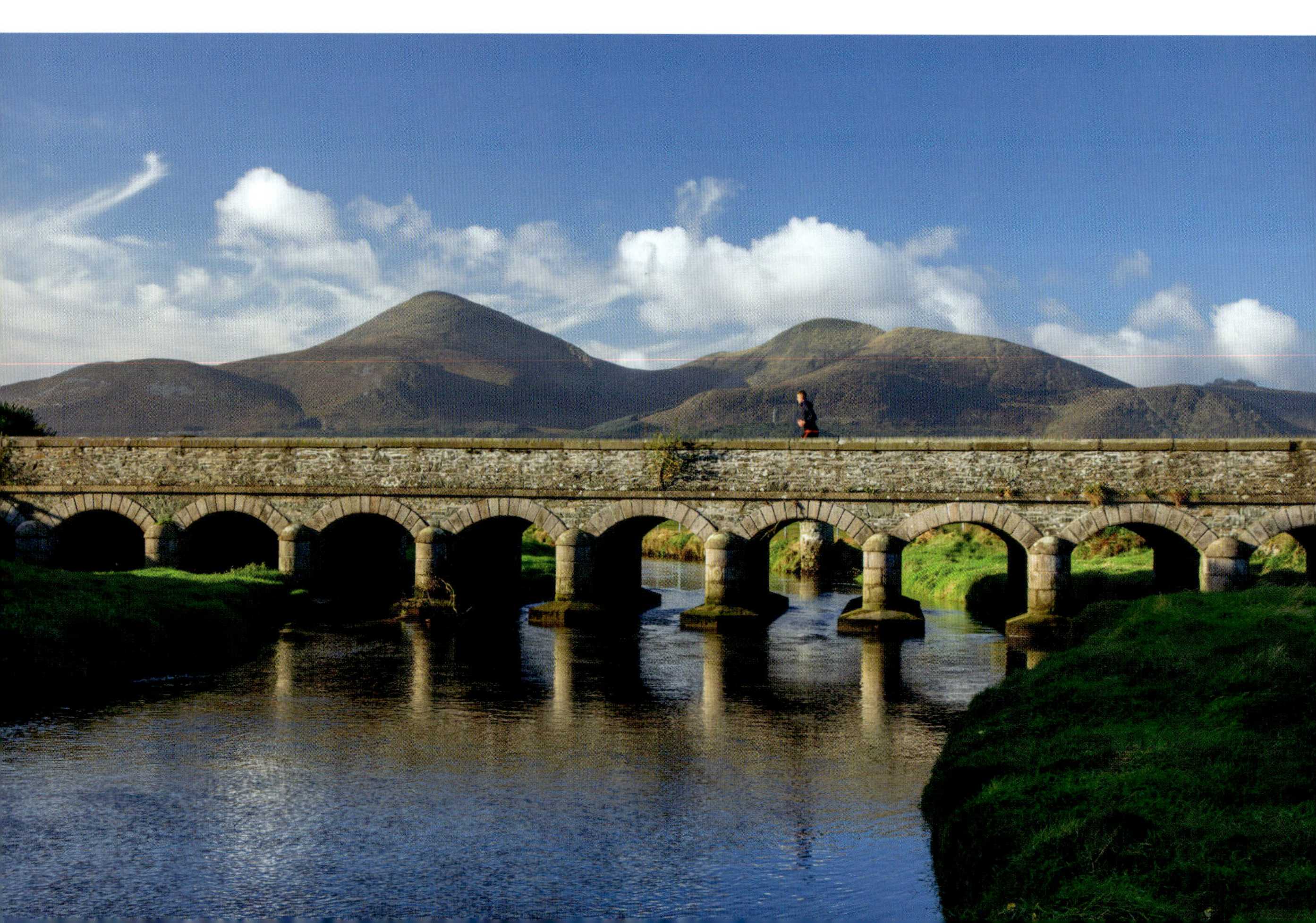

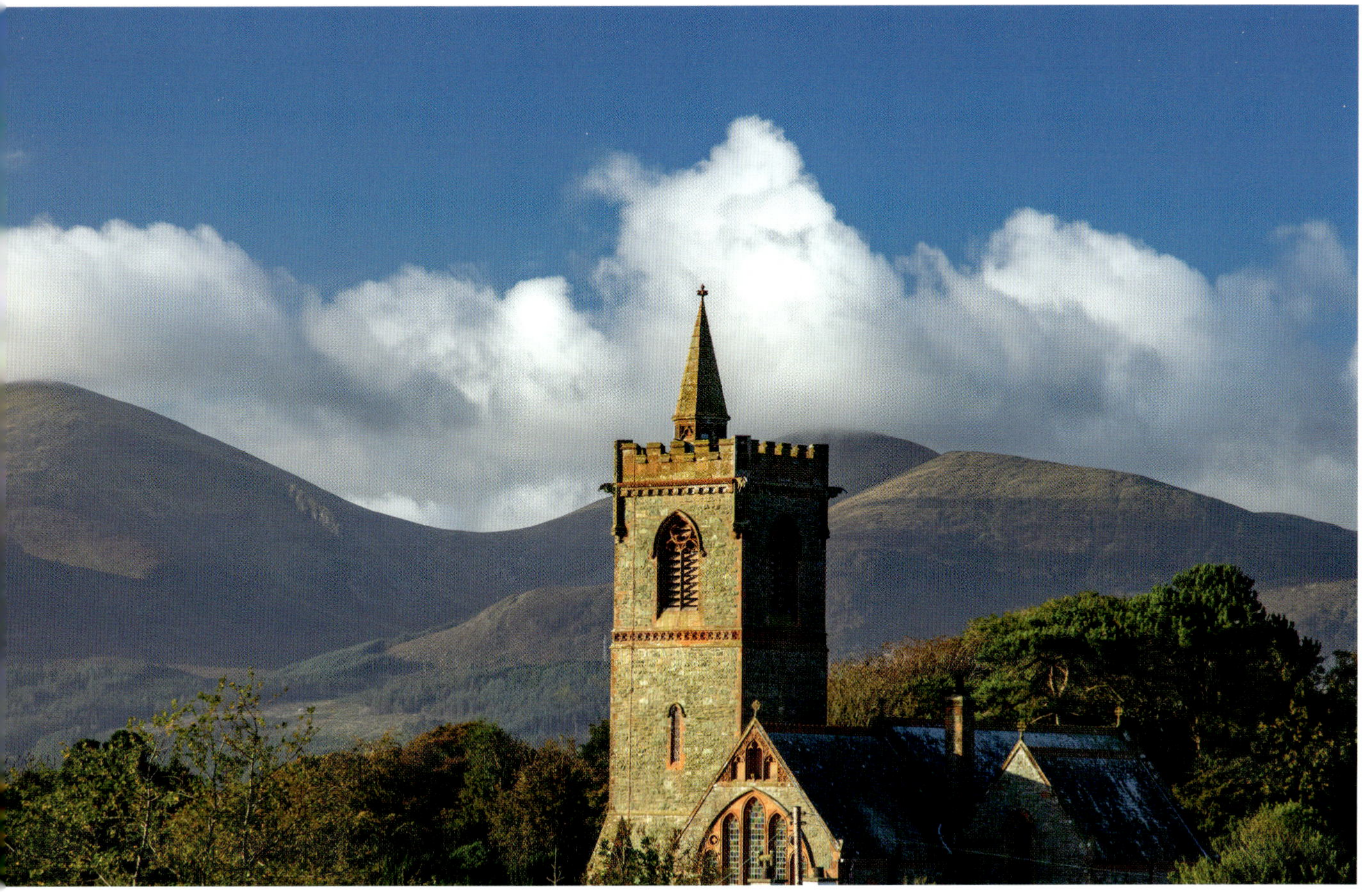

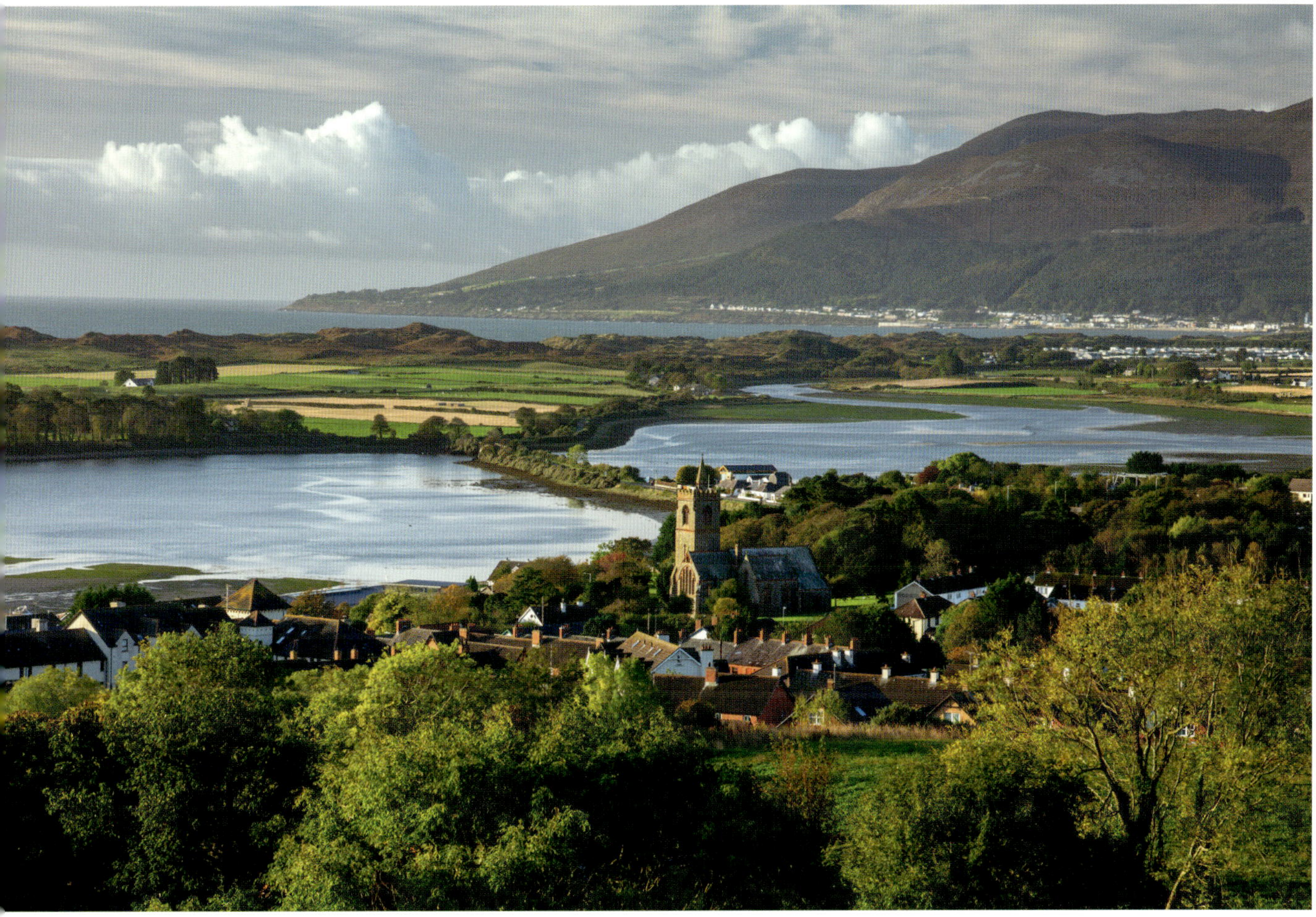

ROSTREVOR

With a population of around 2,500, Rostrevor is an attractive village sandwiched between the southern slopes of the Mournes and the northern shores of Carlingford Lough. It was an important Christian and Celtic site known formerly as both Glen Seicis and Caisleán Ruaidhrí. The forested slopes of Slievemartin tower almost five hundred vertical metres above the village and lend Rostrevor the first part of its contemporary name, deriving from the Irish *ros* meaning 'wooded headland'. The second part of the name is associated with Sir Edward Trevor, who settled in the area in the 17th century.

Rostrevor was a fashionable resort for Victorian tourists, who were transported to the village from the train terminus in Warrenpoint on a horse-drawn tramway. It is now regaining some of that popularity through the walking trails, camping and formal parkland of the Kilbroney estate and Rostrevor Forest Park. The village has also become internationally known for the extensive cross-country and downhill mountain bike trails built in the forest park.

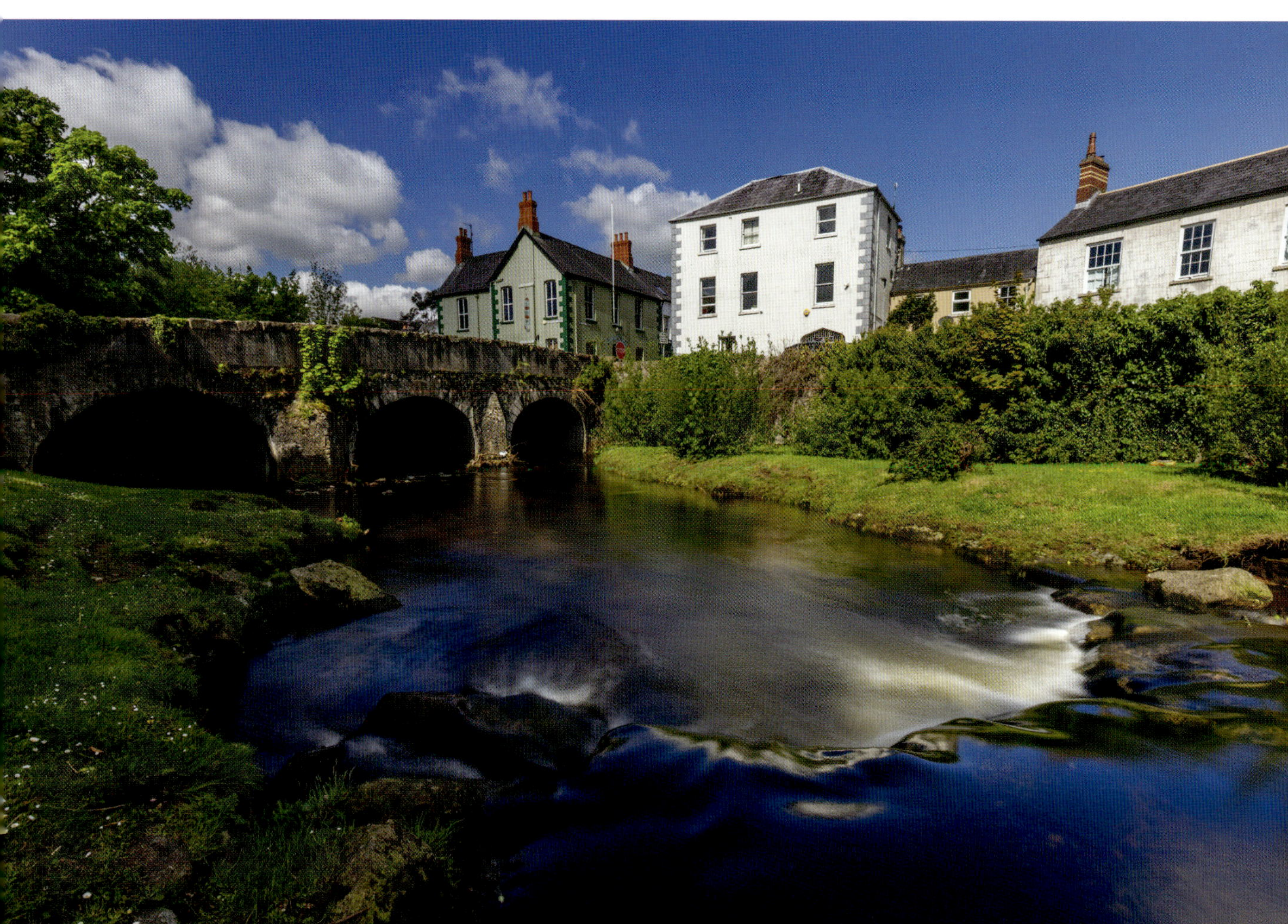

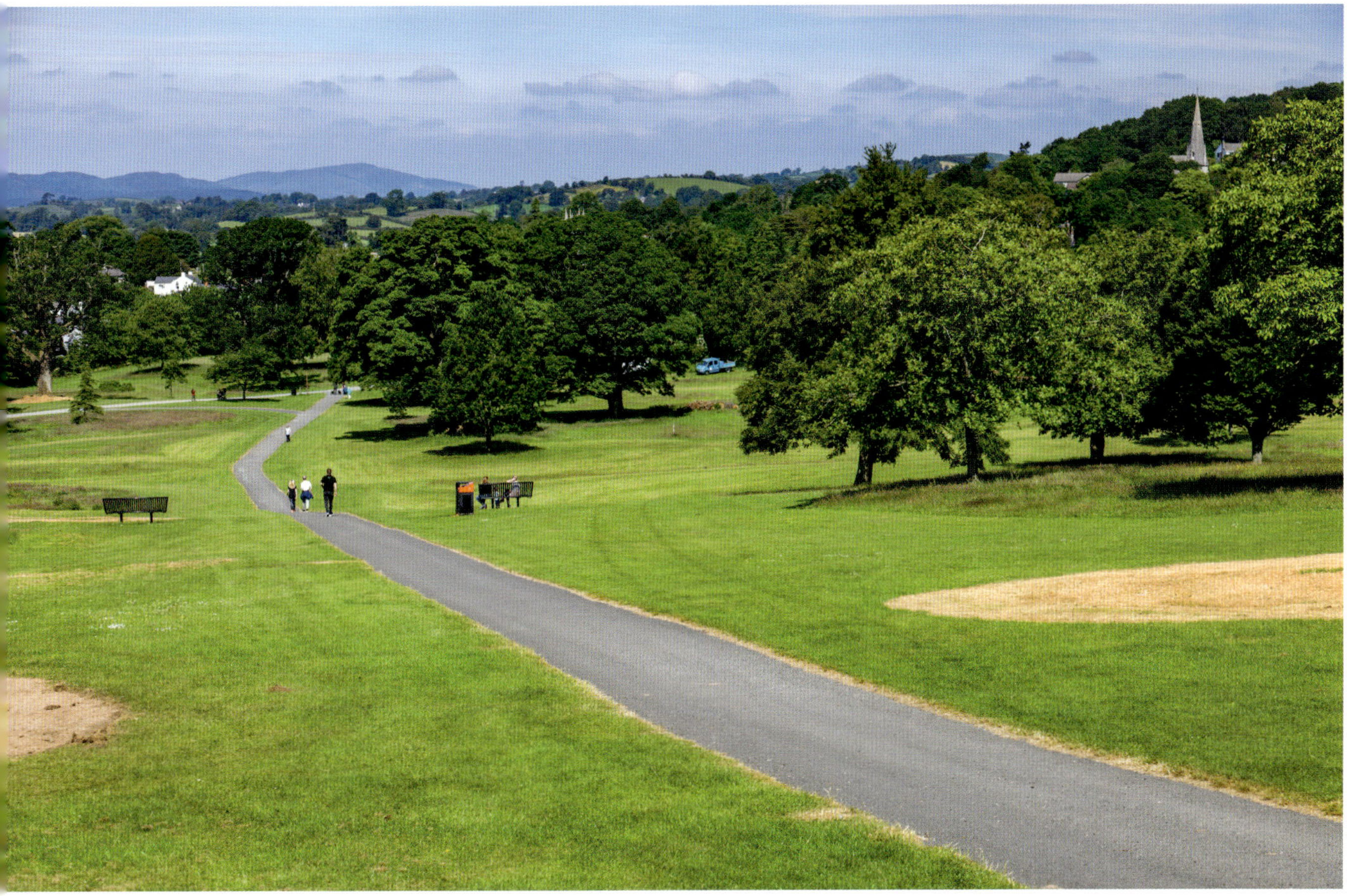

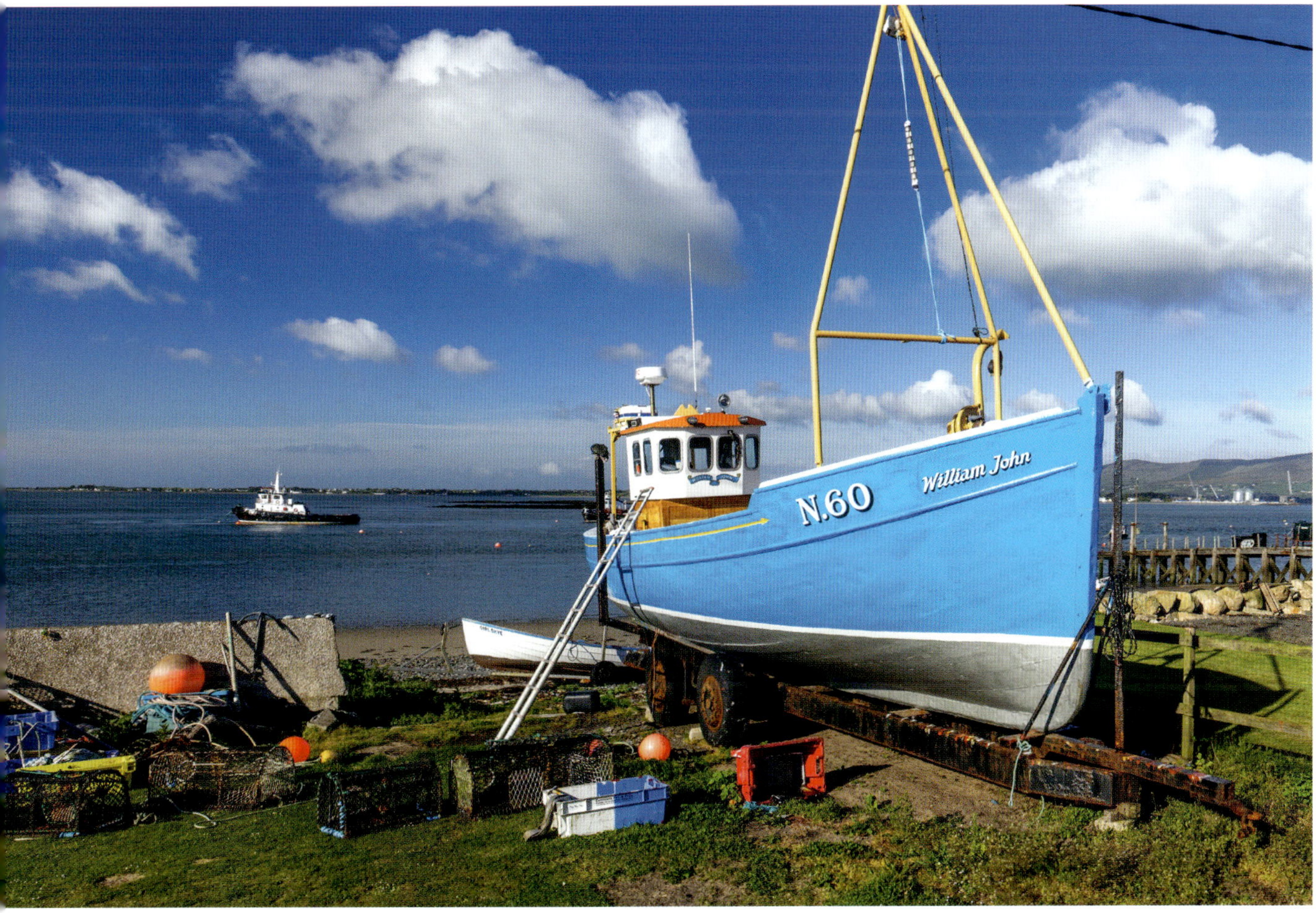

KILKEEL

Kilkeel is the southernmost town in Northern Ireland, situated on the coast at the confluence of the Aughrim and Kilkeel rivers. It takes its name from the nearby 14th century church called *Cill Chaoil*, or 'Church of the Narrow Place', and there are references to Kilkeel as a Christian settlement as far back as the 11th century. The town's economy is dominated by fishing, and many of the 6,500 inhabitants are employed on trawlers or in processing plants. The massive harbour shelters the largest fishing fleet in Northern Ireland. In 1918, several boats from Kilkeel were sunk by a German U-boat under the command of the notorious Otto Von Schrader, although all of the crew survived the ordeal.

Below: A Kilkeel fishing boat returning to harbour.

Right: Annalong cornmill was built in the early 1800s and operated until the 1960s. Before closing, it was one of the last working watermills in Northern Ireland. The building contains many of the original components and is open to the public.

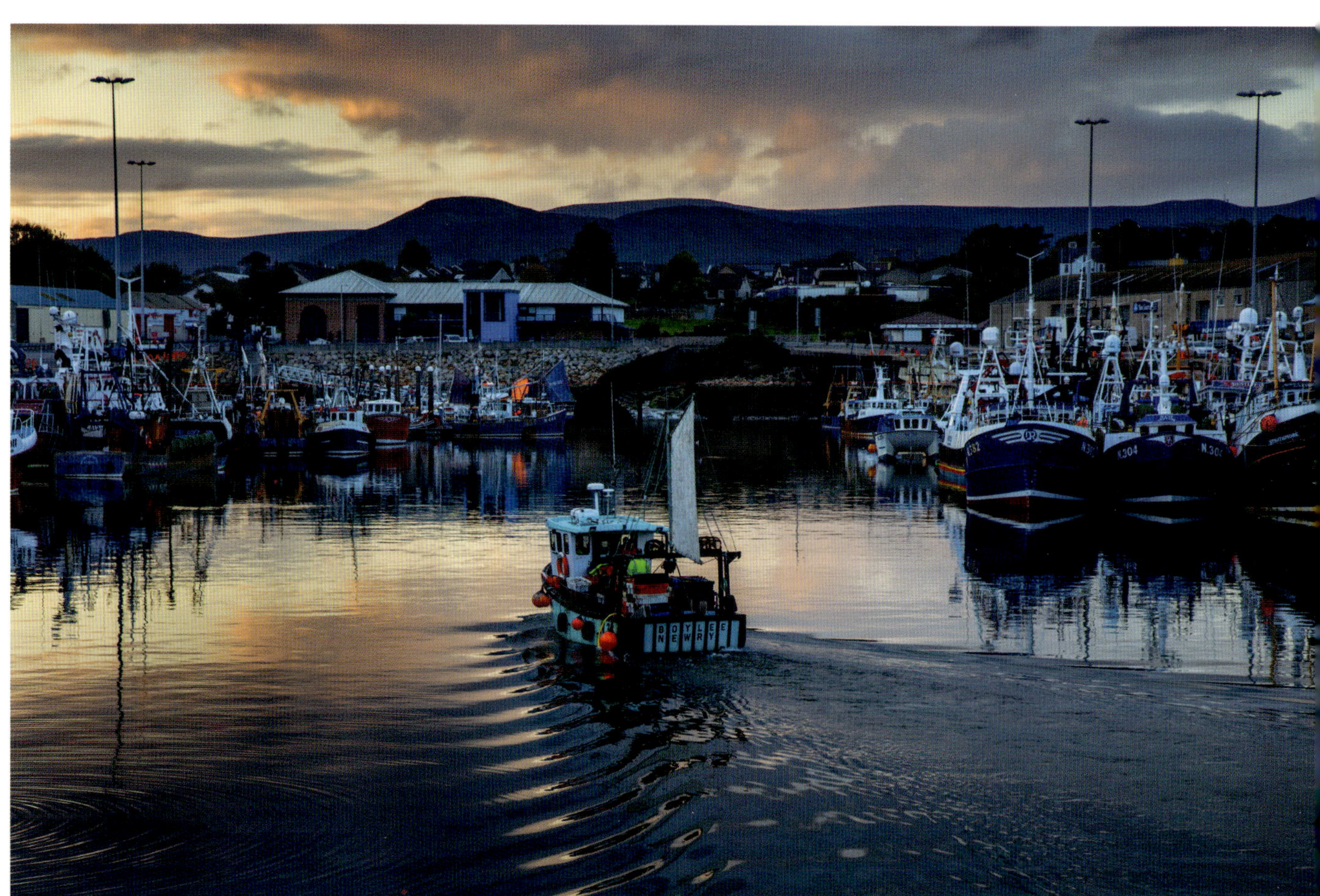

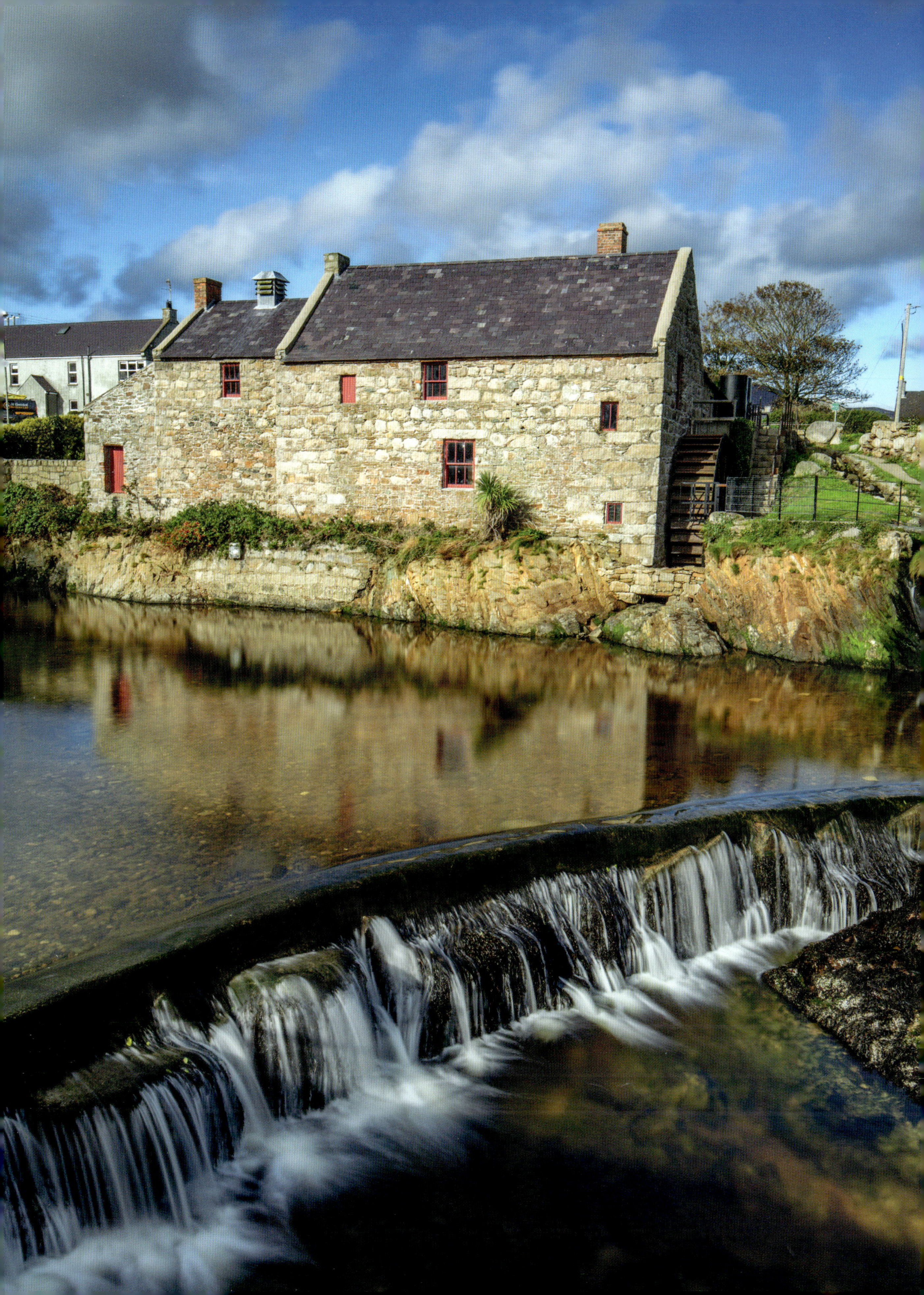

ANNALONG

Simple flint tools found in the vicinity of Annalong and dated to around 5000 BC provide evidence for some of the earliest human settlement in the Mourne area. Only ten kilometres northeast of Kilkeel, along the coast road to Newcastle, this village of some 1,500 people takes its name from the Irish *Áth na Long*, or 'Ford of the Ships'. Indeed, Annalong's importance has always been based around its harbour, which was at first a base for fishing but was developed significantly in the 18th and 19th centuries to accommodate the export of dressed granite. Annalong was the main port for the arrival of building materials during the construction of the Silent Valley Dam. A narrow gauge railway was even built between the harbour and the Silent Valley to move these materials.

Below: Detail of fishing boat in Annalong Harbour.

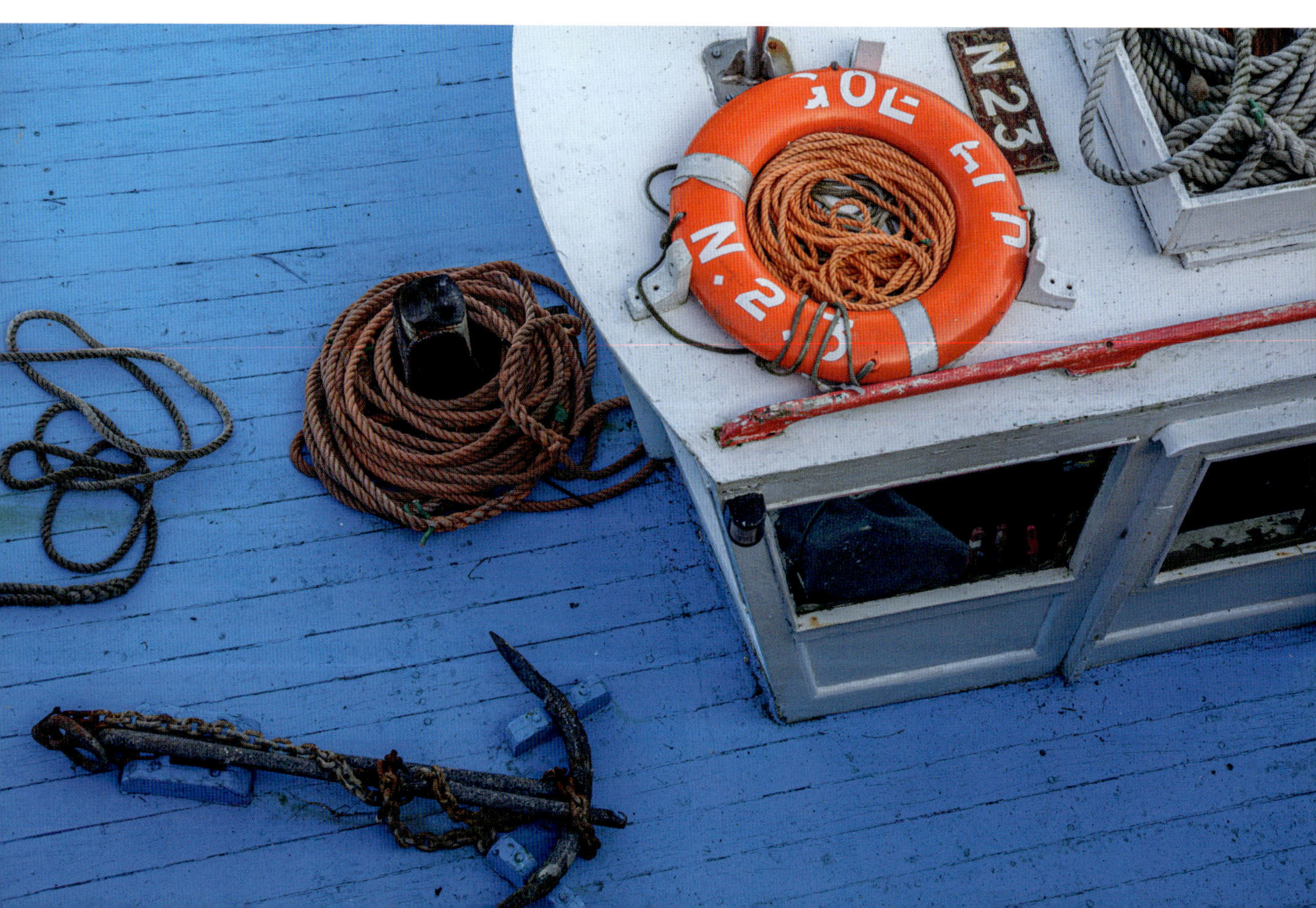

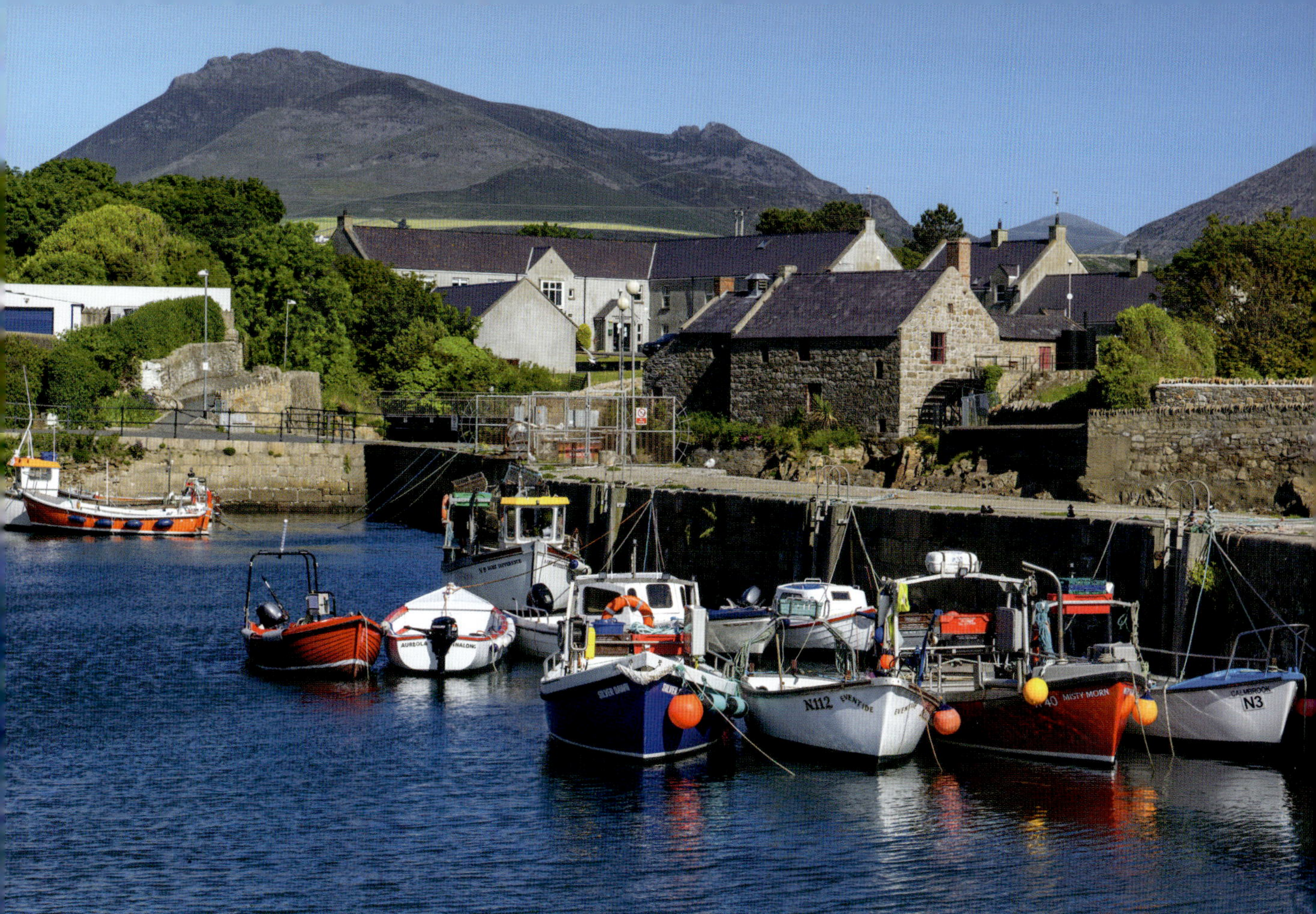

Above: Fishing boats tied up in the shelter of
Annalong Harbour.

HILLTOWN

Hilltown is named after Wills Hill, the 1st Marquess of
Downshire, who founded the village in 1766 so that
local people could be employed in the linen industry. It also became synonymous with the smuggling
industry and was renowned as the inland terminus
of the Brandy Pad, the old smuggler's route from the
coast through the Mourne mountains and beyond.
Today there are still around eight public houses in a
village of less than two thousand people, although at
the height of smuggling, pubs accounted for as many
as half of the houses in the village.

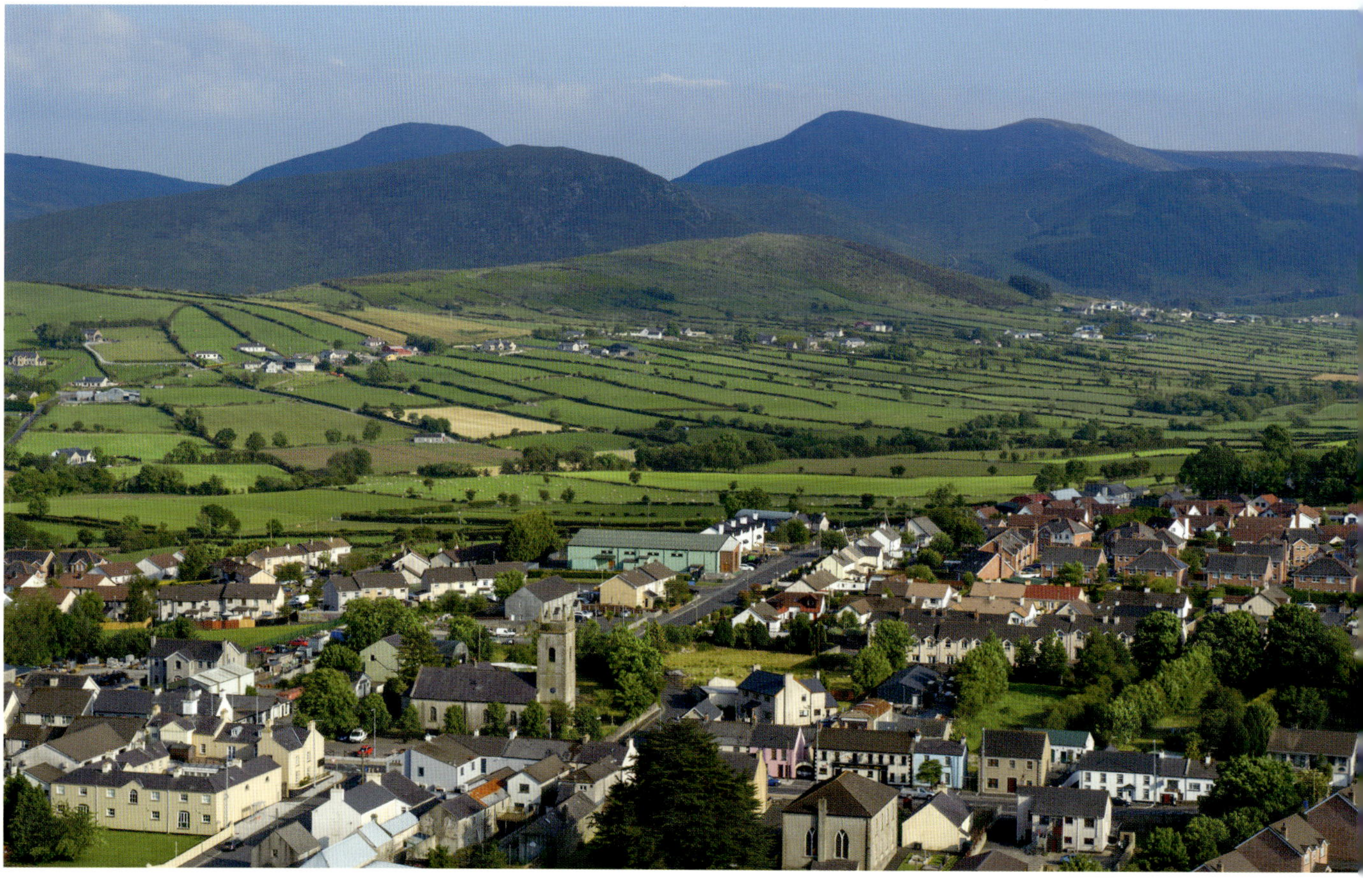

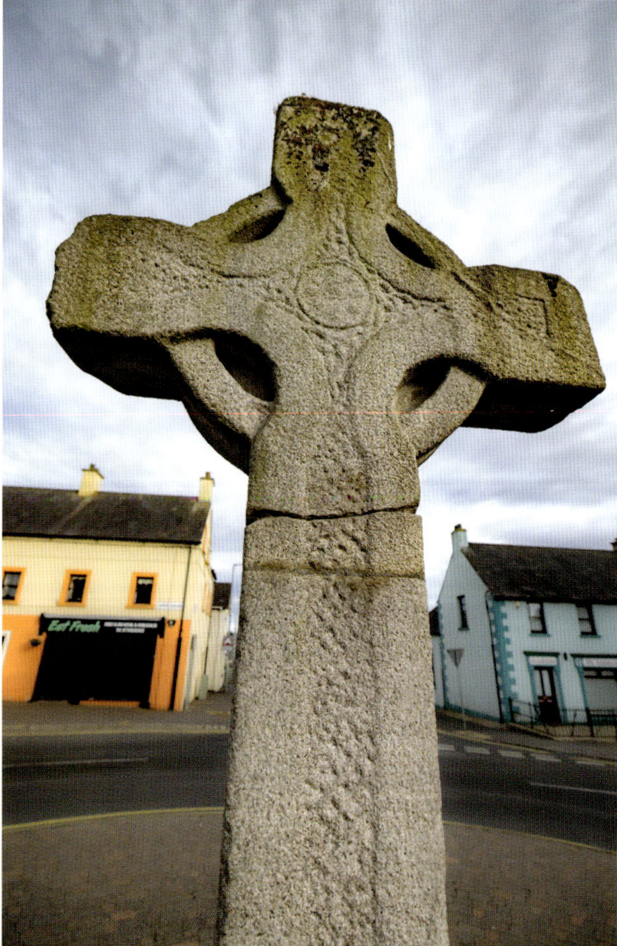

Above: Aerial view of the village of Hilltown with the Mournes in the background.

Left: Drumadonnell High Cross in Castlewellan Main Street is a faithful replica of a 10th century high cross of the same name. The original, which is now housed in Castlewellan Forest Park, is over 2.5m in height and 1.5m wide, and is carved from local granite.

CASTLEWELLAN

Castlewellan town was built by the Annesley family in the 18th century, right next to their Castlewellan demesne. They employed a French architect for its design, and that Gallic influence is clear to see in the wide main street, lined with sycamore trees. There is a granite replica of the 10th century Drumadonnell High Cross in the main square – the original is now in state care. Almost 2,500 people live in the town.

Right: A view of Castlewellan Main Street on a fine spring afternoon.

Below: An aerial view of Castlewellan. Castlewellan Castle and the Peace Maze are visible in the distance.

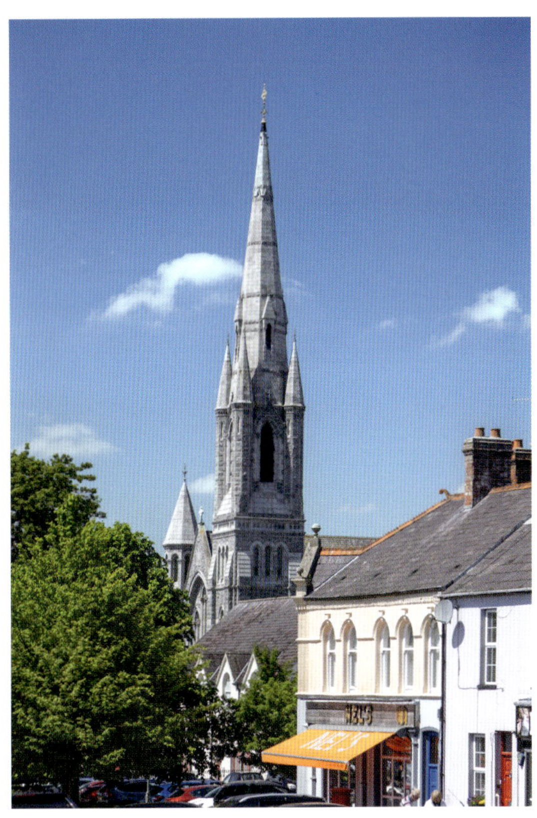

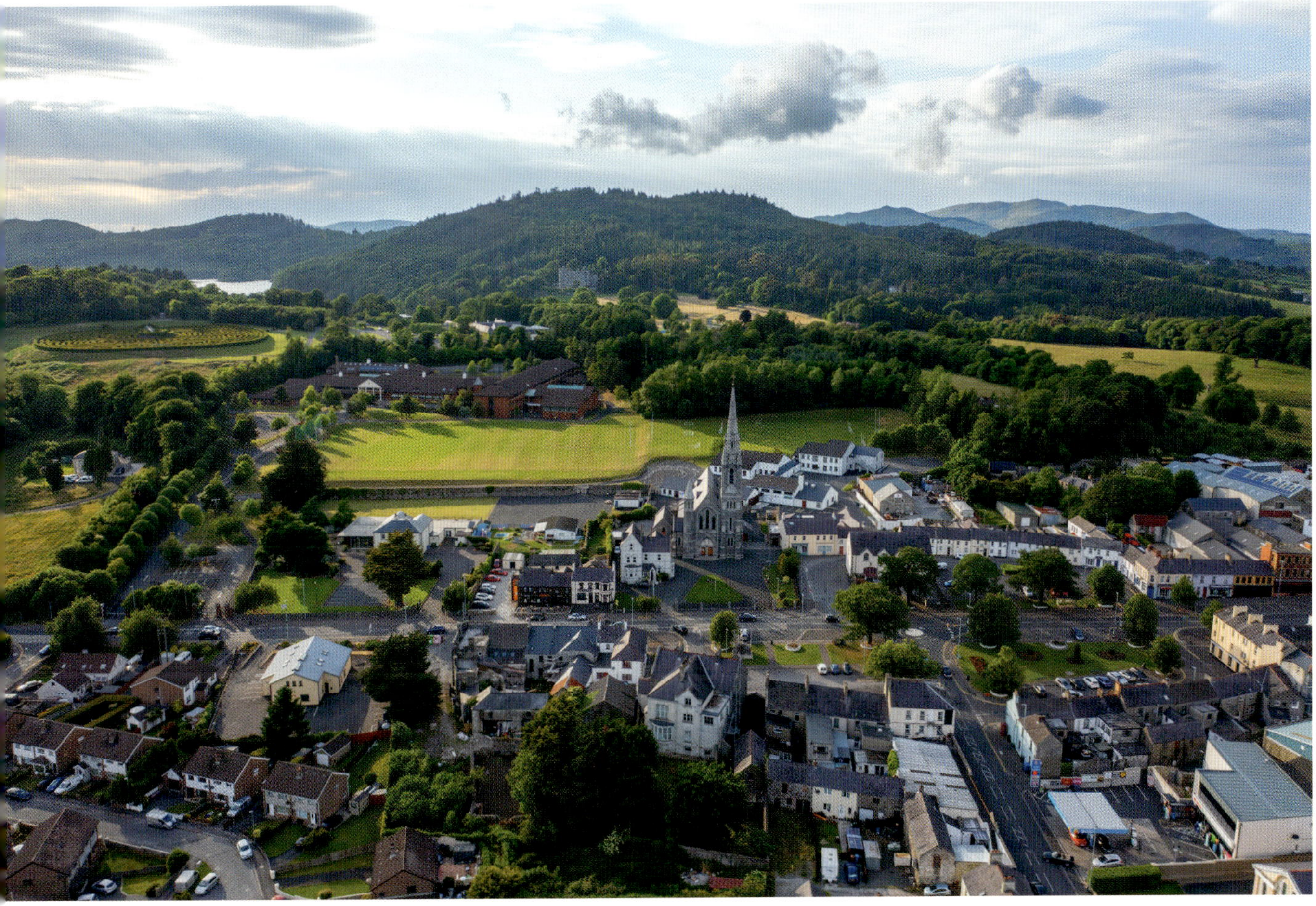

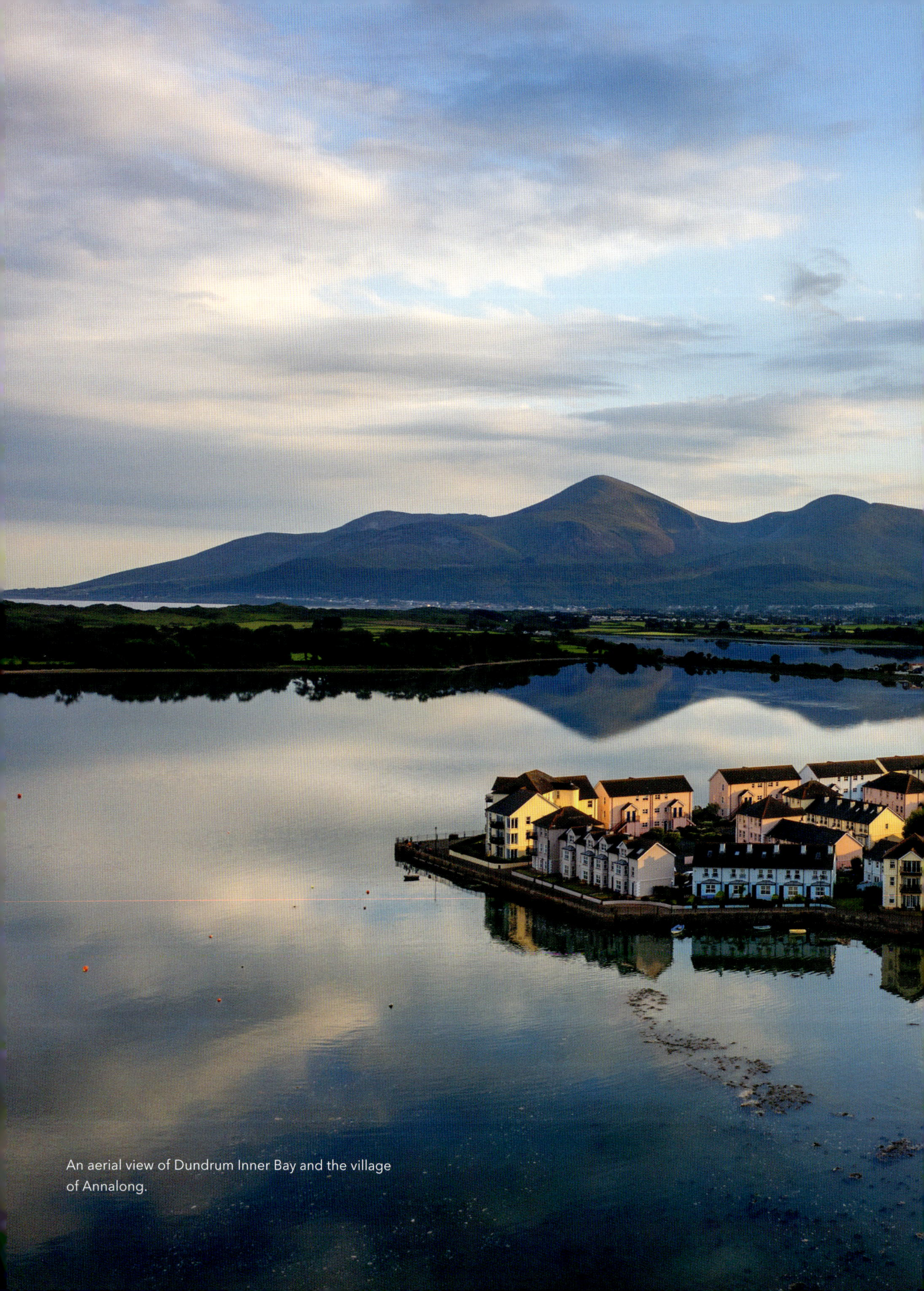

An aerial view of Dundrum Inner Bay and the village of Annalong.

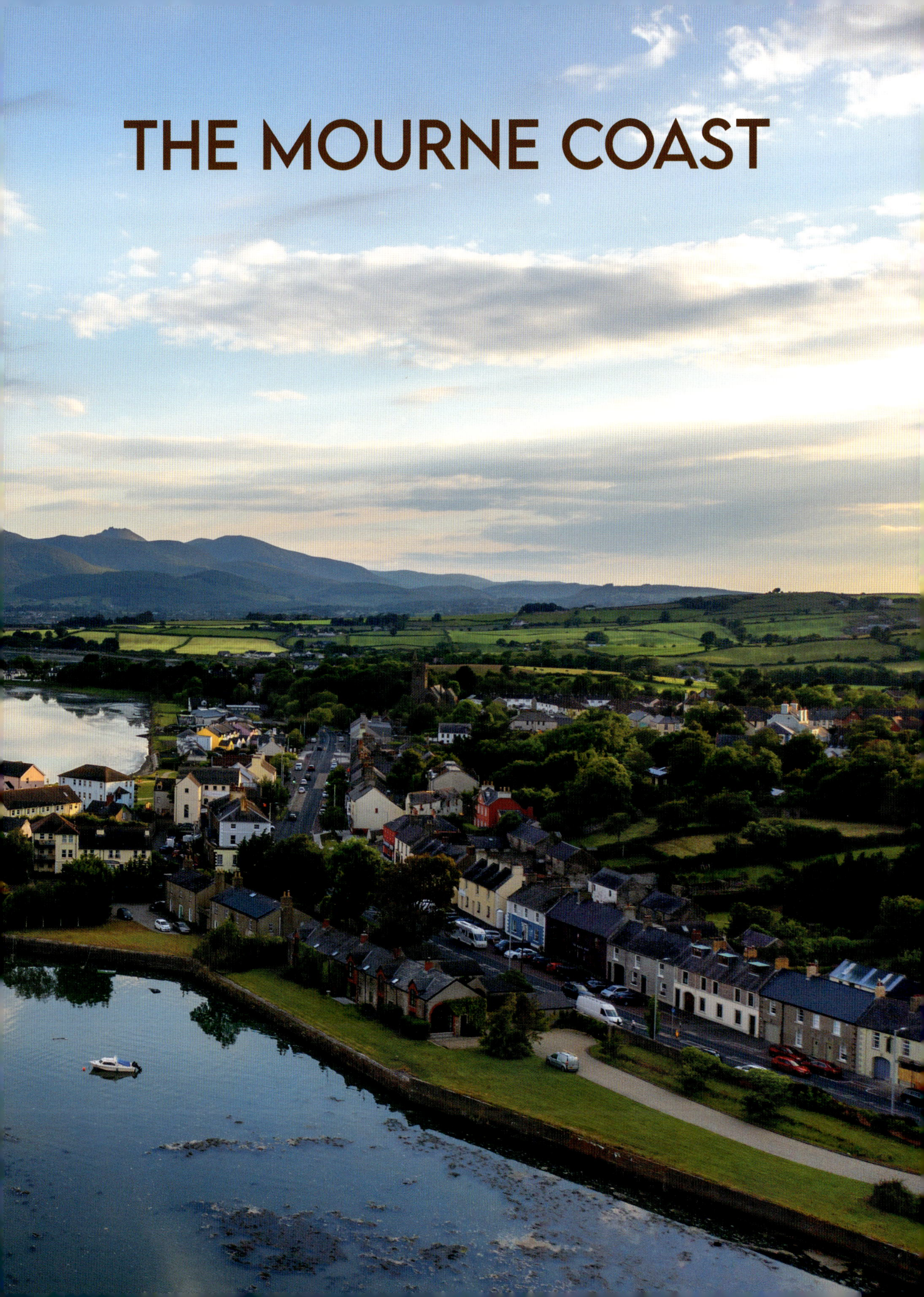

THE MOURNE COAST

From the low, rocky coast and beaches of Lecale and Tyrella in the north, the coast of County Down sweeps around the great arc of Dundrum Bay towards the Mournes. Looking out across this bay is St John's Point Lighthouse, the tallest onshore lighthouse in Ireland at forty metres high. It was originally built in 1844 at only fourteen metres but was redeveloped in the 1880s to its current height and repainted in its distinctive black and yellow hoops in 1902.

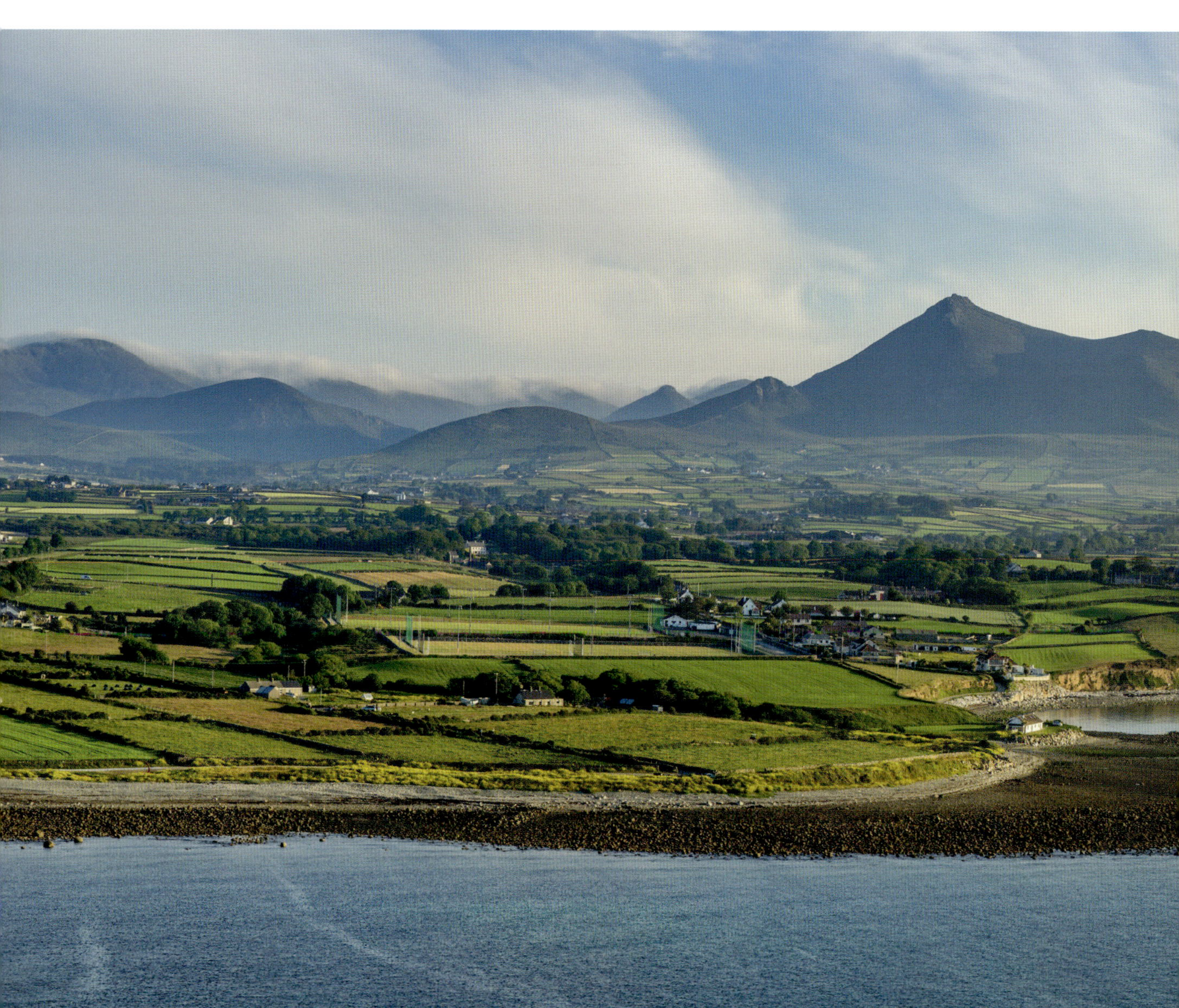

Below left: Looking back towards the Mournes from just off Ballykeel Point.

Below right: Swimmers brave the waters of the Irish Sea just south of Newcastle, overlooked by a modern mural painted on the sea wall.

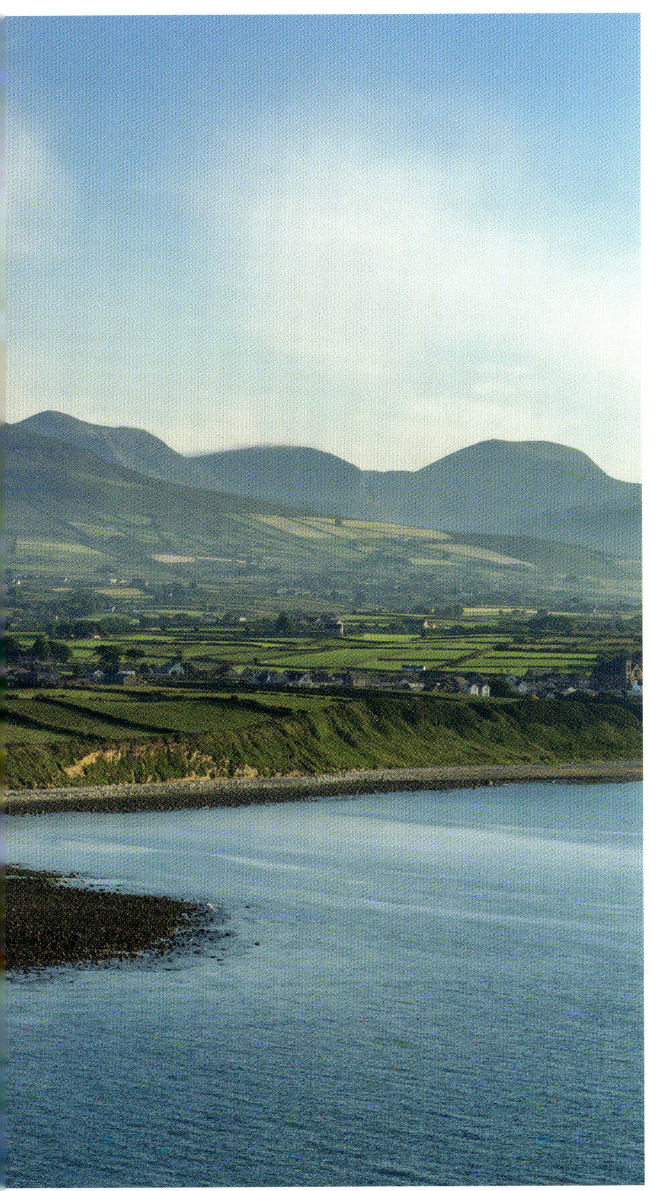

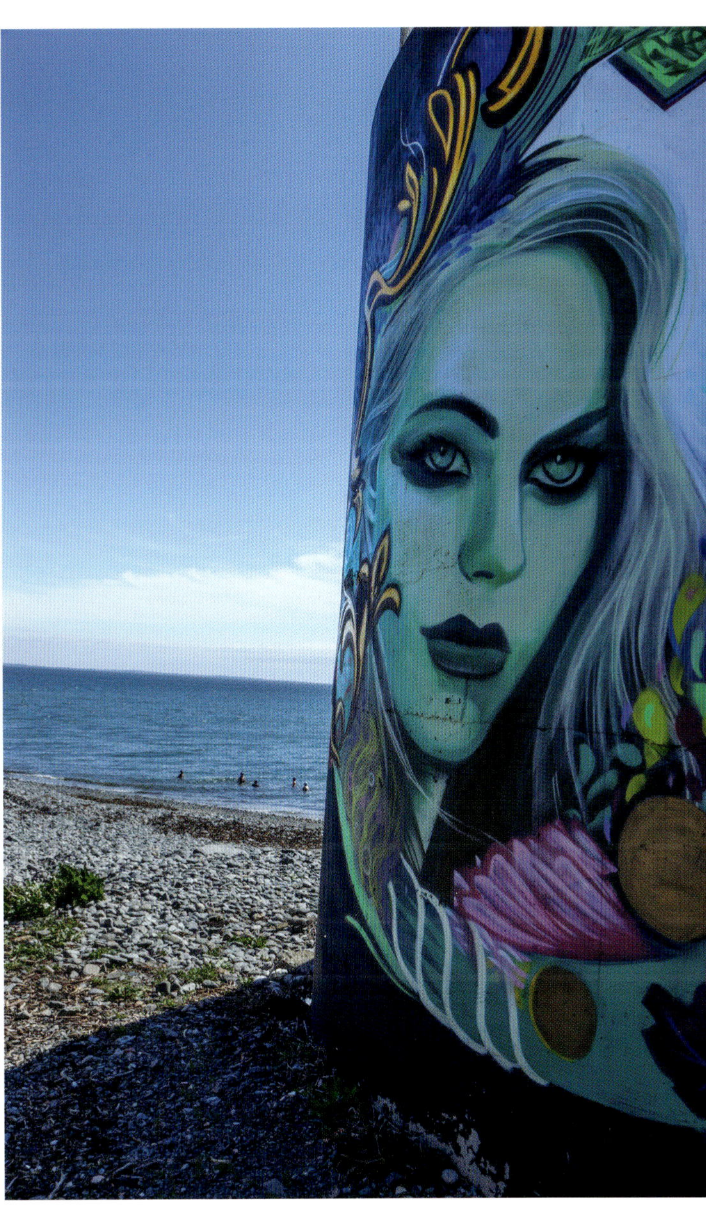

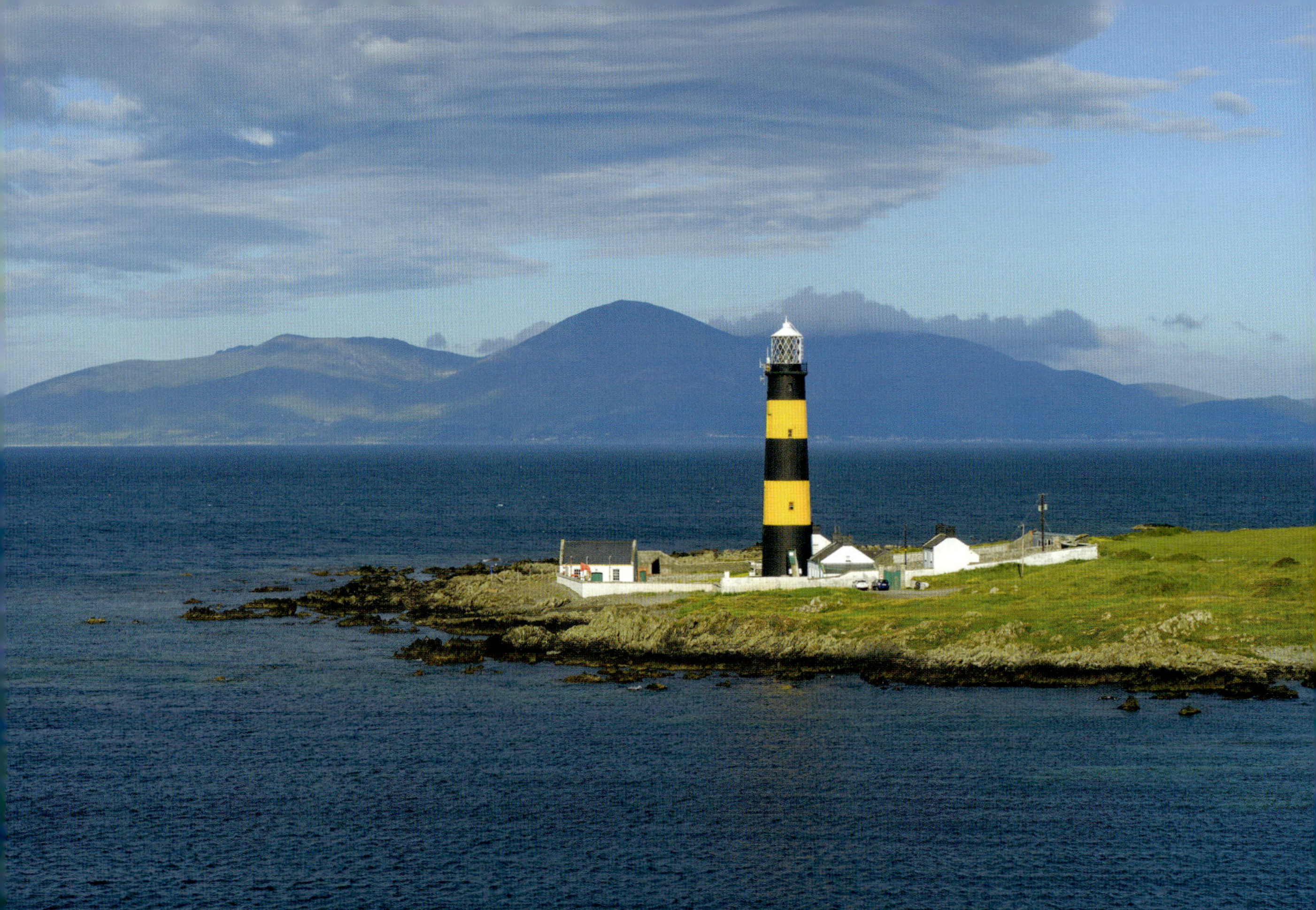

The nearby beach of Tyrella is one of Northern Ireland's most charming and popular family beaches, with idyllic white sand and clear, shallow waters. The south-facing coast here is one of sandy beaches interspersed with modest rocky headlands, giving way to the much longer expanse of Ballykinlar Beach and dune system. Just behind these dunes is the sprawling former military base, which closed in 2018.

The coast is now broken by the mouth of an estuary that winds through the dunes, giving passage to Dundrum Inner Bay and the harbour and quay at Dundrum. Dundrum Inner Bay is an important habitat for birds, with large areas of saltmarsh and extensive sand and mud flats exposed at lower tides – ideal for many species of wintering waders. On the western side of the estuary, the beach and dune system continues all the way to Newcastle. This is probably the most important dune and heath ecosystem in Ireland and is conserved and maintained as the Murlough National Nature Reserve by the National Trust. The dune systems here and at Ballykinlar are up to six thousand years old and are based on glacial gravel deposits.

Murlough supports a huge diversity of flora and fauna, with more than six hundred species of butterfly and moth, including the rare marsh fritillary. This ecosystem may seem quite natural, but it has been shaped considerably by human interference. During the medieval period, rabbit warrens were encouraged as a source of food and pelts, but myxomatosis crashed the rabbit population and has allowed scrub – including non-native sycamore and sea-buckthorn – to take hold. Currently, controlled grazing is being used to try to halt the spread of scrub and open up grass and heath.

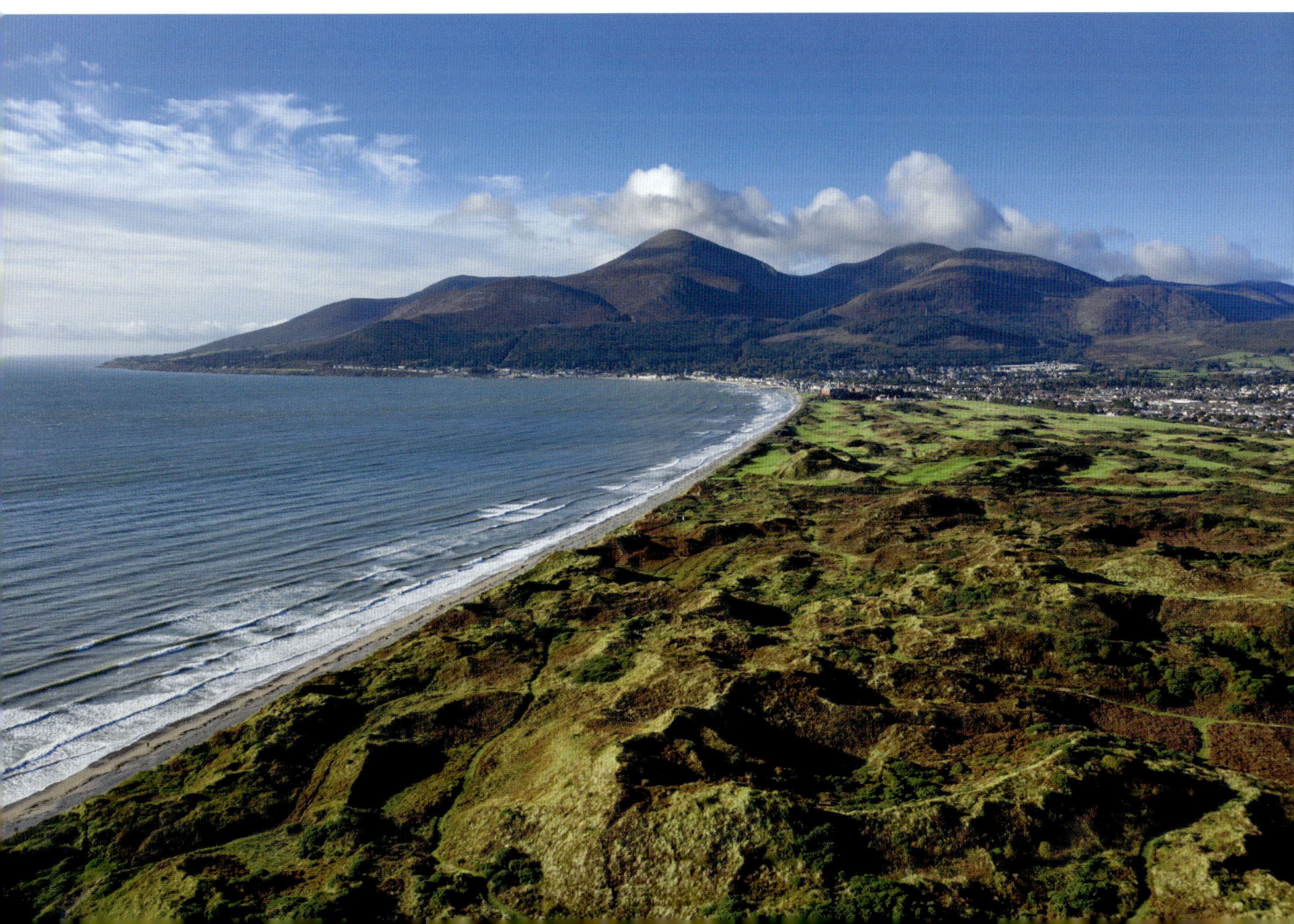

From Newcastle southwards, the coast of Mourne becomes more rocky and inaccessible, as the slopes of Slieve Donard come right down to the shore in a skirt of low cliffs. This remote coastline was frequently used in the 19th century by smugglers landing illicit cargoes of alcohol, tobacco, tea and silks. The contraband would then be spirited away through the mountains on tracks such as the Brandy Pad.

Along this section of the coast is the infamous Bloody Bridge, an old, ivy-covered

Below: The dune system of Murlough National Nature Reserve on the shores of Dundrum Bay.

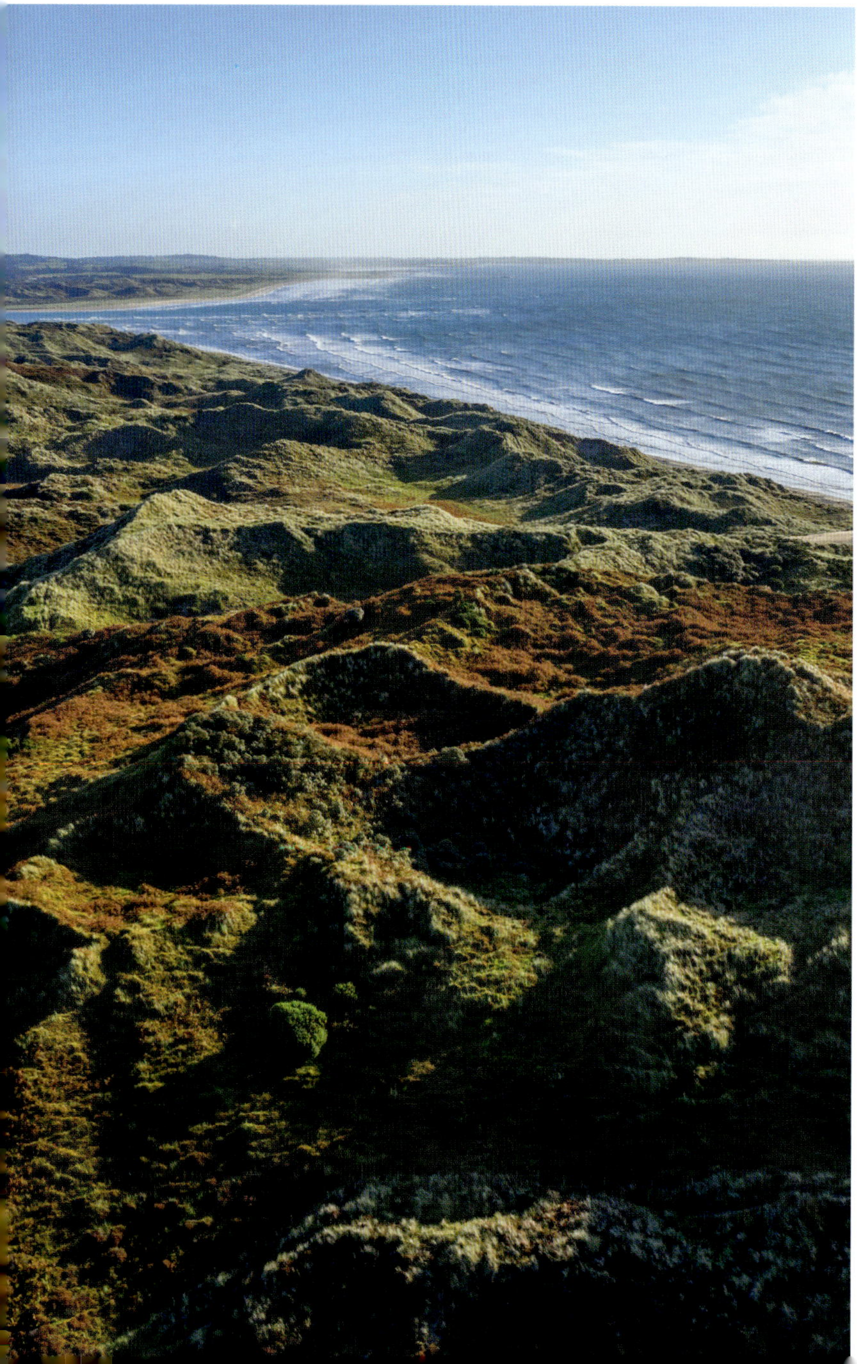

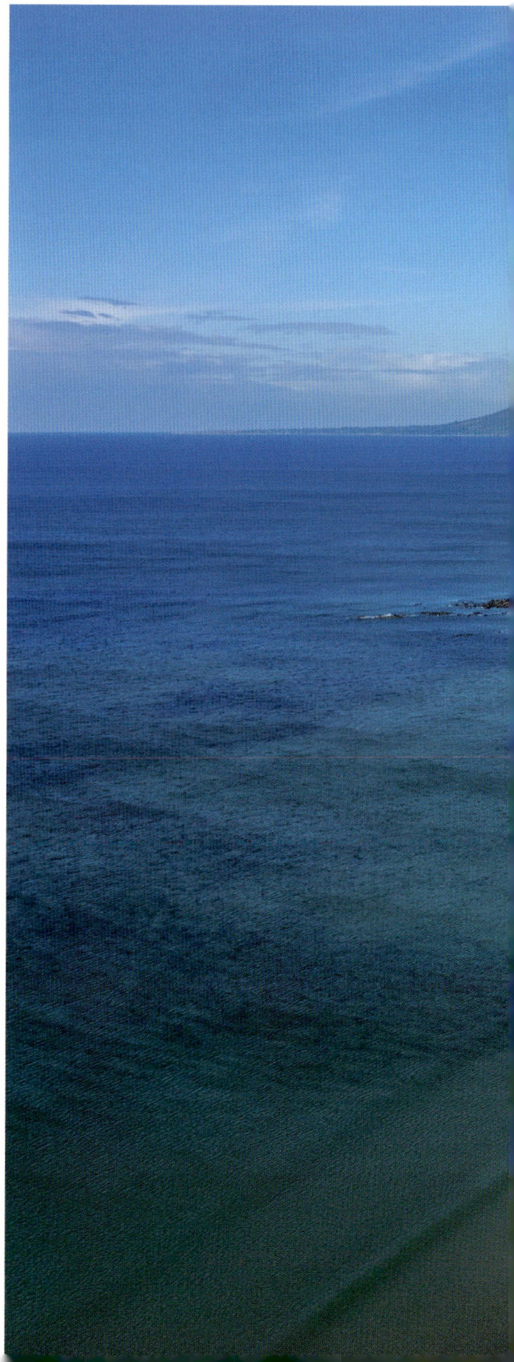

stone span now marooned beside a modern road bridge. Just what happened here on 23 October, 1641, is not entirely certain. It seems that a number of Protestant prisoners, perhaps ten, were being taken to Downpatrick as part of a prisoner exchange, but when it was discovered that the men for whom they were to be exchanged had already been hanged, they were massacred.

South of Slieve Donard, the coast relaxes once more, fringing the fertile coastal plains,

Below: The beautiful white sands of Tyrella seen from the air.

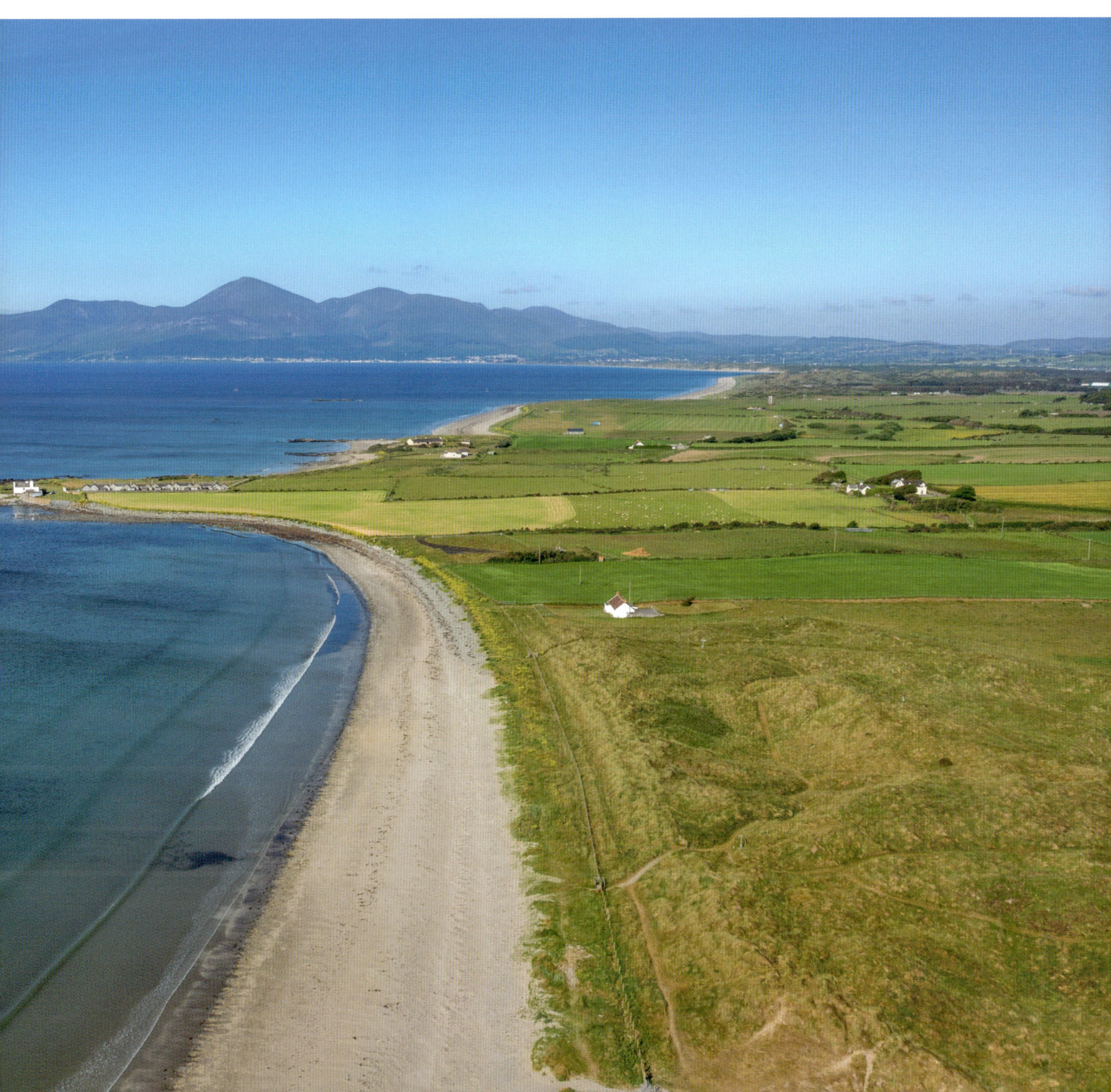

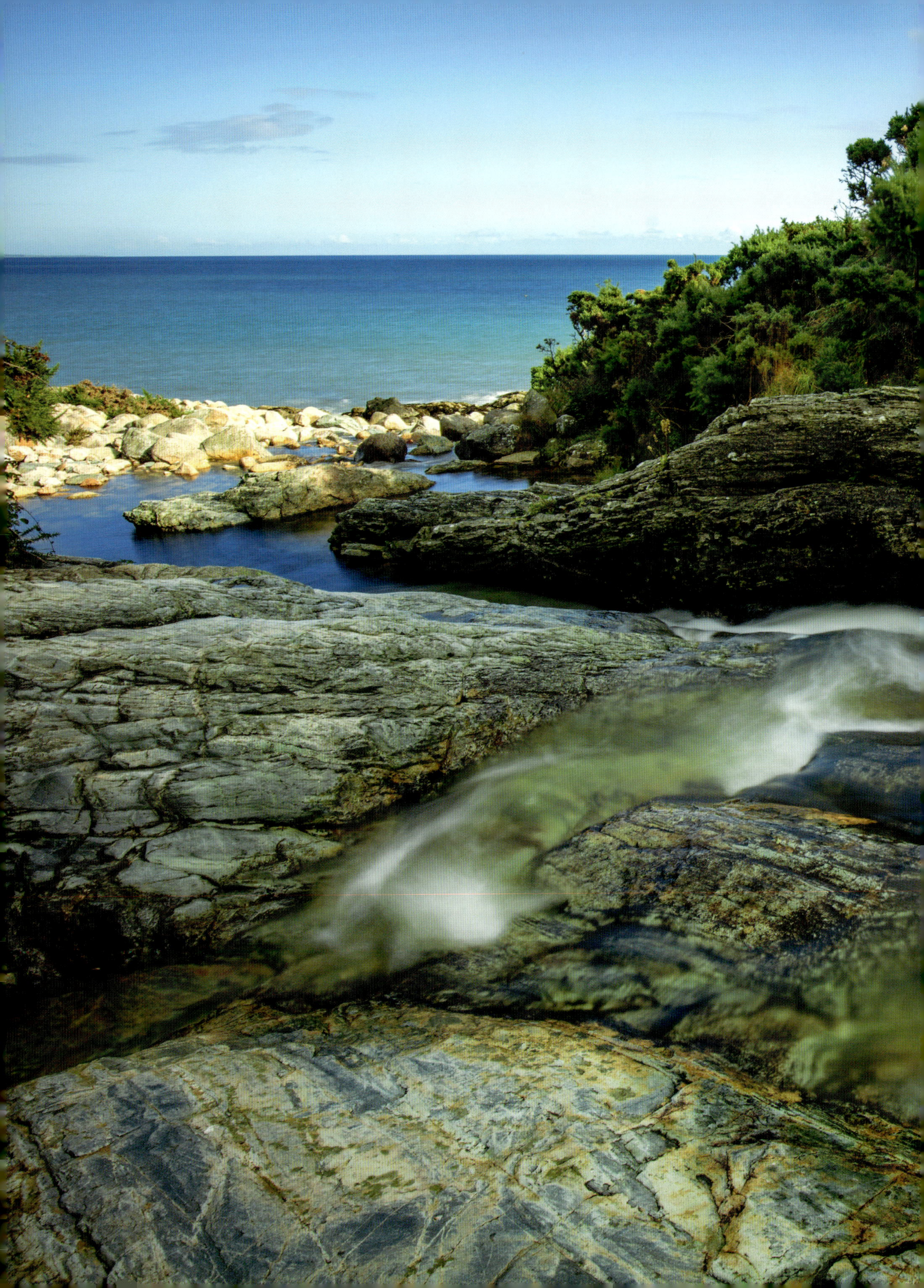

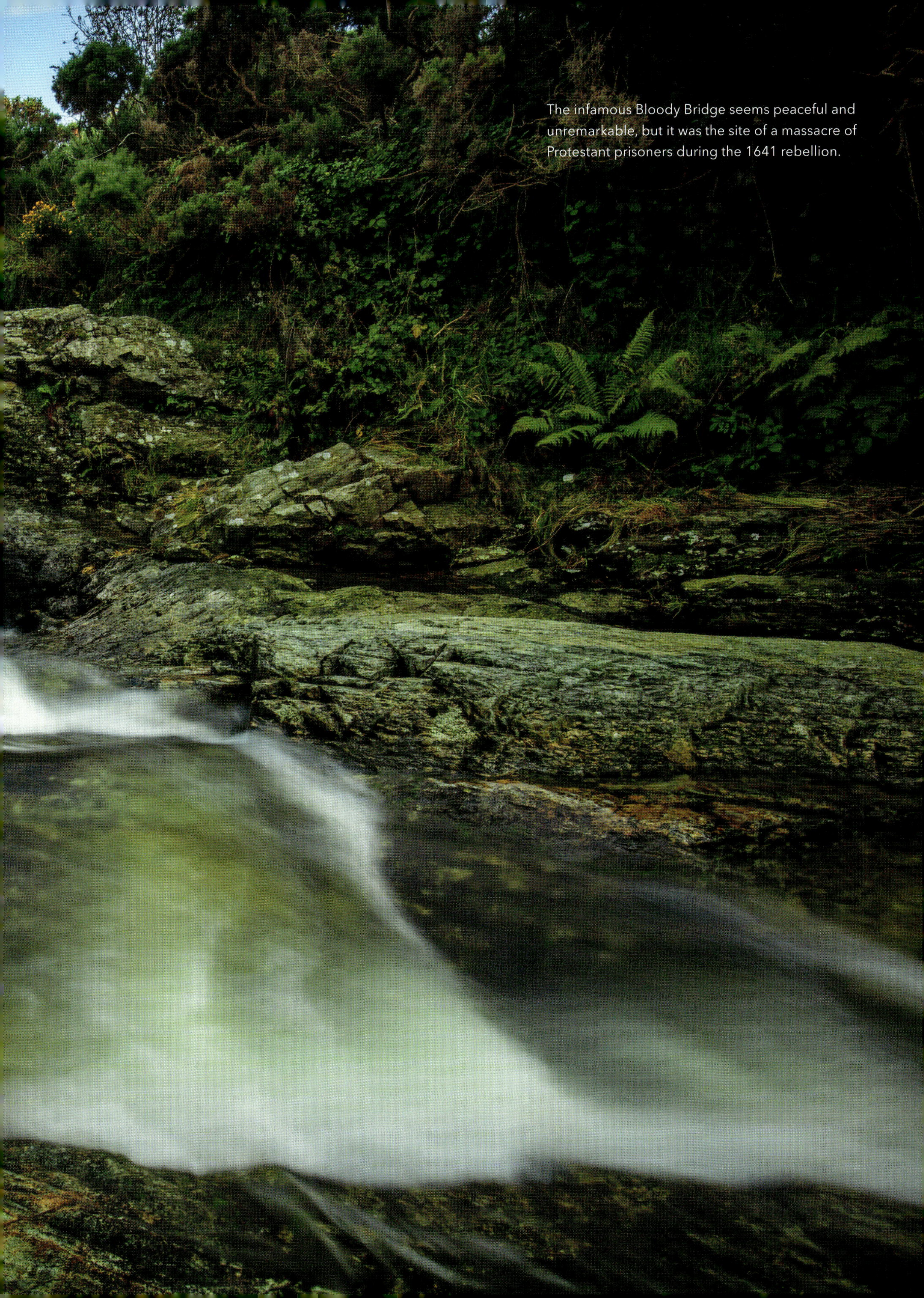

The infamous Bloody Bridge seems peaceful and unremarkable, but it was the site of a massacre of Protestant prisoners during the 1641 rebellion.

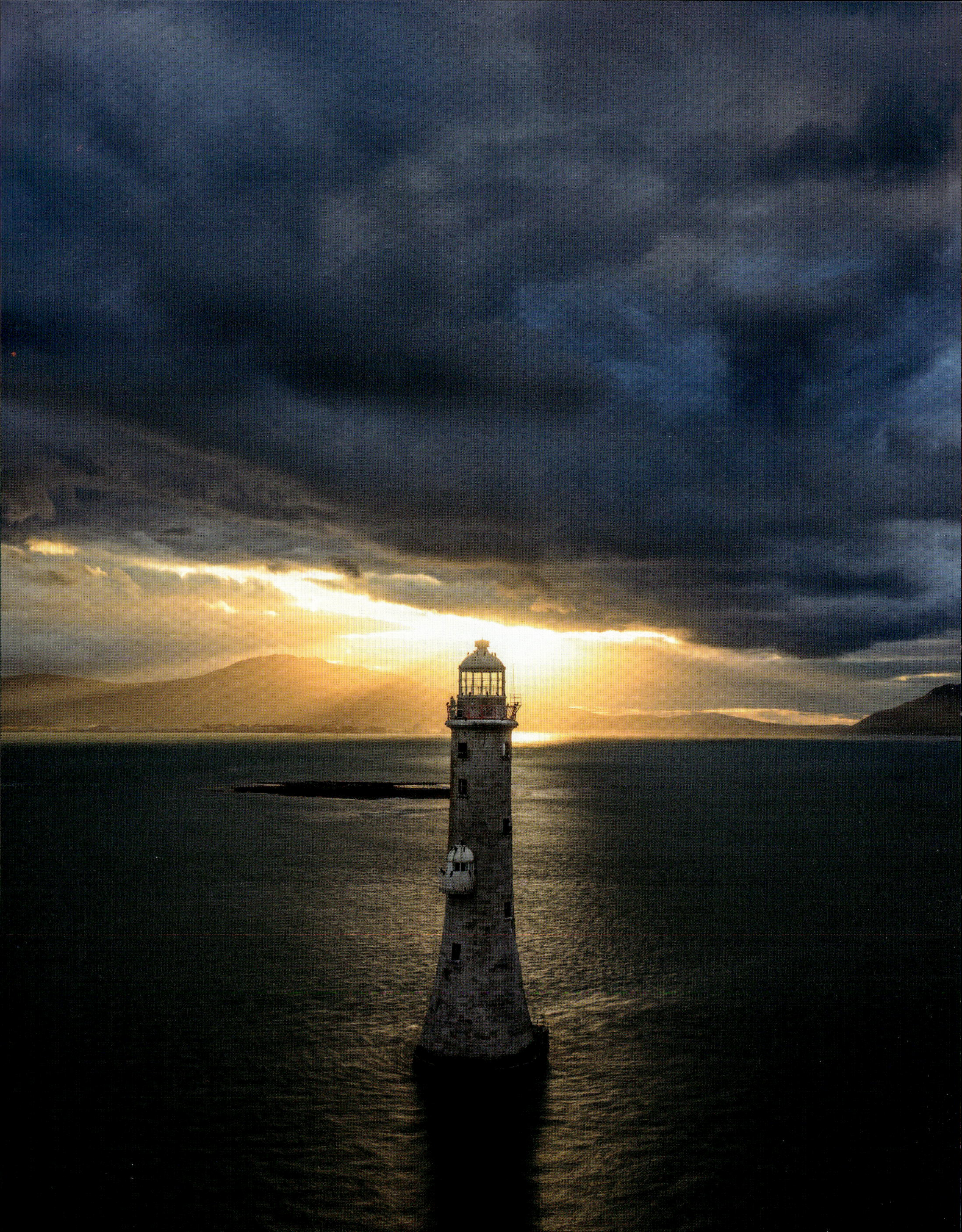

as it sweeps around past the fishing harbours of Annalong and Kilkeel. Today Kilkeel is the centre of commercial fishing in the Mourne region, and indeed it boasts the largest fishing fleet in Northern Ireland. However, Annalong and Newcastle also once had significant fleets. In January 1843, forty-six fishermen from Newcastle and twenty-seven from Annalong were lost in Dundrum Bay when they were caught out by a storm that struck unexpectedly from the northwest.

Not far to the southeast of Kilkeel is Cranfield Point, where the coast turns to the northwest and into the enormous sea inlet of Carlingford Lough. Just over a kilometre offshore from Cranfield Point is the spectacular Haulbowline Lighthouse, built in 1824 on a partially submerged shelf of rock. It is thirty-four metres high and marks the seaward entrance to a narrow shipping channel that has unfortunately been the scene of tragedy. On 3 November,

Left: A late evening storm bears down on the Haulbowline Lighthouse.

Below: Looking south across the fertile coastal plains towards Kilkeel.

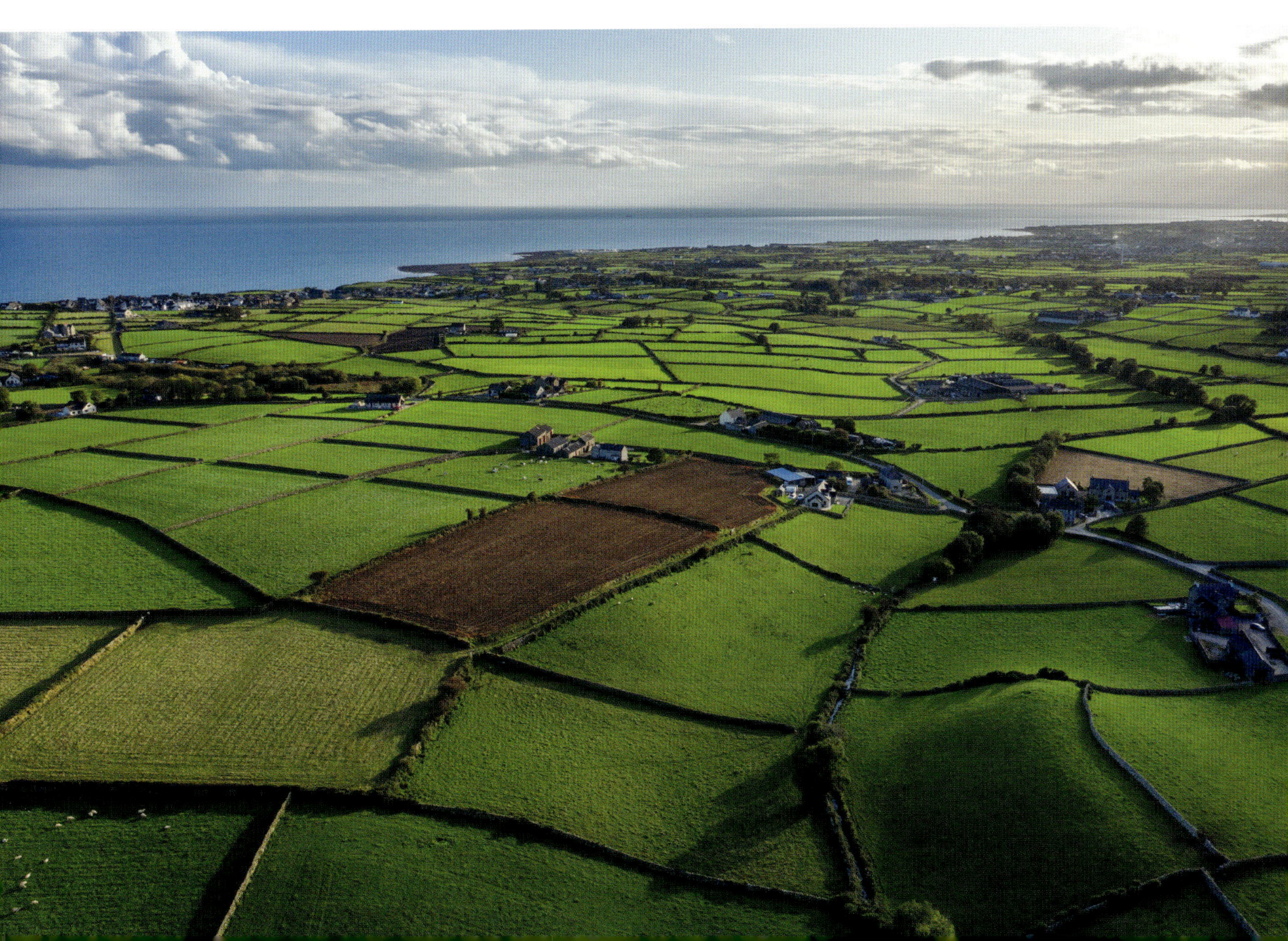

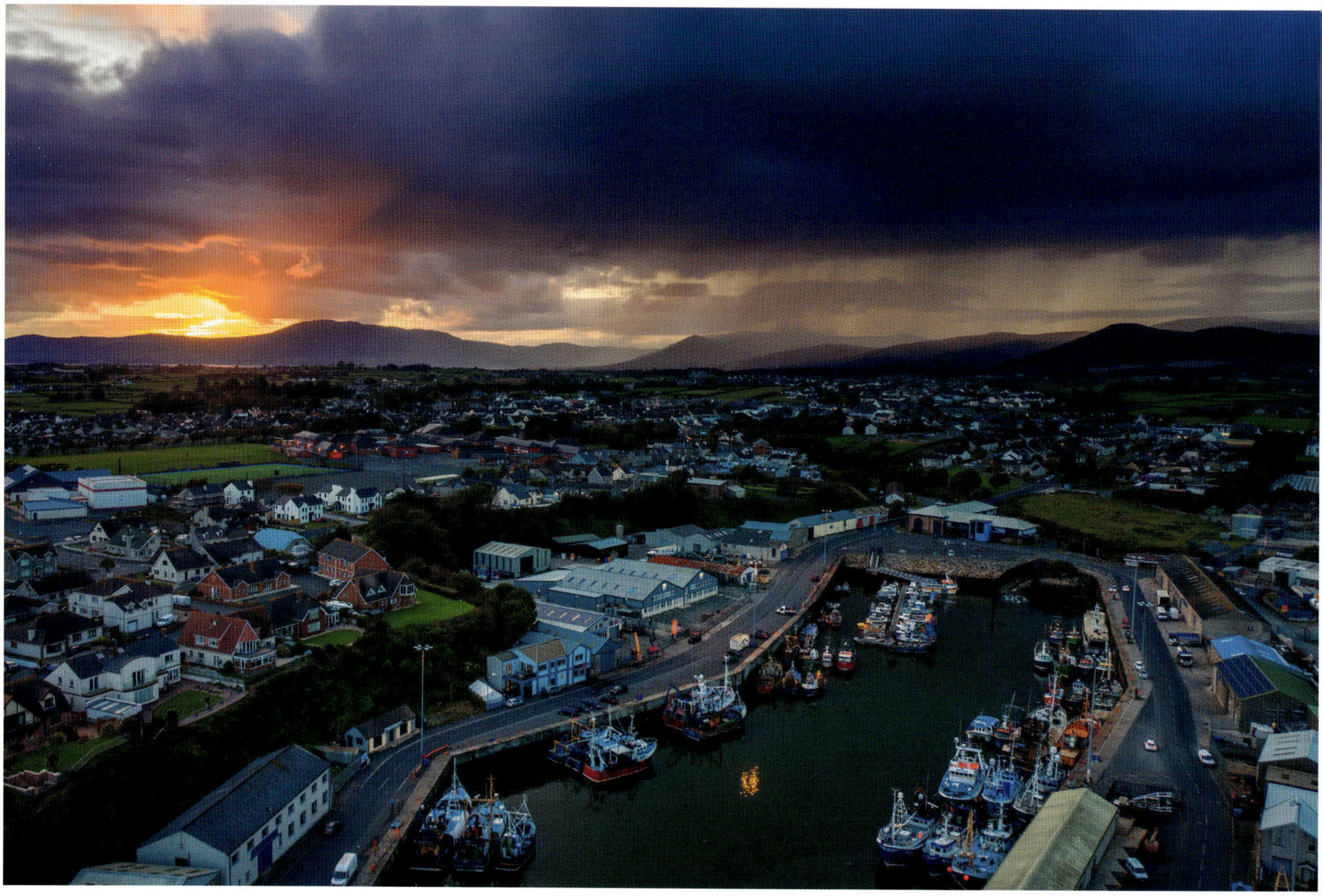

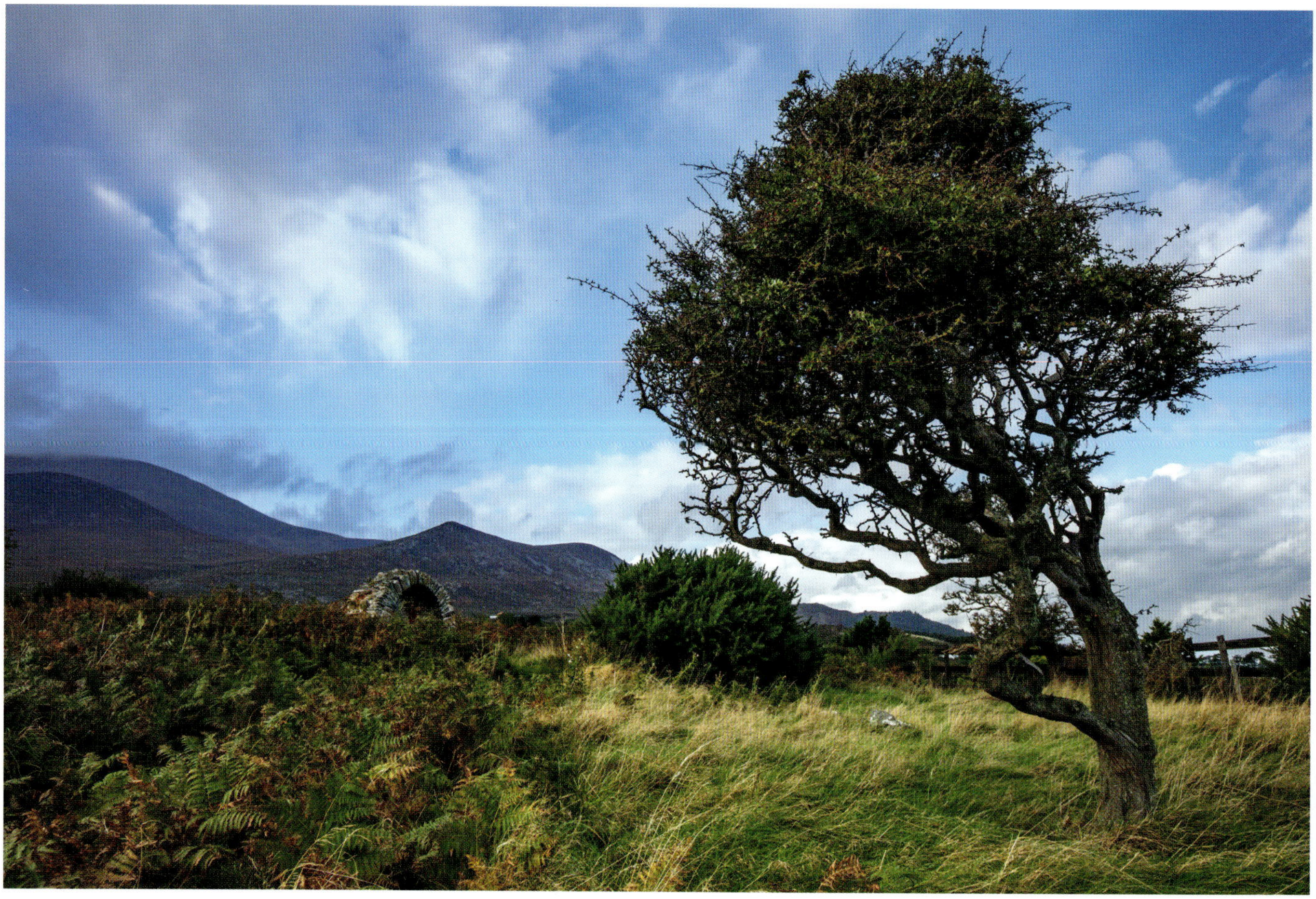

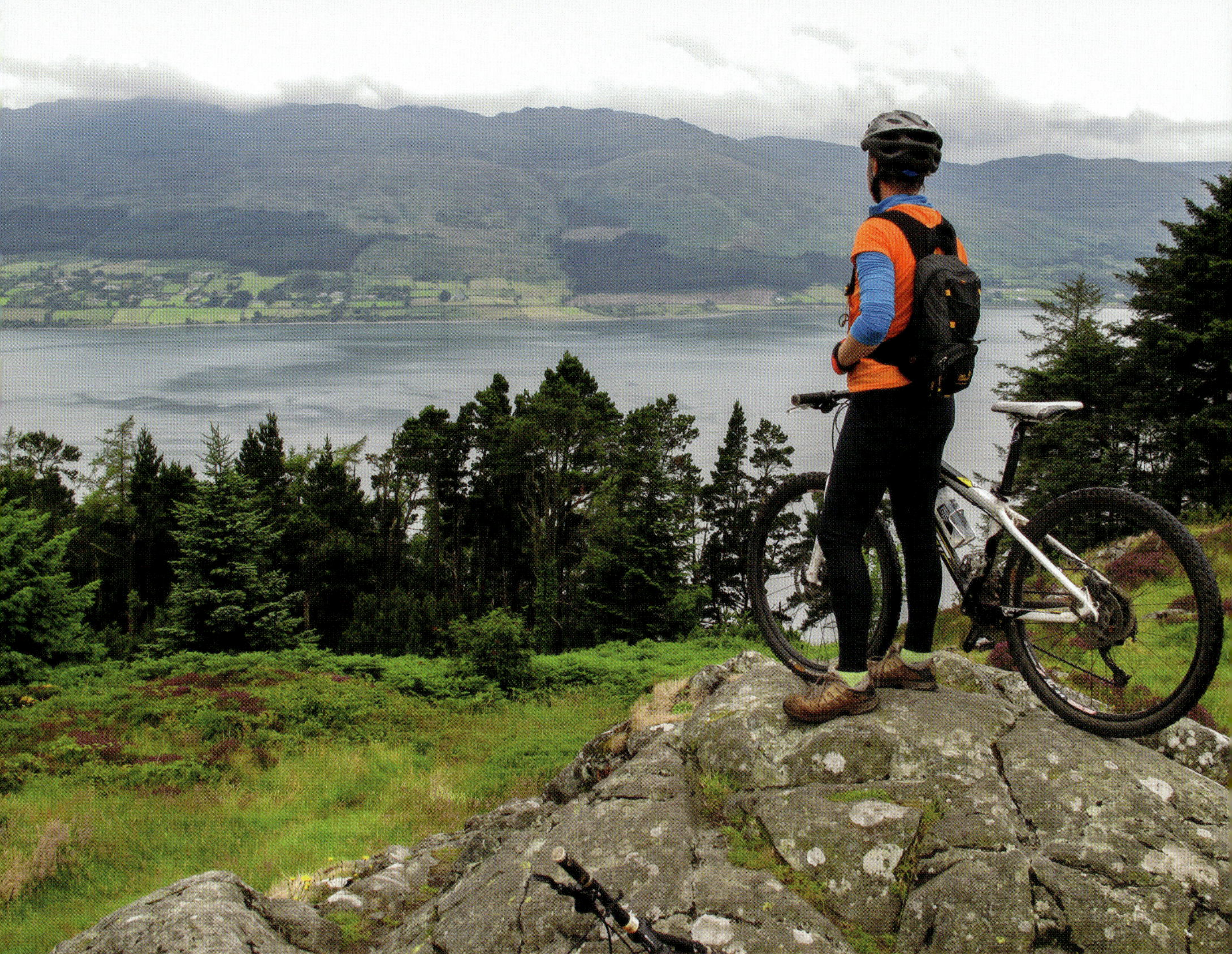

1916, the SS *Connemara*, a passenger ferry, and the SS *Retriever*, a collier returning from Garston, collided close to the lighthouse with the loss of ninety-four lives and just one survivor.

Carlingford's name derives from the Old Norse word *Kerlingfjǫrðr*, meaning 'narrow sea-inlet of the hag'. It is a true fjord or flooded glacial valley. Extensive salt marsh and mud flats on the northern side of the lough attract many species of wading bird, whilst several small offshore islands host important breeding colonies of terns.

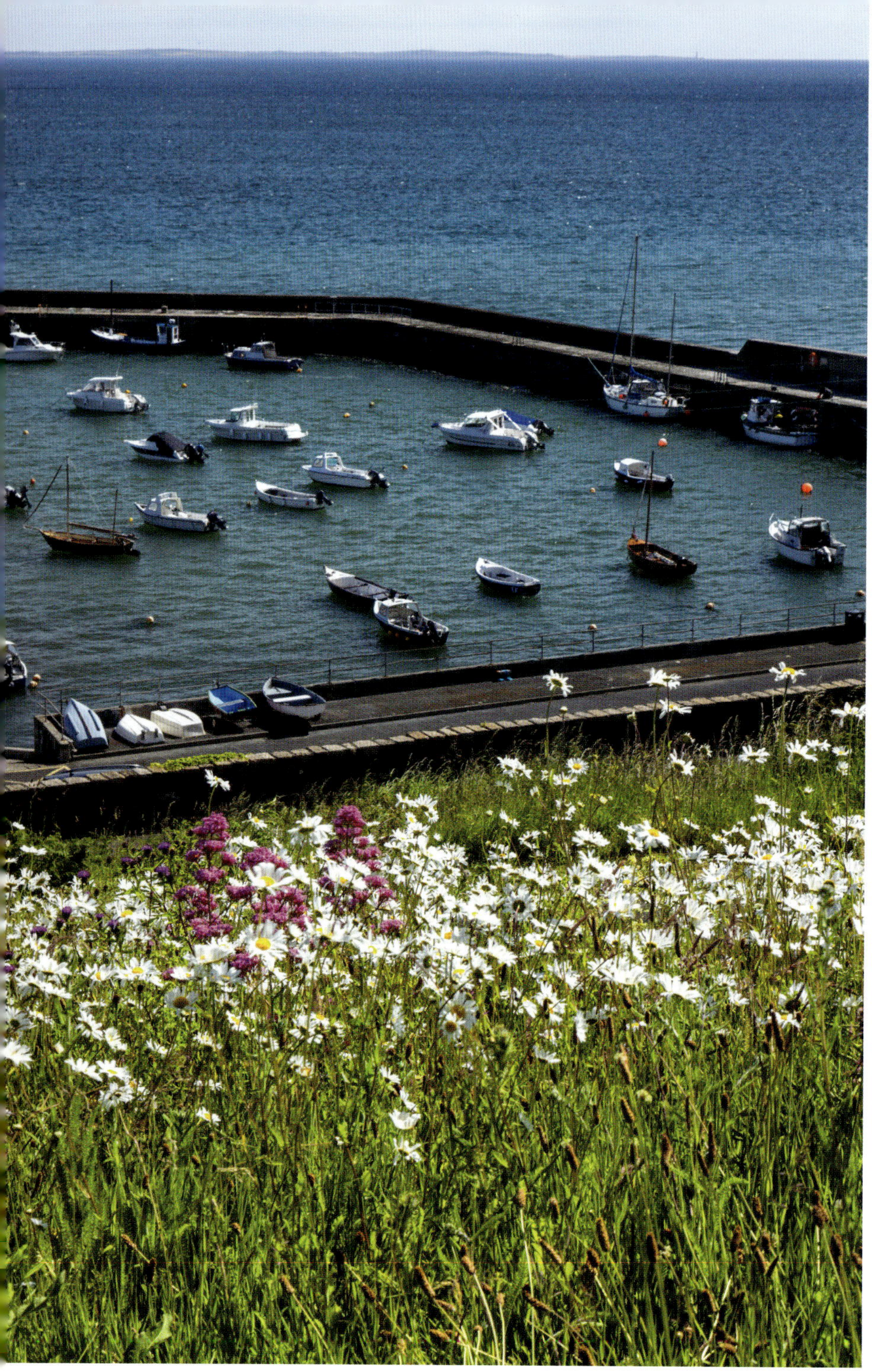

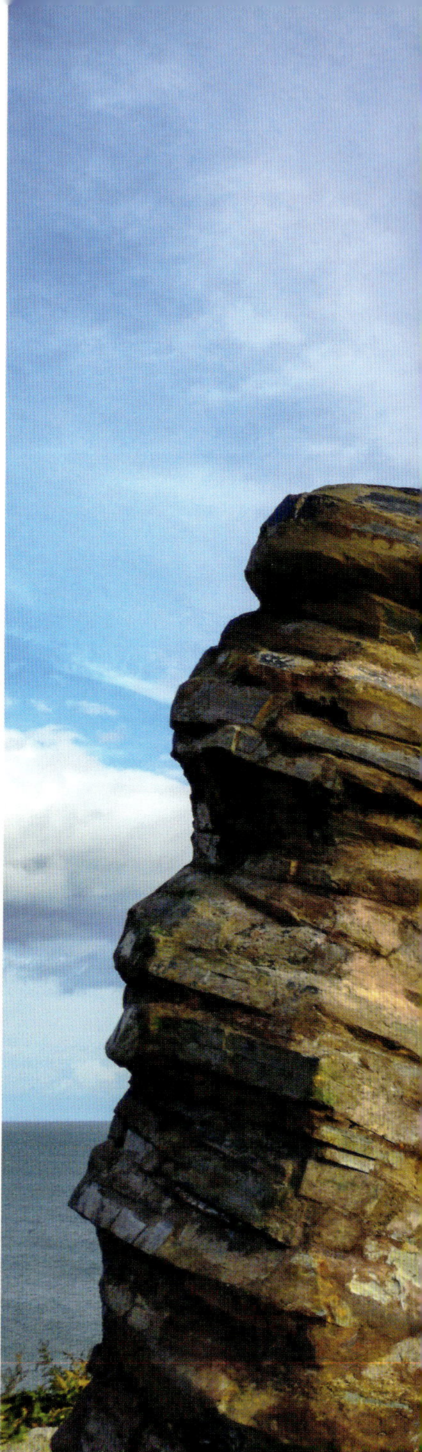

Above: Looking down on Newcastle harbour from a
hillside meadow.

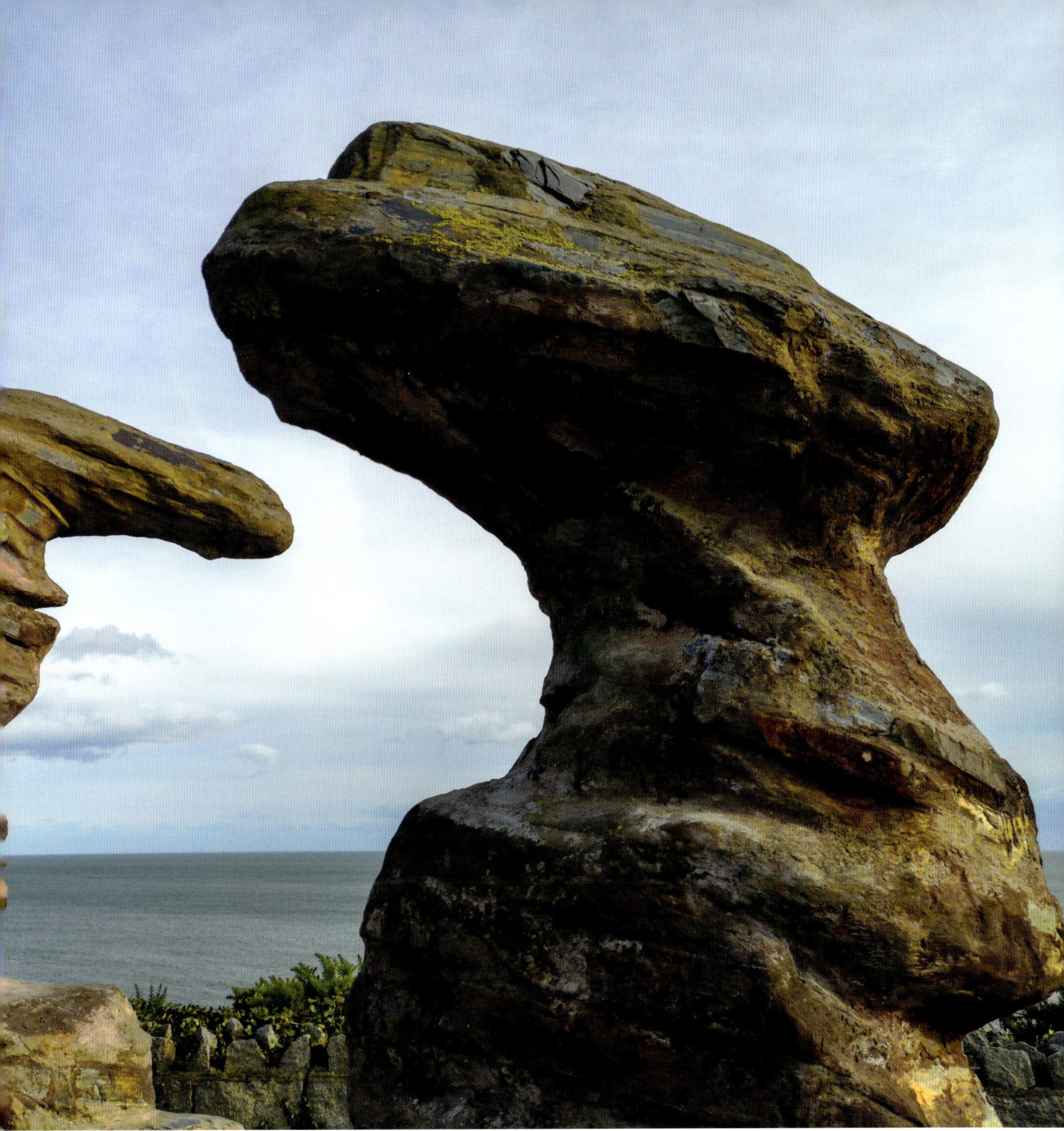

Above: A sculpture by German artist Ralf Sander, entitled 'The Smugglers Head', at Bloody Bridge.

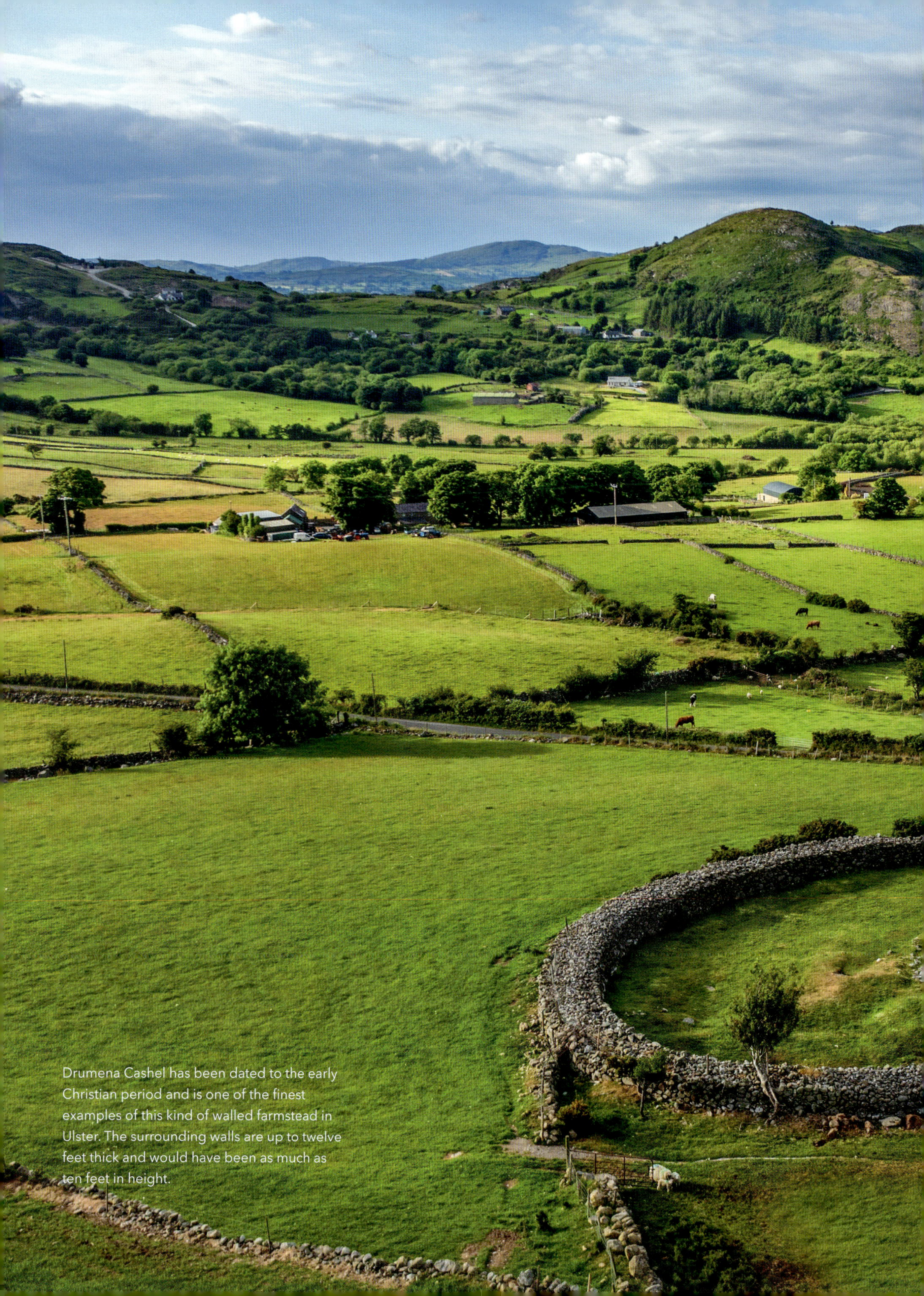

Drumena Cashel has been dated to the early Christian period and is one of the finest examples of this kind of walled farmstead in Ulster. The surrounding walls are up to twelve feet thick and would have been as much as ten feet in height.

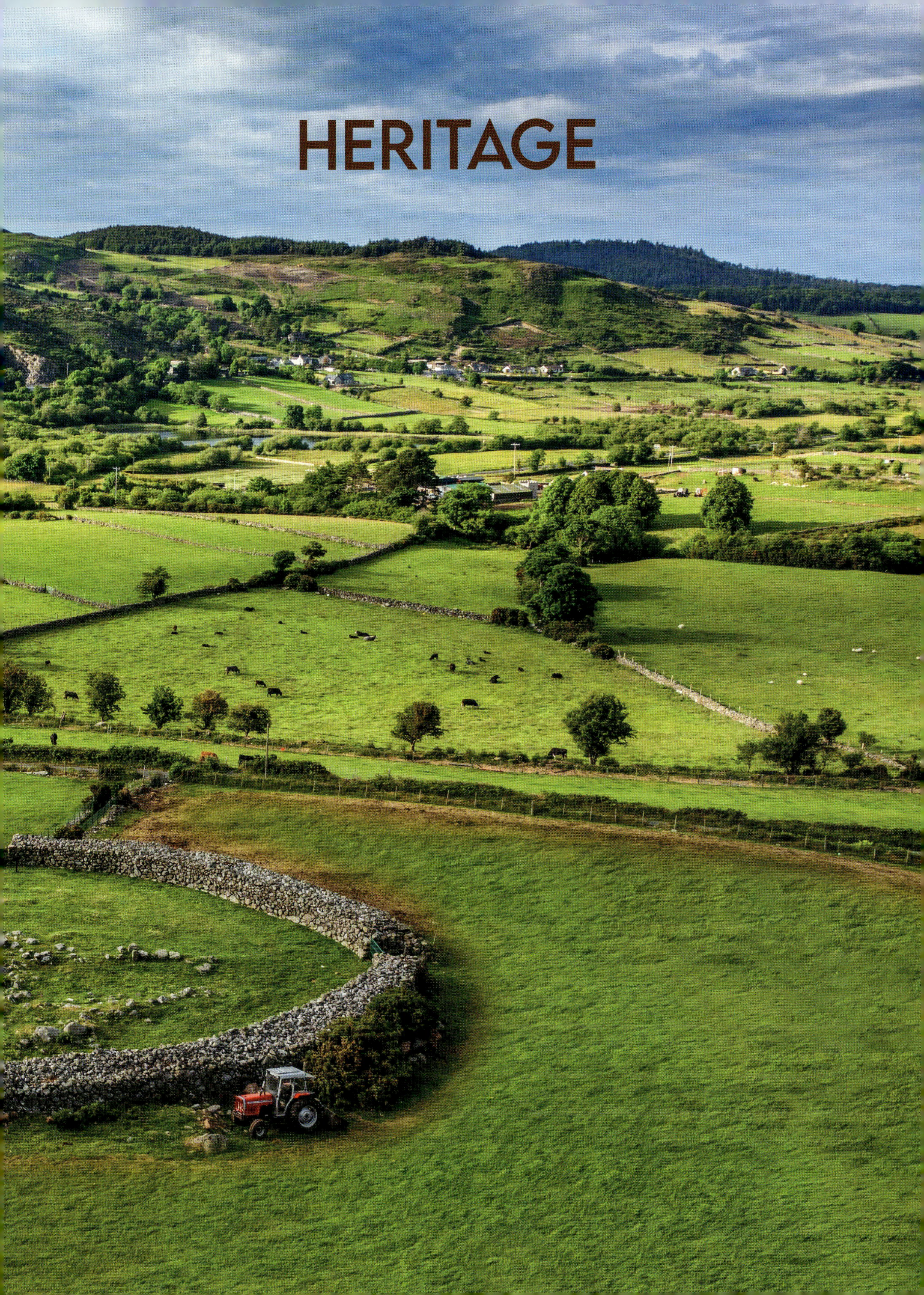
HERITAGE

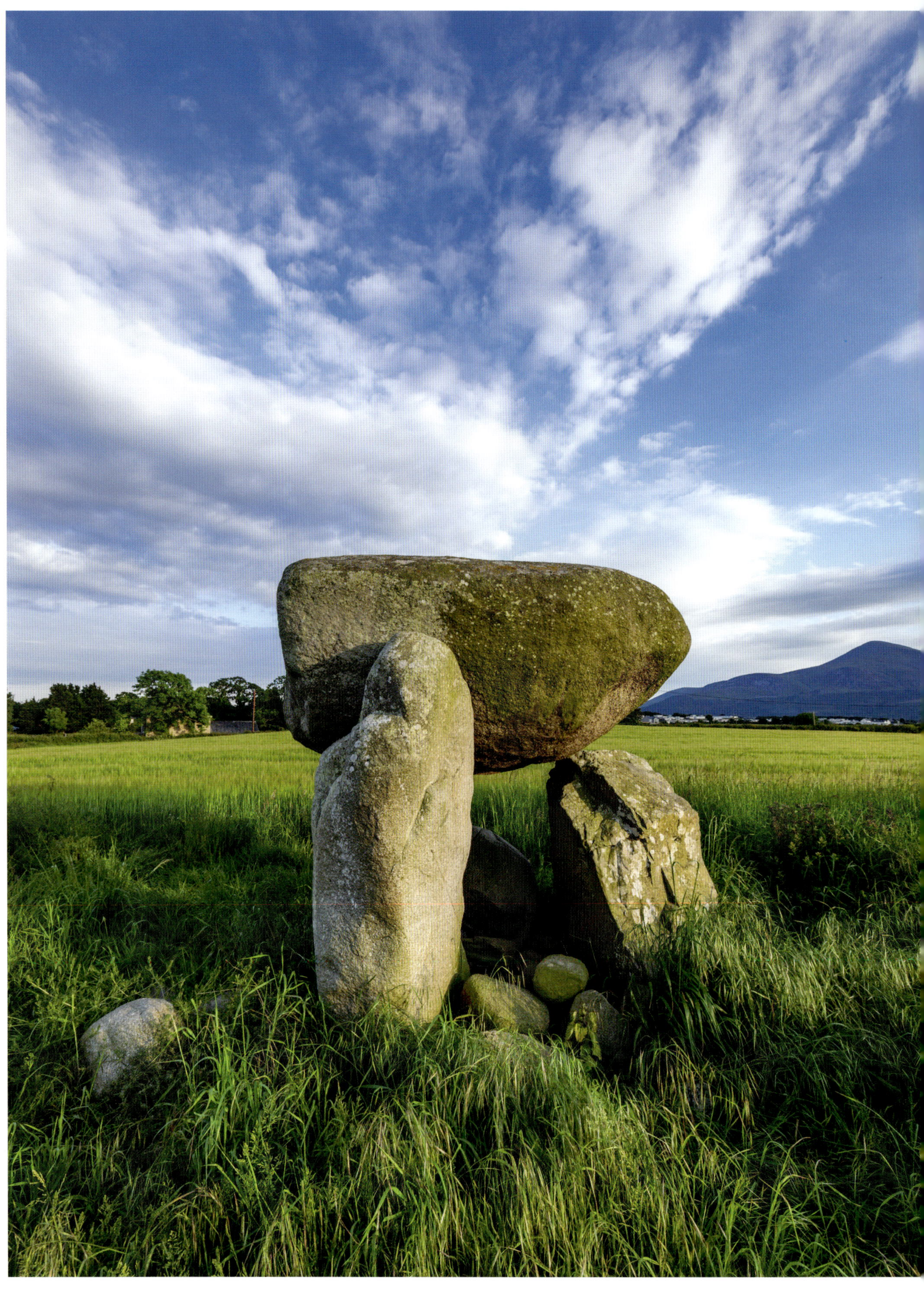

Simple flint tools unearthed near the village of Annalong provide the earliest evidence of human settlement in the Mournes; these date from the Mesolithic period, between 4000 and 6000 BC. But it was the arrival of Neolithlic farmers after 4000 BC that saw humans begin to write their story in the Mourne landscape.

Radiocarbon dating of charcoal found in sediments of the Leitrim River Valley, in the northwest of the Mournes, has suggested early Neolithic peoples used slash and burn techniques to clear the forest cover for farming and livestock pasture. It is thought that early inhabitants regarded the summits of the high mountains as a link between the earth and the afterlife, and it was common for them to build burial chambers on certain prominent peaks. The passage tomb known as the Great Cairn on the summit of Slieve Donard dates from this period. There are also several excellent examples of portal tombs or dolmens

Left: Slidderyford Dolmen, a fine example of a Neolithic burial tomb located just south of Dundrum village.

Below: The entrance to the souterrain within Drumena Cashel. These dark passages are thought to have been used to store food and may also have been used as a defensive refuge in times of danger.

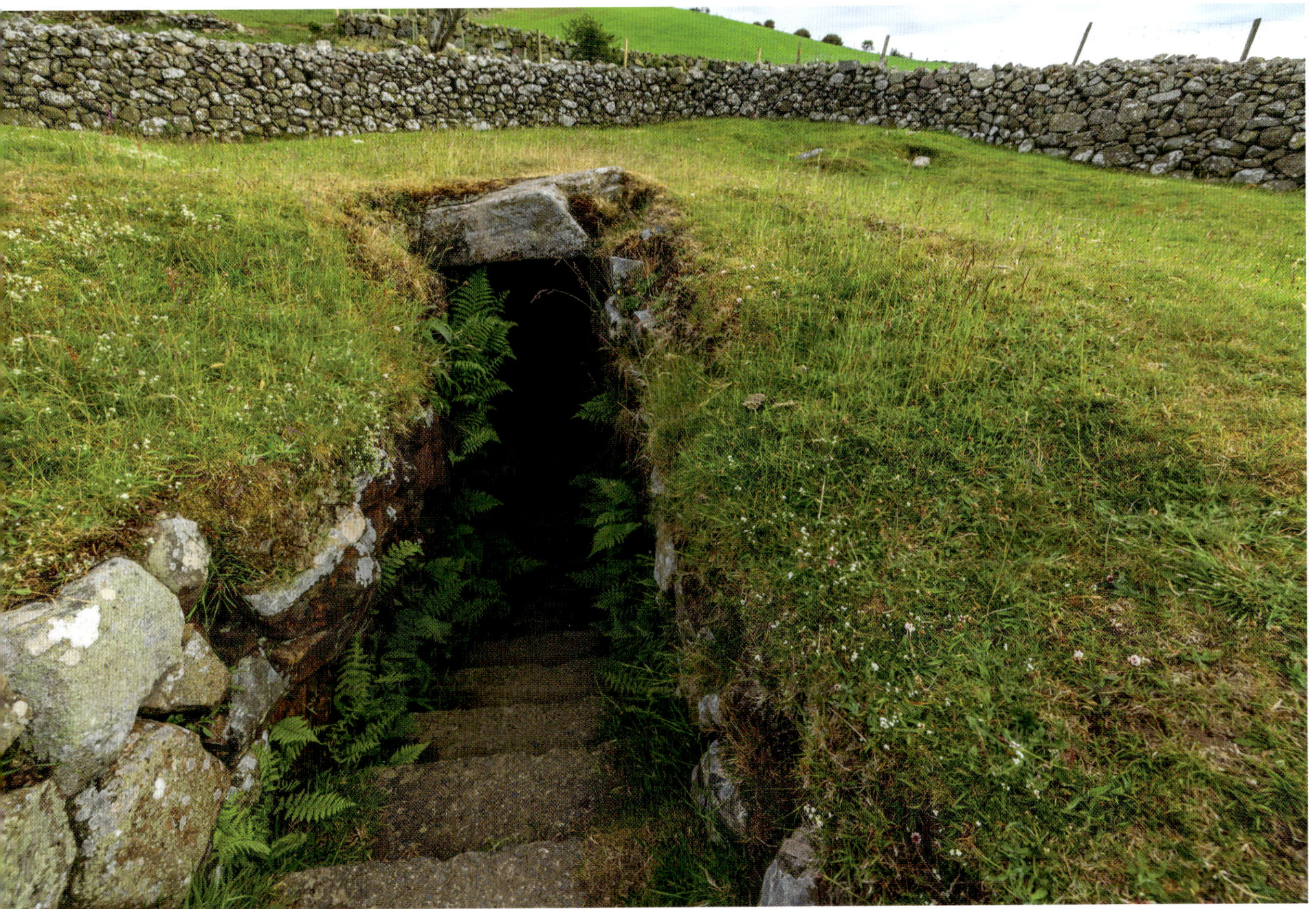

in the Mourne area, including Slidderyford and Legananny. Just how they were able to manually move and manoeuvre such enormous rocks into position is not fully understood.

Numerous Bronze Age (2400–600 BC) archaeological sites exist in the Mournes. These early Celtic peoples left behind hill forts, stone circles and standing stones. Prominent burial tombs were also still being used, and the Lesser Cairn on the summit of Slieve Donard dates from this period. Research undertaken on gold artifacts has suggested that the Mourne mountains may have provided the majority of the gold used in Ireland at this time.

Iron Age remains are less evident, but things pick up again during early Christian times.

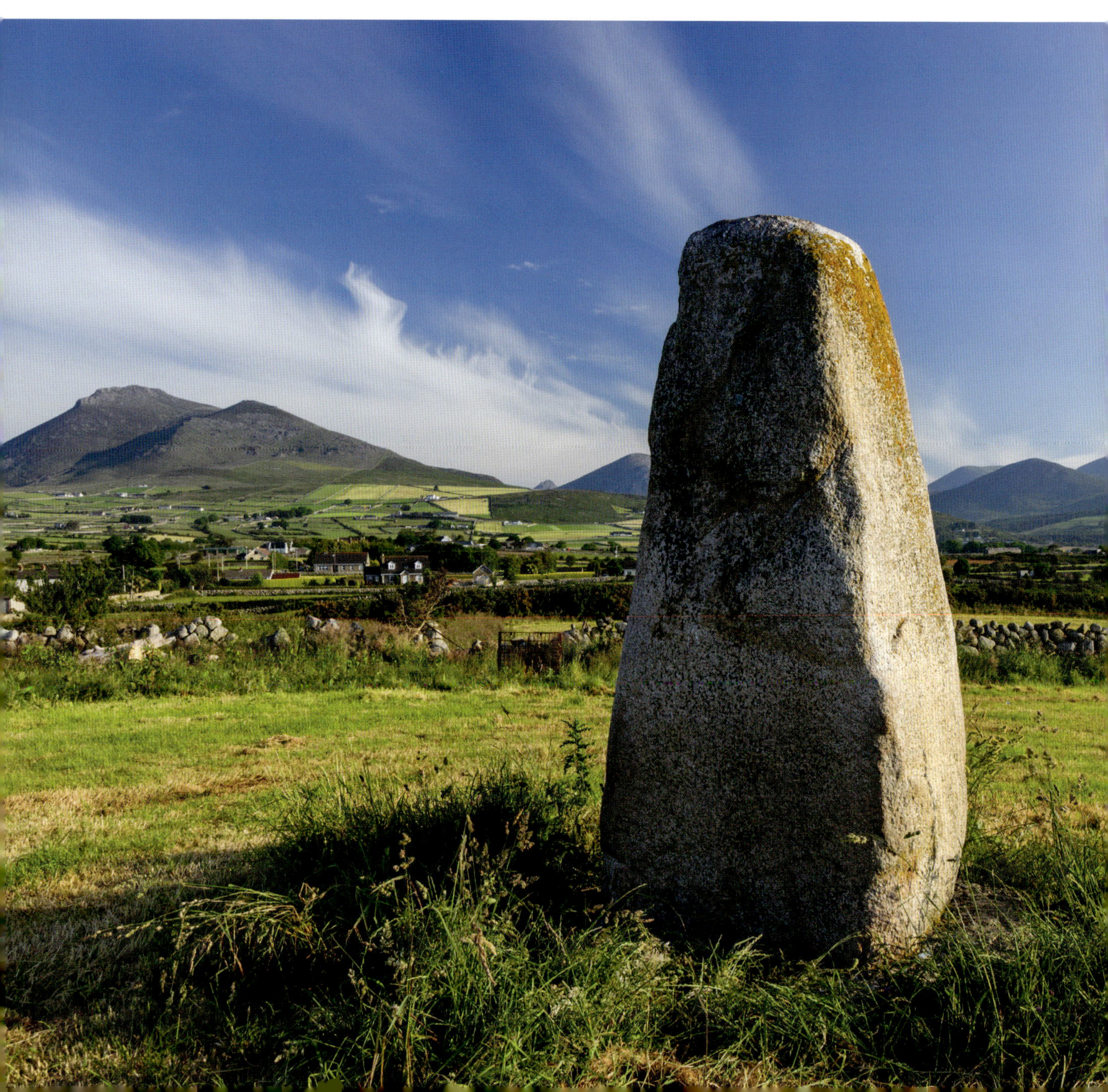

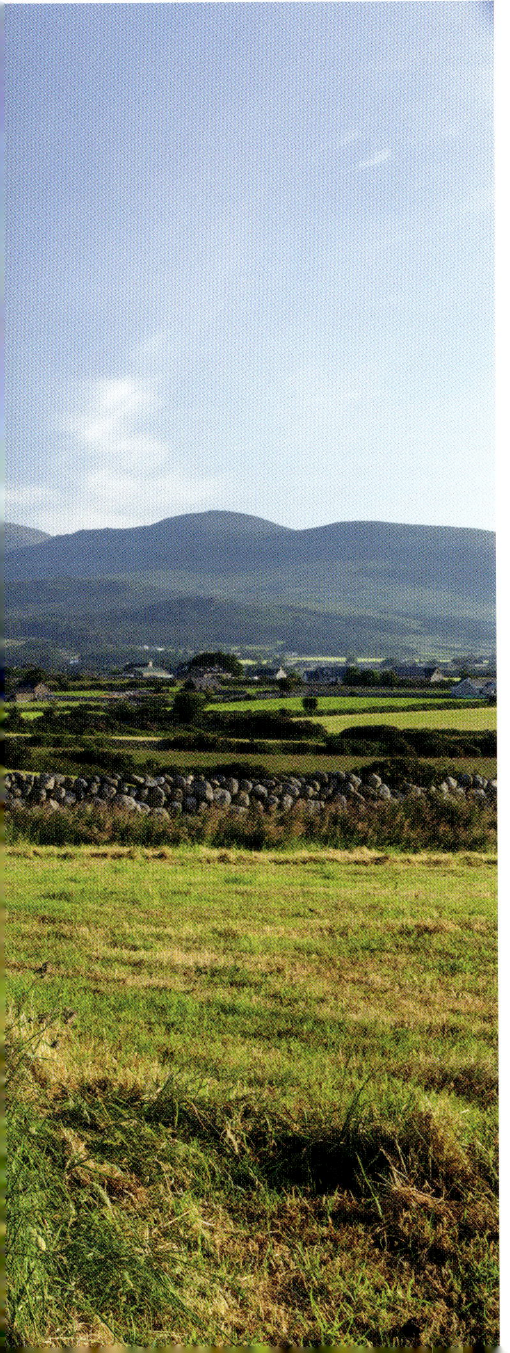

 The ruins of Maghera round tower near Bryansford. The tower is thought to date from the 10th century; much of it collapsed due to storm damage in the 18th century.

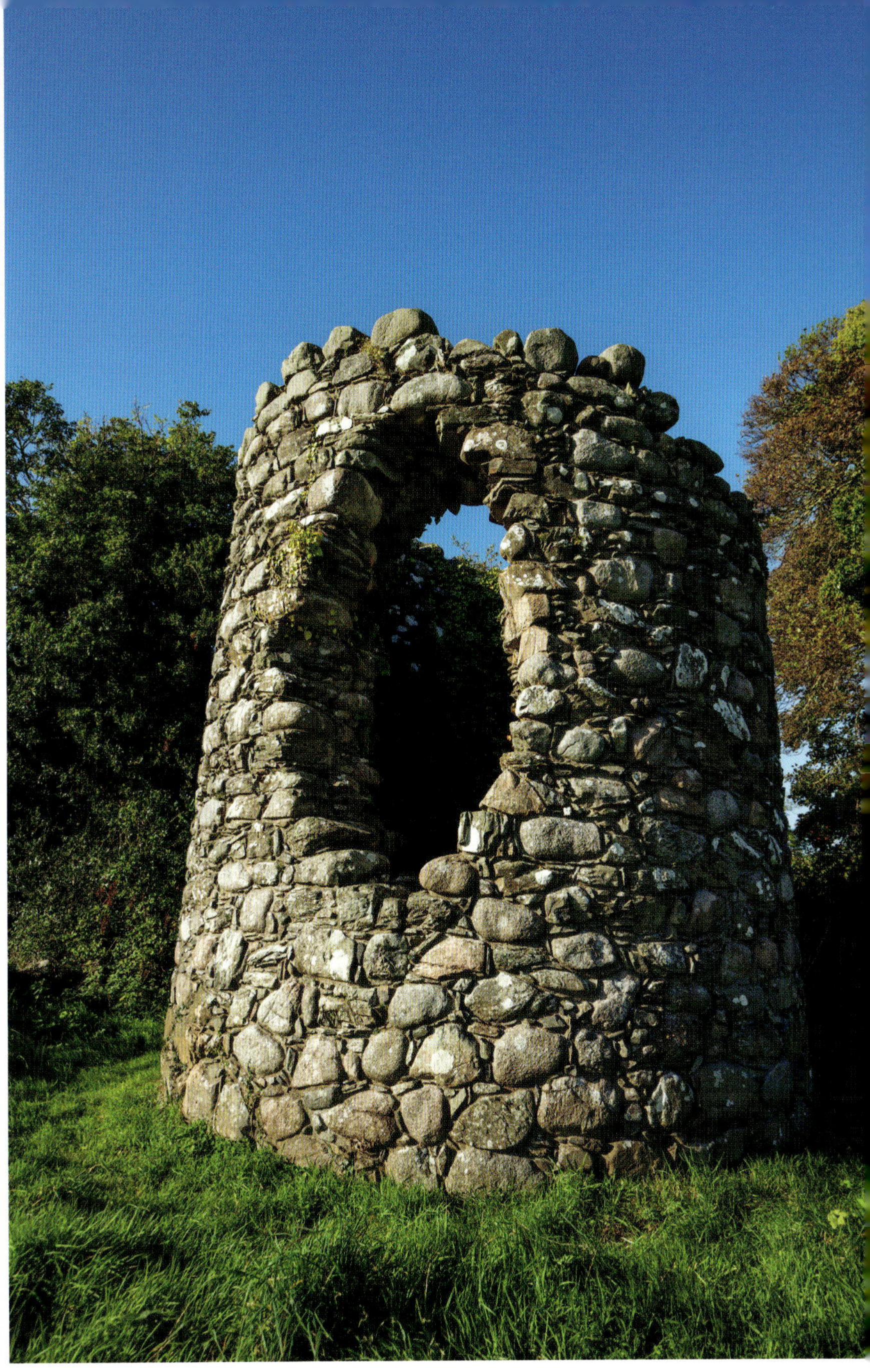

 The Long Stone is approximately 2.5 metres tall and is located in the townland of Longstone, just outside Annalong. It is thought to be the only remaining stone of a Neolithic burial chamber.

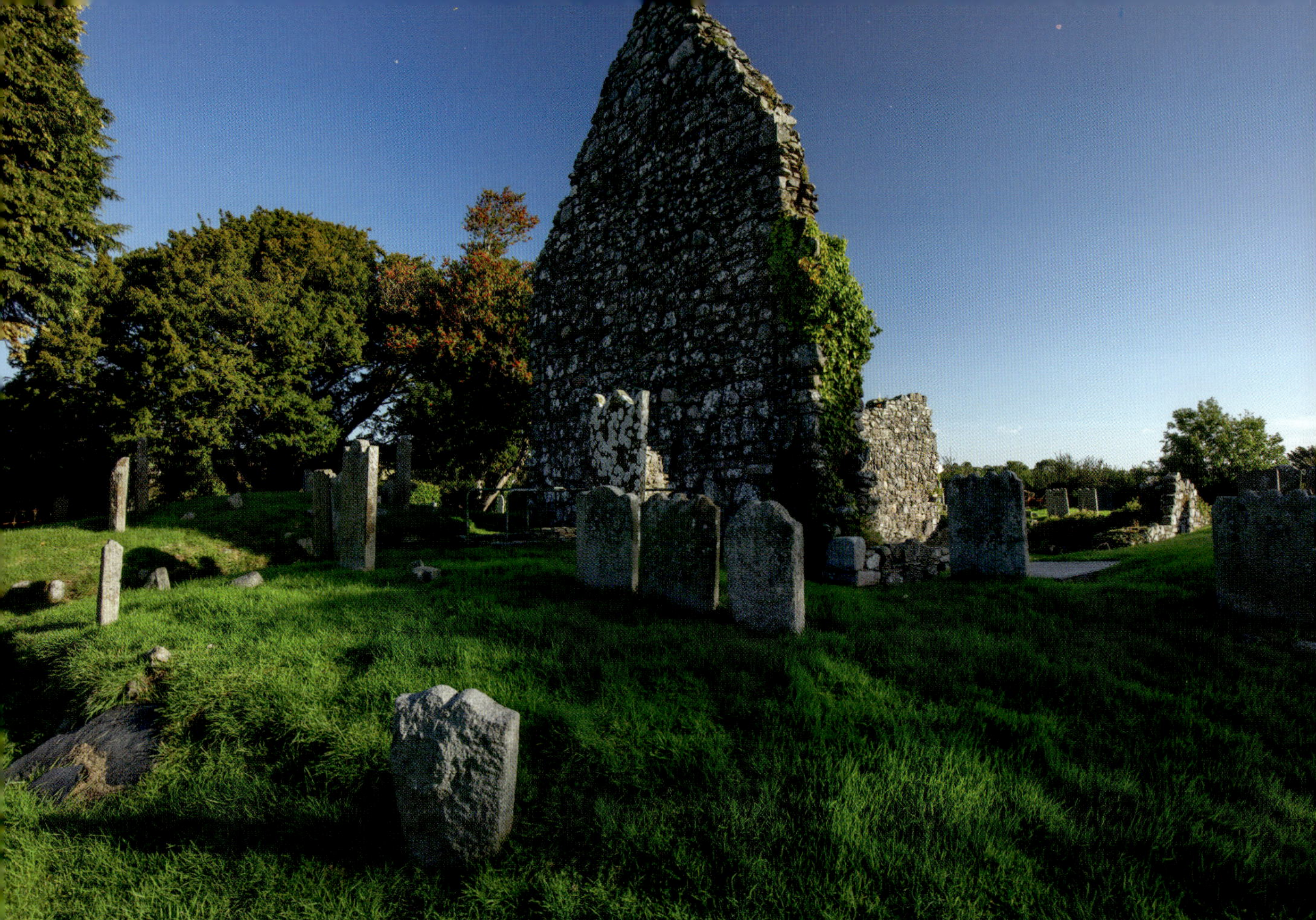

Drumena Cashel, between Castlewellan and Hilltown, dates from this period. Stone and turf 'booley' huts were used on the higher ground of the Mournes, as farmers moved their livestock onto the mountains to graze in the summer, returning to the low ground again in the winter. Around this time, select blocks of granite were quarried in the Mournes for millstones and also to build some notable early Christian monuments, such as the 9th century High Cross in Downpatrick. The stone tower and old church at Maghera are associated with St Donard, who is said to have used the Great Cairn on Slieve Donard as a monastic cell and the Lesser Cairn as an oratory, and so giving his name to the mountain.

In 1177, the famous Anglo-Norman knight John de Courcy led an incursion into eastern Ulster, occupying

Above: The ruined gable wall of the old church at Maghera is thought to date from the 13th century.

Above right: The remains of Clough Castle, once an important Anglo-Norman structure from the late 12th century.

Right: The partially restored remains of an 800-year-old lime kiln on the grounds of Dundrum Castle.

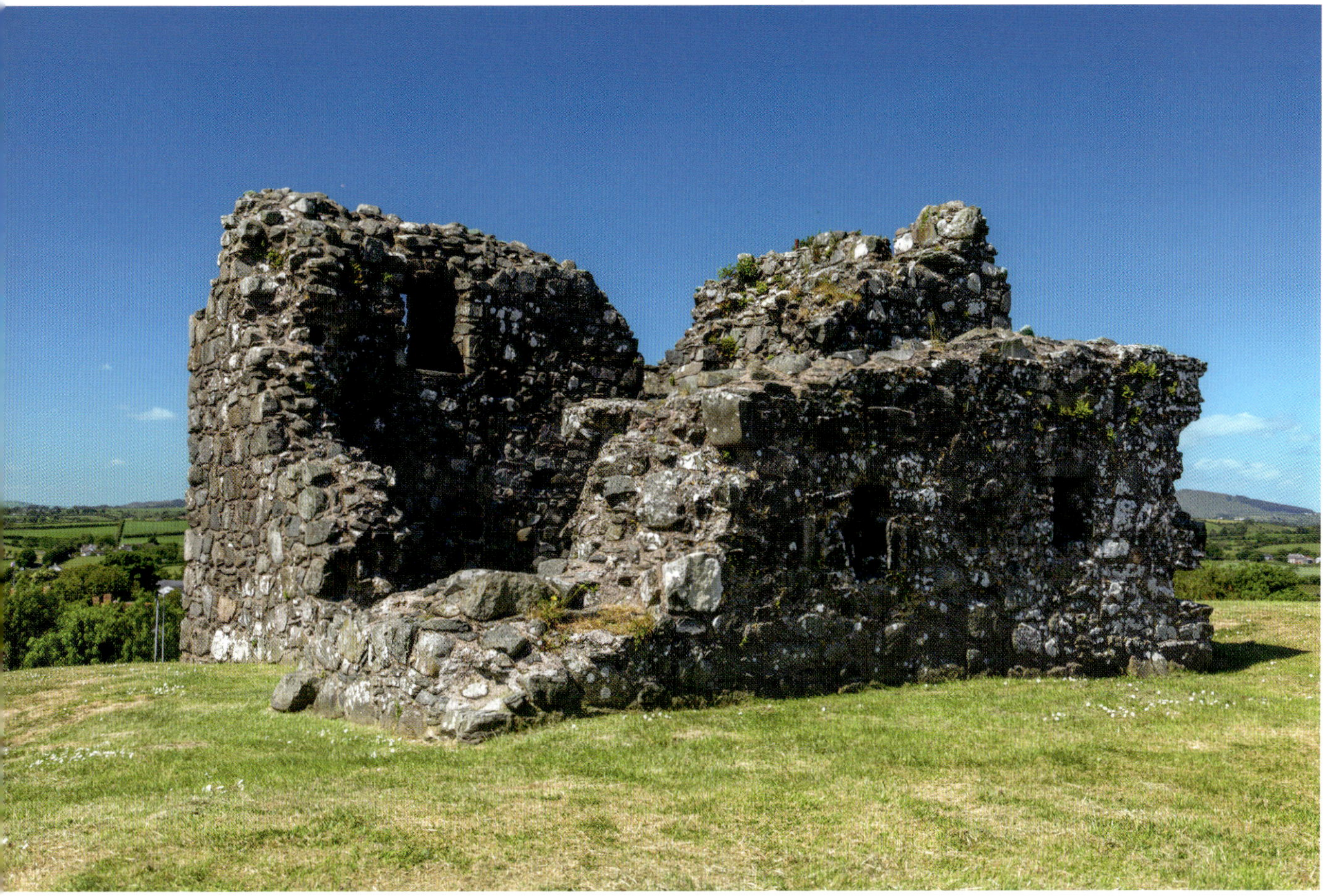

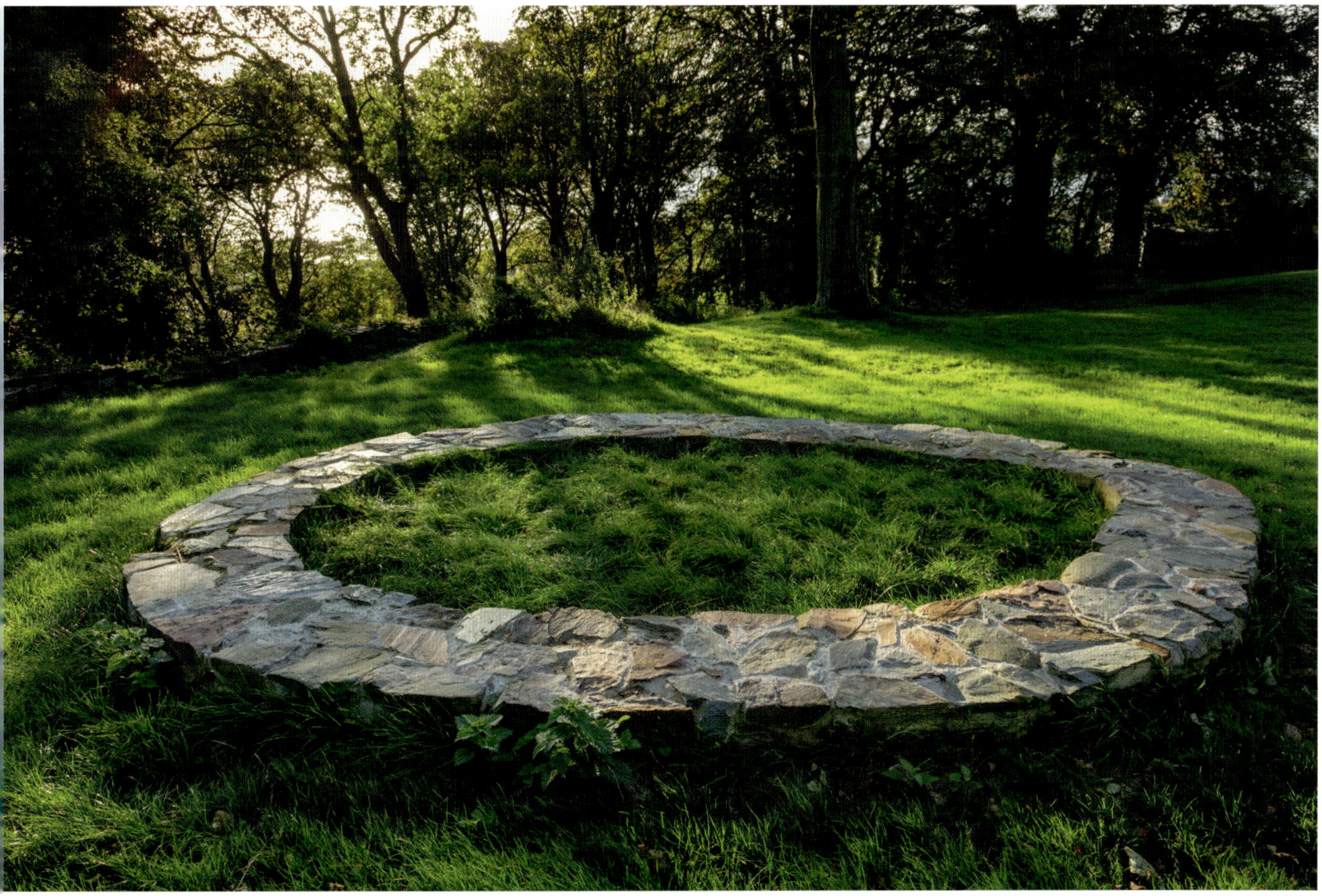

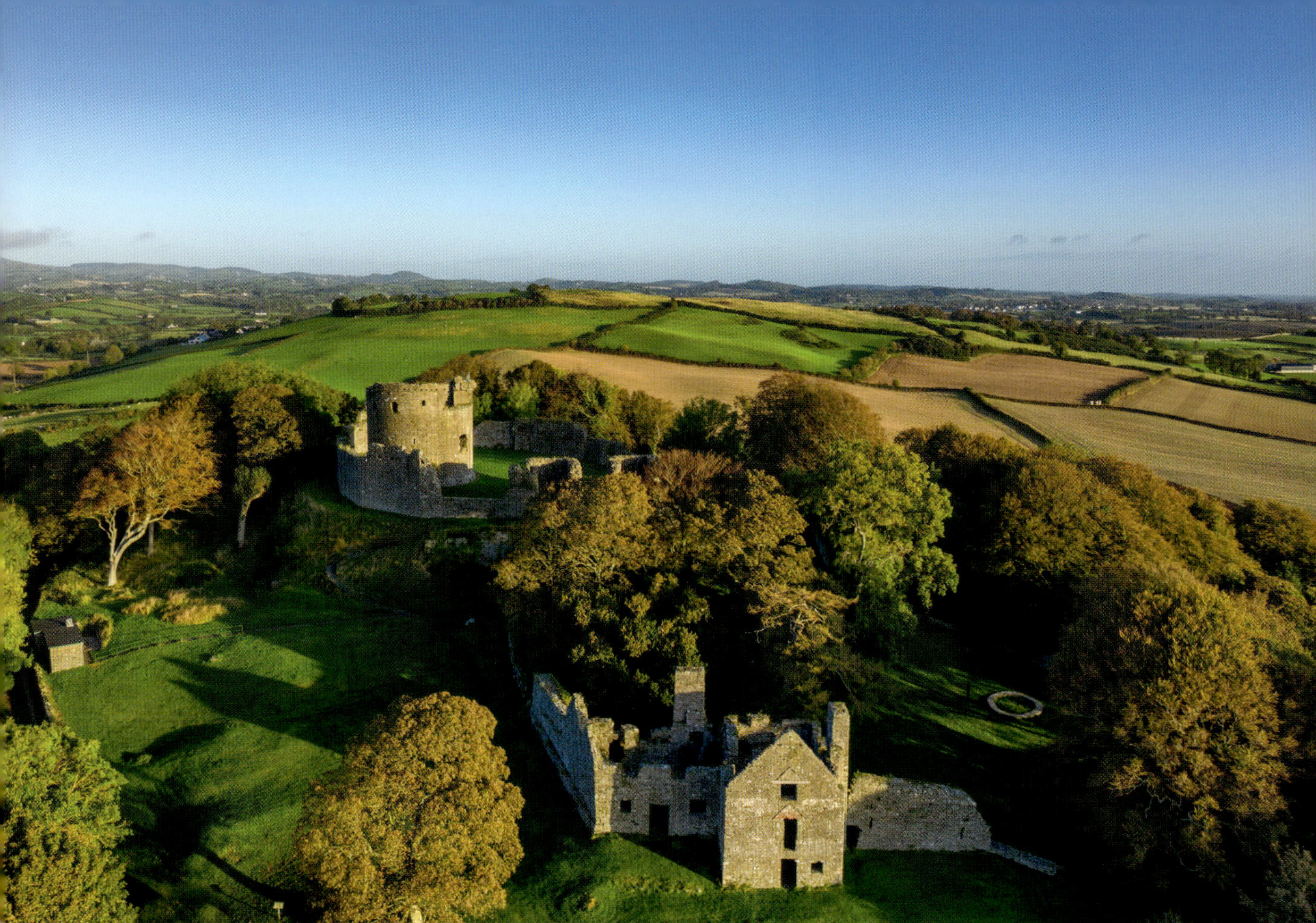

much of southern and eastern Down, including the Mournes. Throughout the 12th and 13th centuries, the Anglo-Normans brought advanced stone-building techniques with them – most specifically their expertise in building defensive structures.

With its key strategic position on the eastern seaboard, it is unsurprising that Anglo-Norman castles from this period can still be seen in the Mourne area. The best examples are the castles at Dundrum, Greencastle and Clough, which are all thought to have been built originally by John de Courcy. In fact, the castle at Dundrum was so well fortified that when de Courcy returned from exile in 1205 with a force of Norse soldiers, he was unable to retake his former stronghold. These castles were significantly strengthened and adapted during a second wave of castle building in the 16th century. During this time, tower houses were also built at several locations, of which the best surviving example is Narrow Water Castle outside Warrenpoint.

Above: An aerial view of Dundrum Castle, built in the early 13th century by John de Courcy. Sited on a prominent hill overlooking Dundrum Bay, the castle commands fine views in all directions and was an important strategic asset for several centuries.

During the Georgian period of the 18th century, the Kilbroney estate was developed, along with the Tollymore estate and its imaginative stone follies and bridges. The Annalong Cornmill was also built around this time. The Victorian era and the Industrial Revolution saw the building of Castlewellan Castle and the expansion of the local business of granite quarrying into a serious export industry. The harbours in Newcastle, Annalong and Kilkeel were expanded to accommodate larger vessels, and the Victorian housing along the seafront in Newcastle became the homes of wealthy merchants. In the late 19th and early 20th centuries, planners and engineers turned to the Mournes as a source of water to satisfy the rapidly expanding demands of Belfast. The project to divert water from the Mournes led to the construction of the Silent Valley and Ben Crom dams, as well as the Mourne Wall itself.

Today, the granite industry of the Mournes has faded to a niche market; fishing, agriculture and tourism are now mainstays of the local economy. New developments have largely

Below: Hanna's Close just outside Kilkeel is one of the best preserved examples of a *clachan* in Ireland. These restored traditional cottages date from around the 1640s and are now run as holiday rentals.

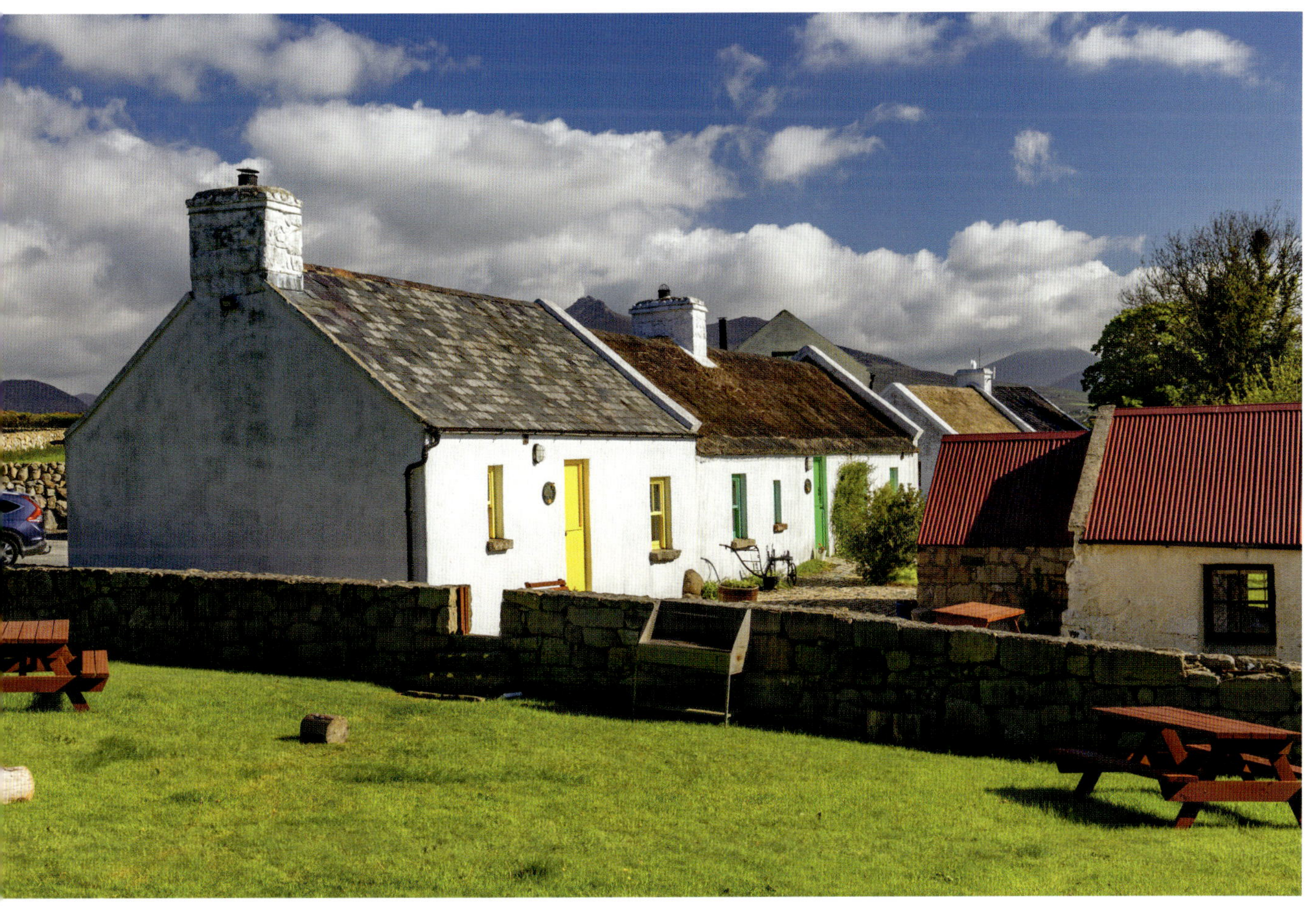

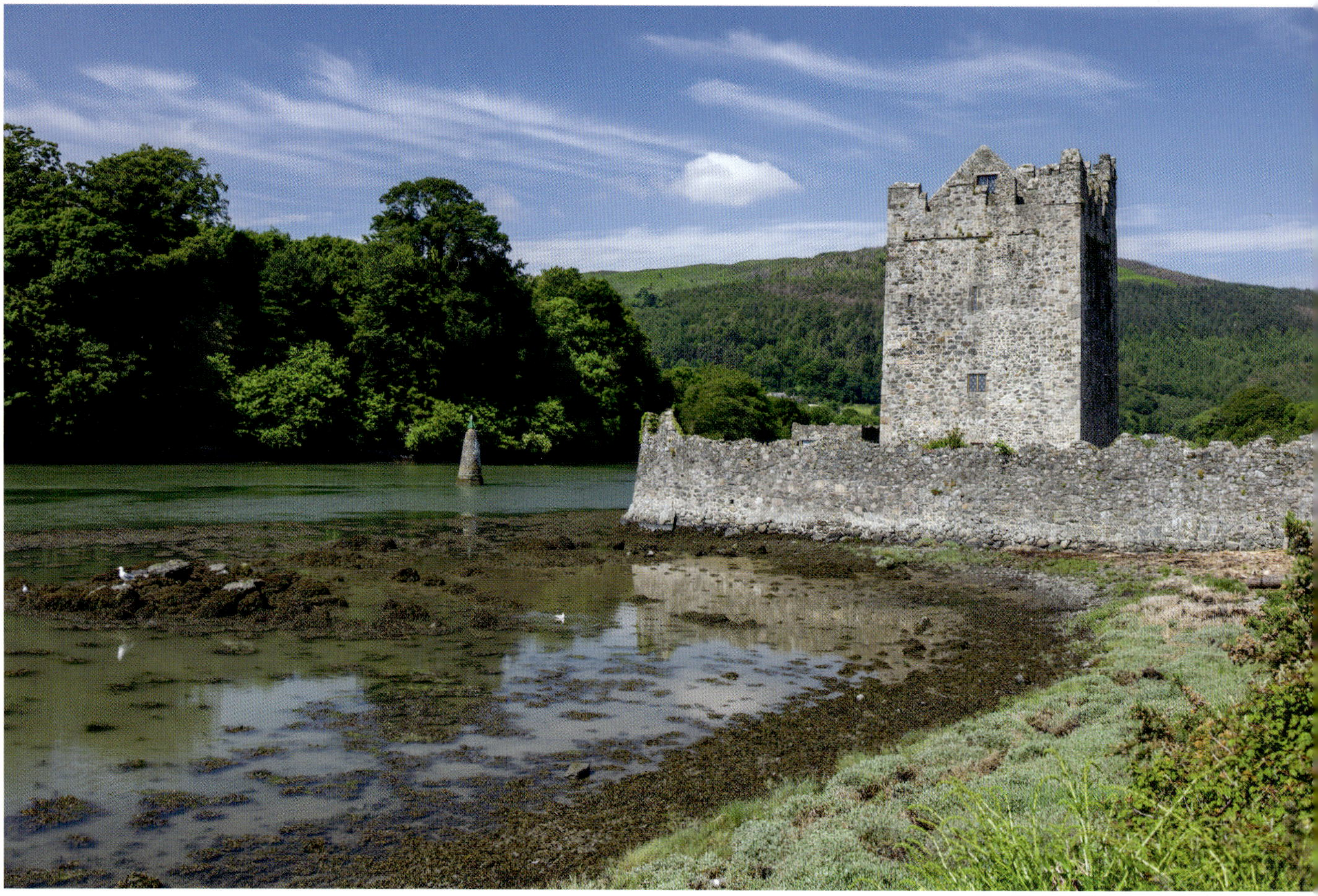

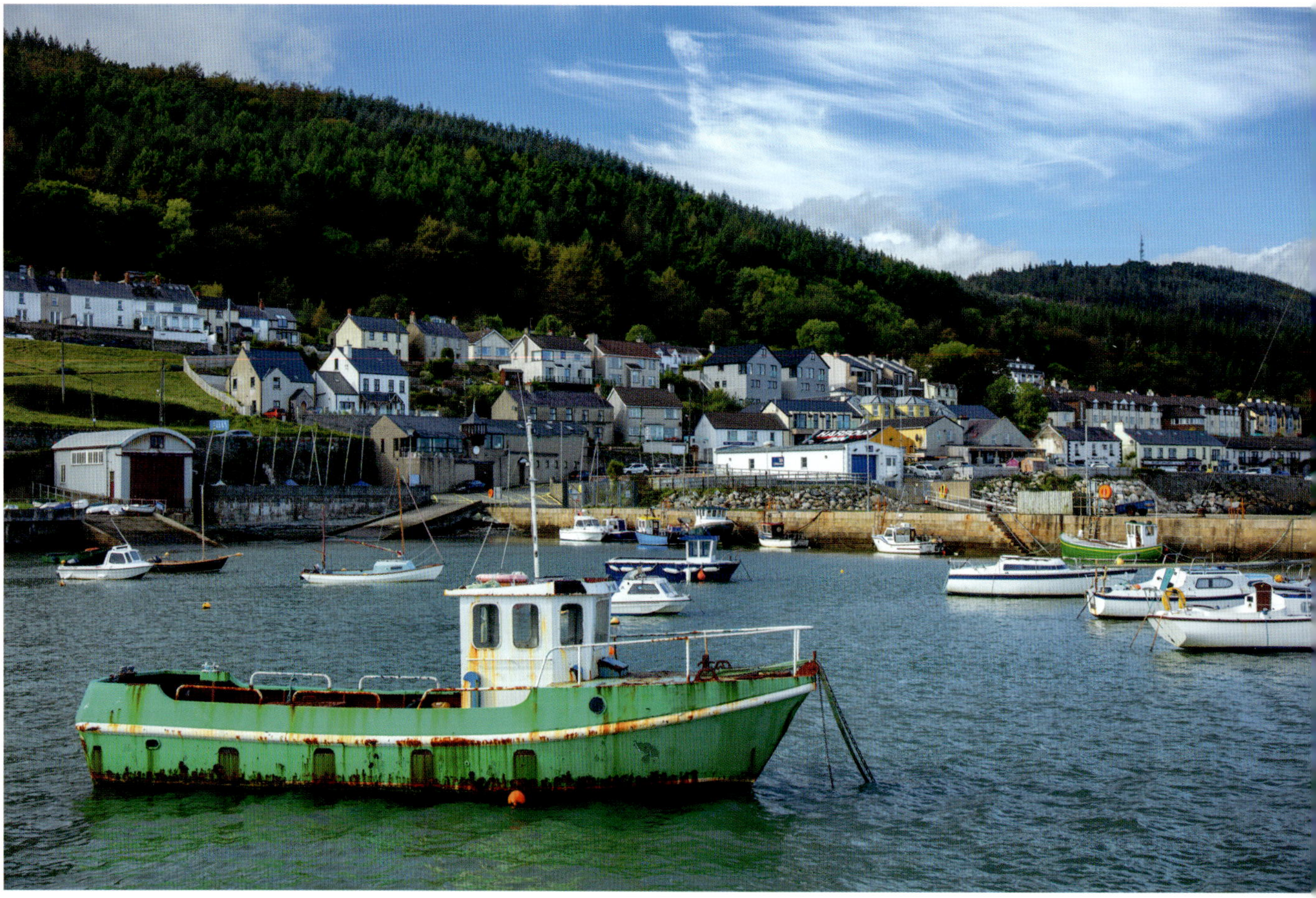

been replaced by the concerns of heritage conservation and management. Following the creation of the Mourne Area of Outstanding Natural Beauty in 1986, authorities have been concerned that new buildings should respect the Mourne landscape. Building and restoration in the vernacular style has been encouraged, and to date the area has not been regarded as a suitable location for the development of windfarms.

In 2002, government proposals were announced to make the area into Northern Ireland's first national park. Although lauded by many, the idea has not been universally welcomed. Just like many of the national parks in Britain, local people live and work within the proposed boundaries, and they are concerned that rules designed to promote conservation may unfairly hinder development. So far, these proposals have not progressed beyond a consultation stage.

Above left: Dating from the 16th century, Narrow Water Castle just outside Warrenpoint was once an important Anglo-Norman stronghold guarding the inner reaches of Carlingford Lough.

Below left: Newcastle harbour.

Below: Stepping stones on the Shimna River in Tollymore Forest Park.

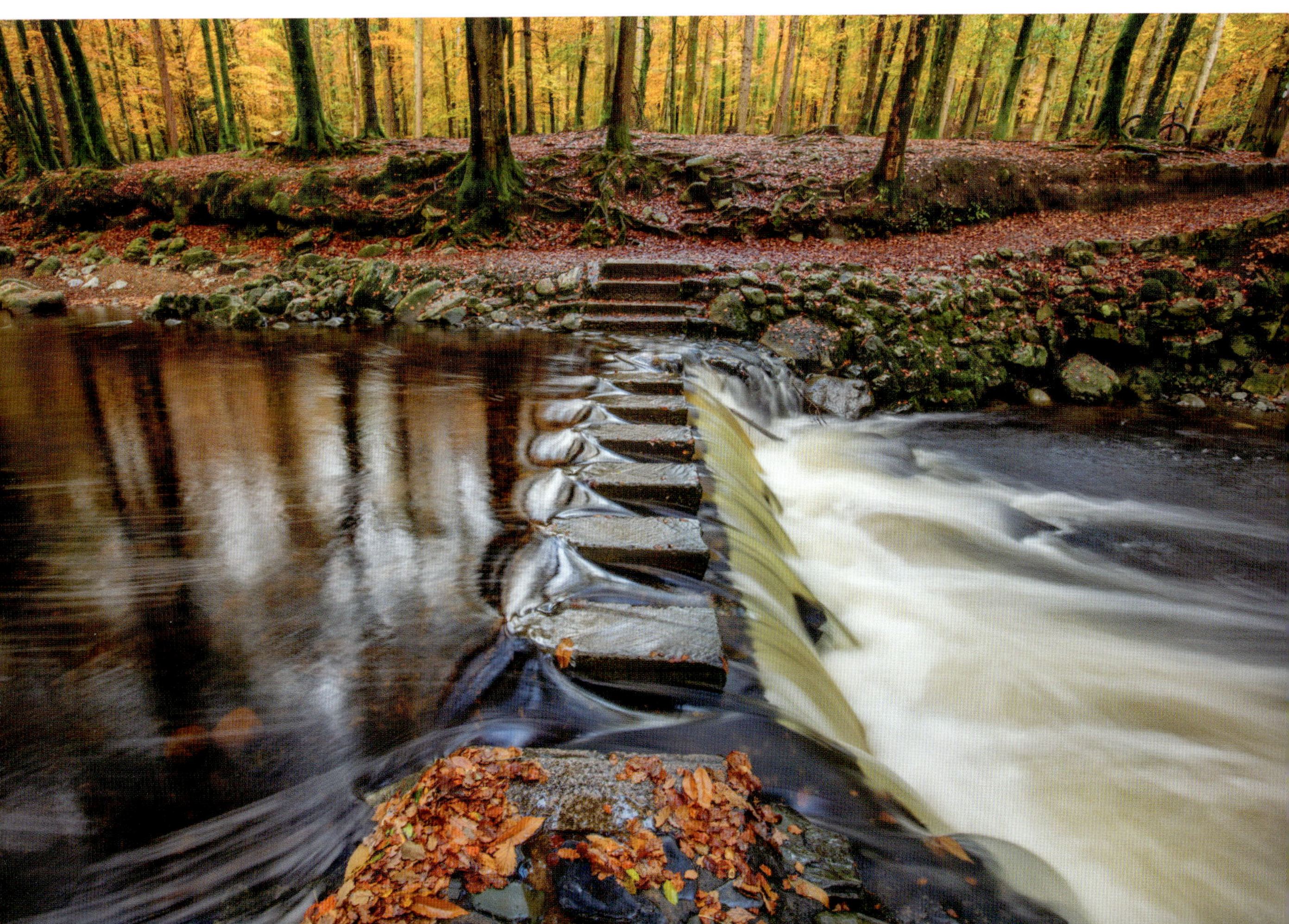

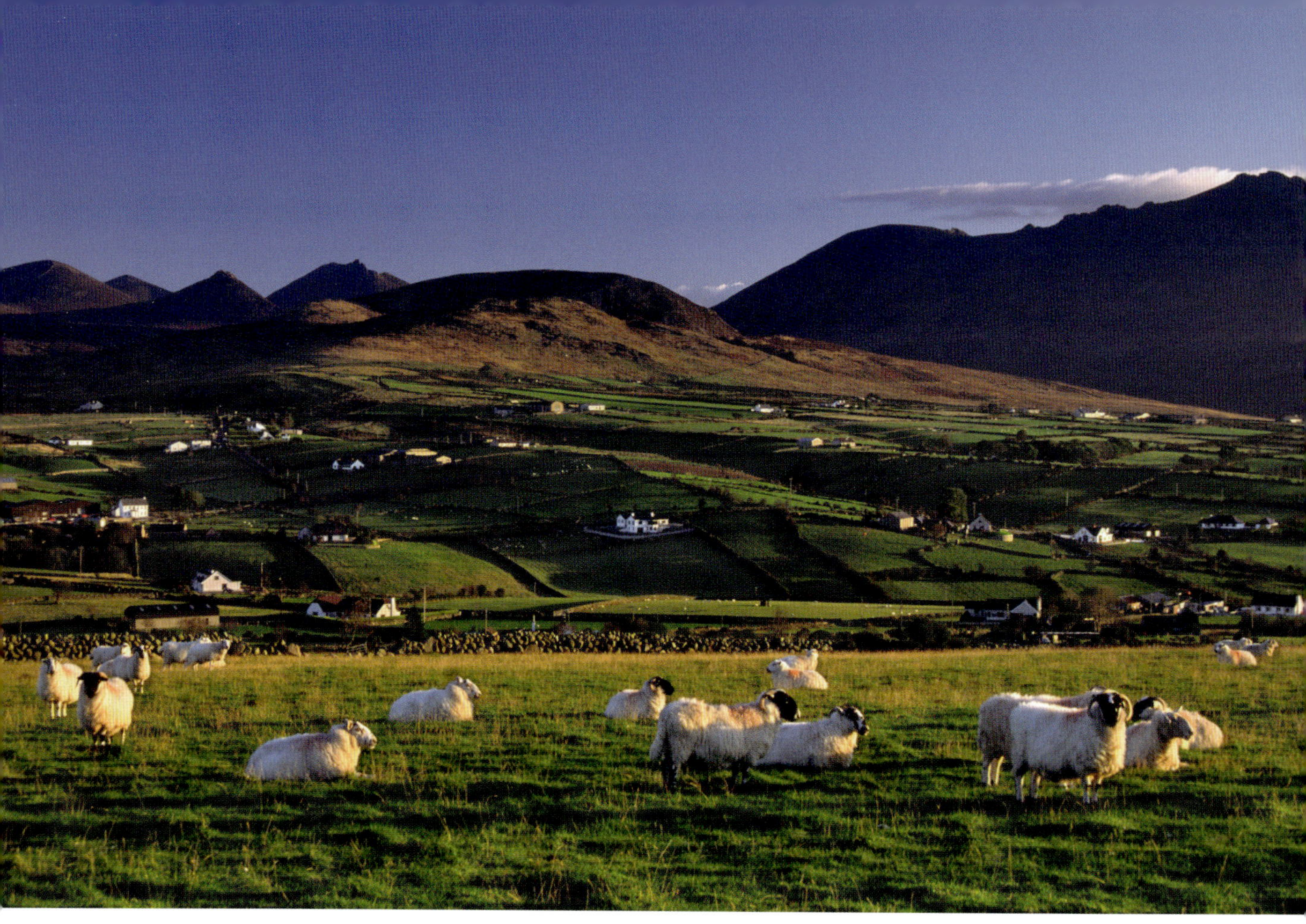

THE STONE WALLS
OF MOURNE

More than anything – with perhaps the exception of the graceful sweep of the mountains and their curious summit crenelations – the character of the Mourne landscape is defined by its patchwork of iconic dry-stone walls. For the earliest farmers, it wasn't just the forest they needed to clear but also the debris and spoil of successive Ice Ages. Generation after generation engaged in the back-breaking task of clearing the litter of granite boulders to make fields cultivable. The boulders were then used to build field and territory boundary walls as well as shelters.

Known locally as 'ditches', traditional Mourne dry-stone walls have changed little over the years. The simple technique used in their construction differs from those used in most other parts of Britain and Ireland: they are normally constructed as a 'single skin', with only a single stone thickness, gradually tapering with large boulders at the base and much smaller rocks at the top. Unlike most other stone walls, the gaps are not filled in, allowing the wind to pass through. This method lends itself to the use of very large rocks and also the aid of machinery, so new walls are still being constructed using these techniques. The best examples can be seen on the coastal plain between the southern slopes of the Mournes and the villages of Annalong and Kilkeel.

Left: From Aughrim Hill to the south of the High Mournes. This view is characteristic of the Mourne landscape: patchworks of rolling farmland and dry-stone walls with a backdrop of craggy summits.

Below: The characteristic and unique stone walls of the Mournes.

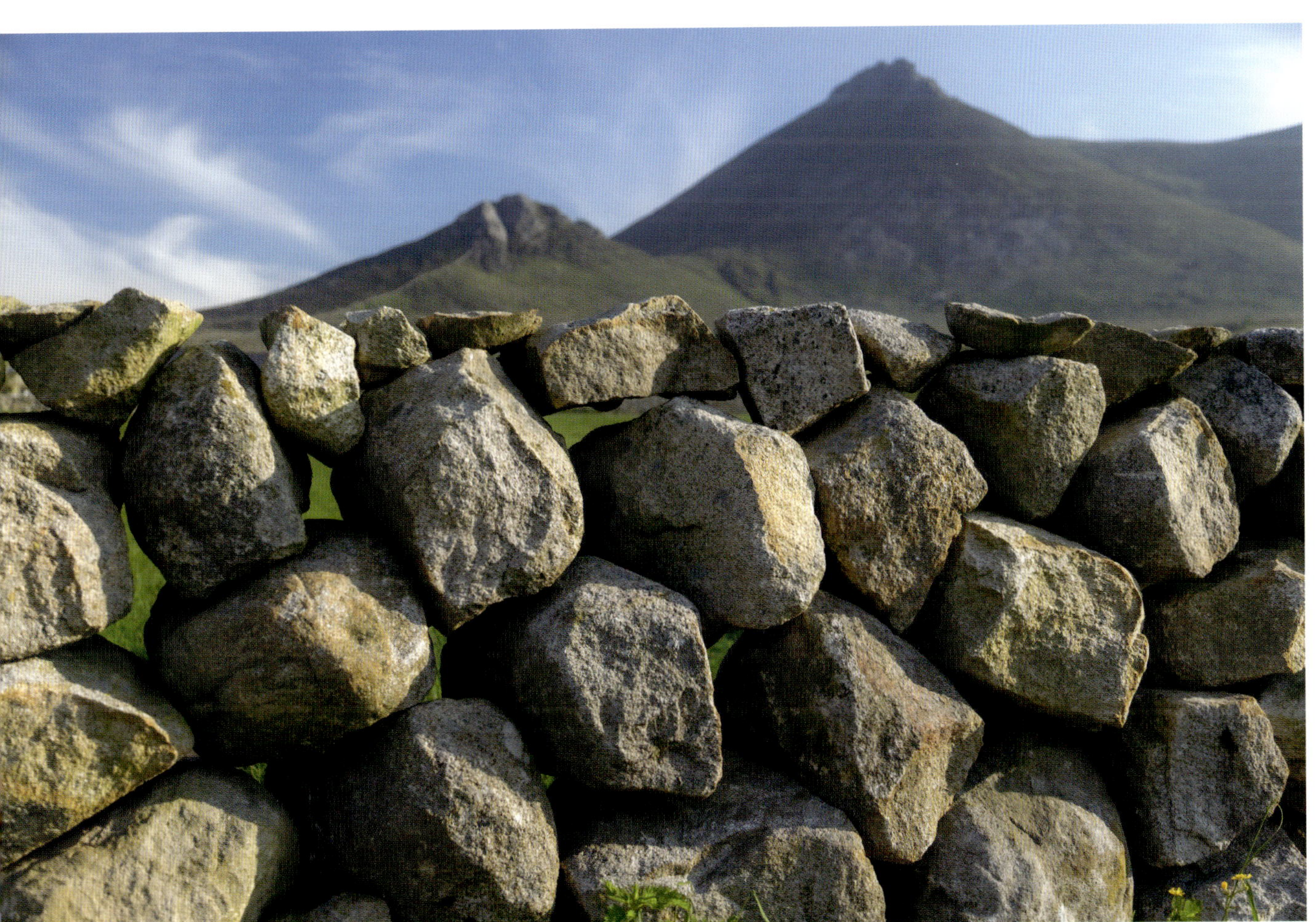

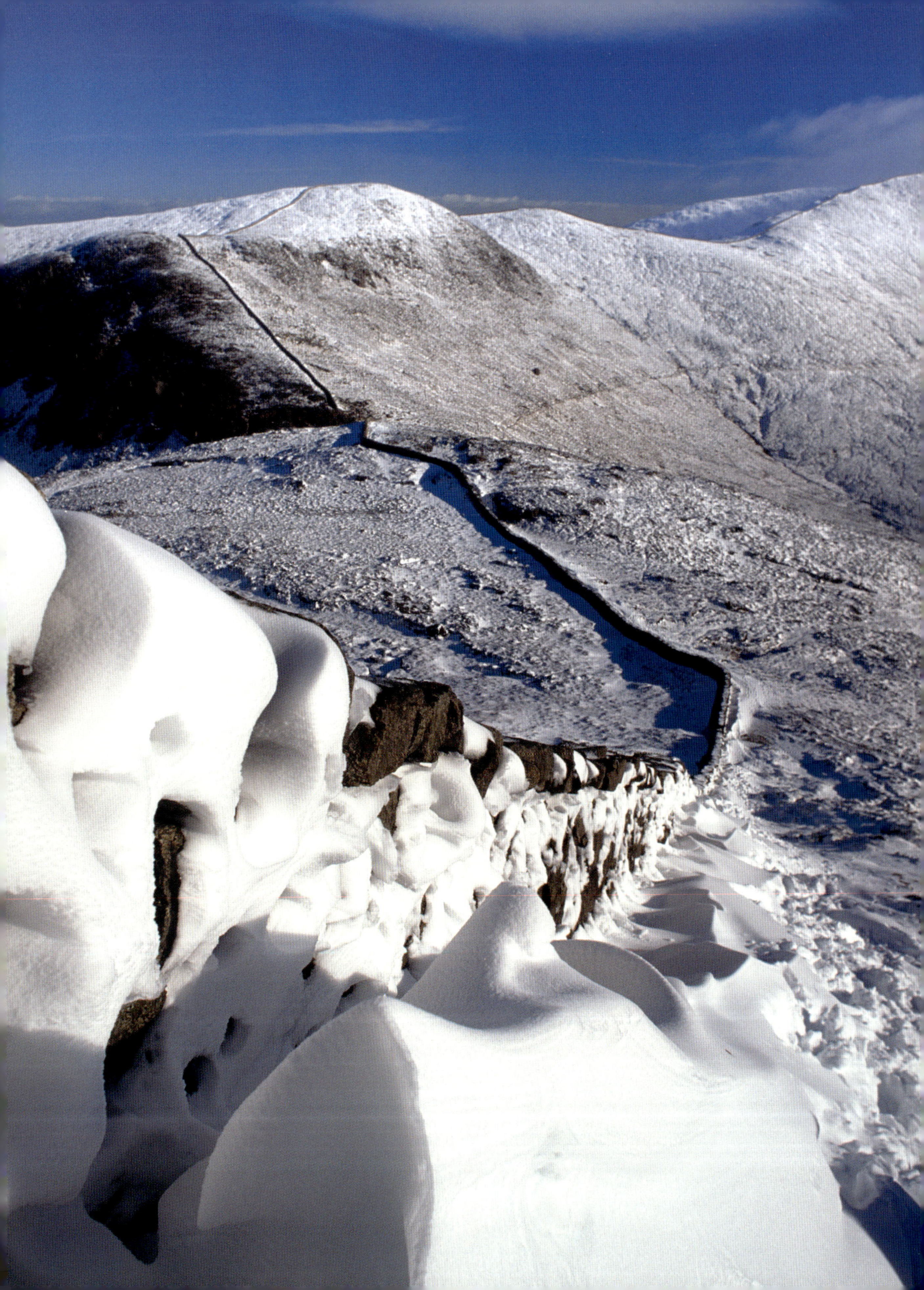

INDEX

Left: Wind-drifted snow several feet deep piled up in the lee of the Mourne Wall.

Also available from

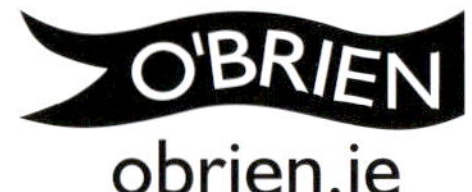

O'BRIEN
obrien.ie

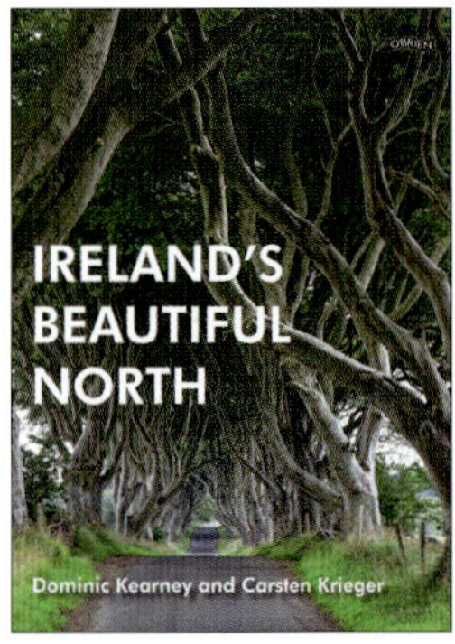

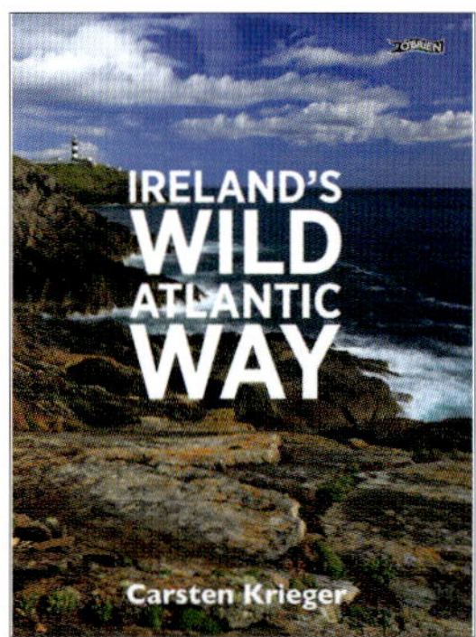

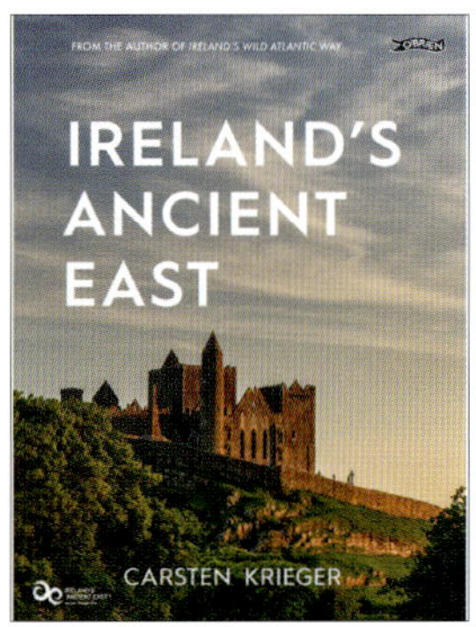

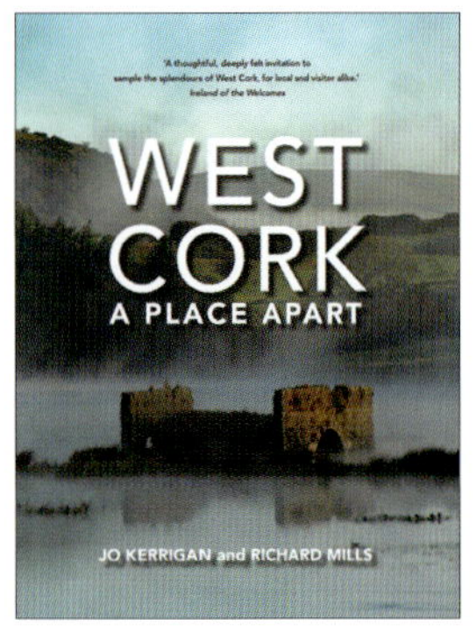

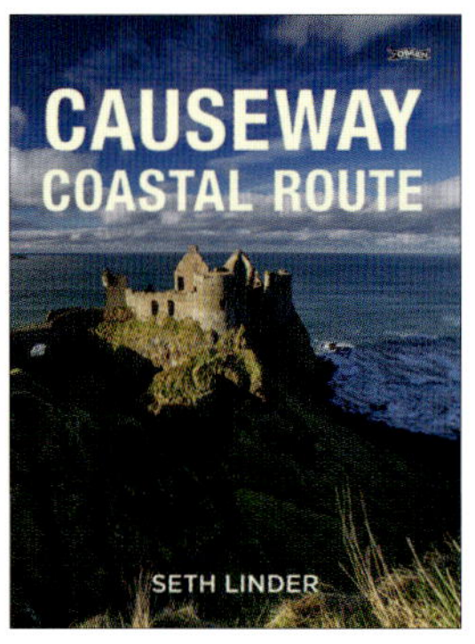

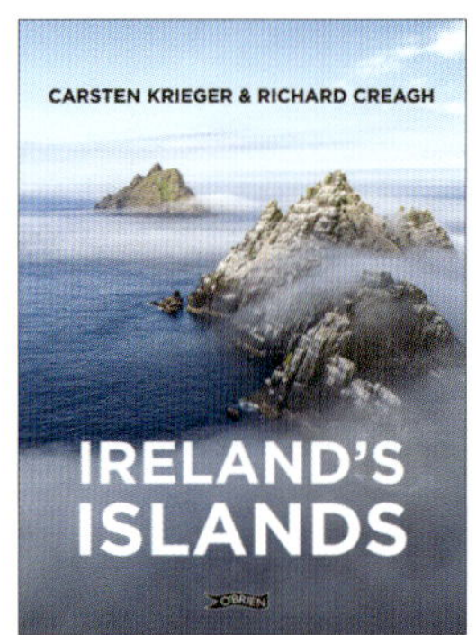